The Poverty of Nations

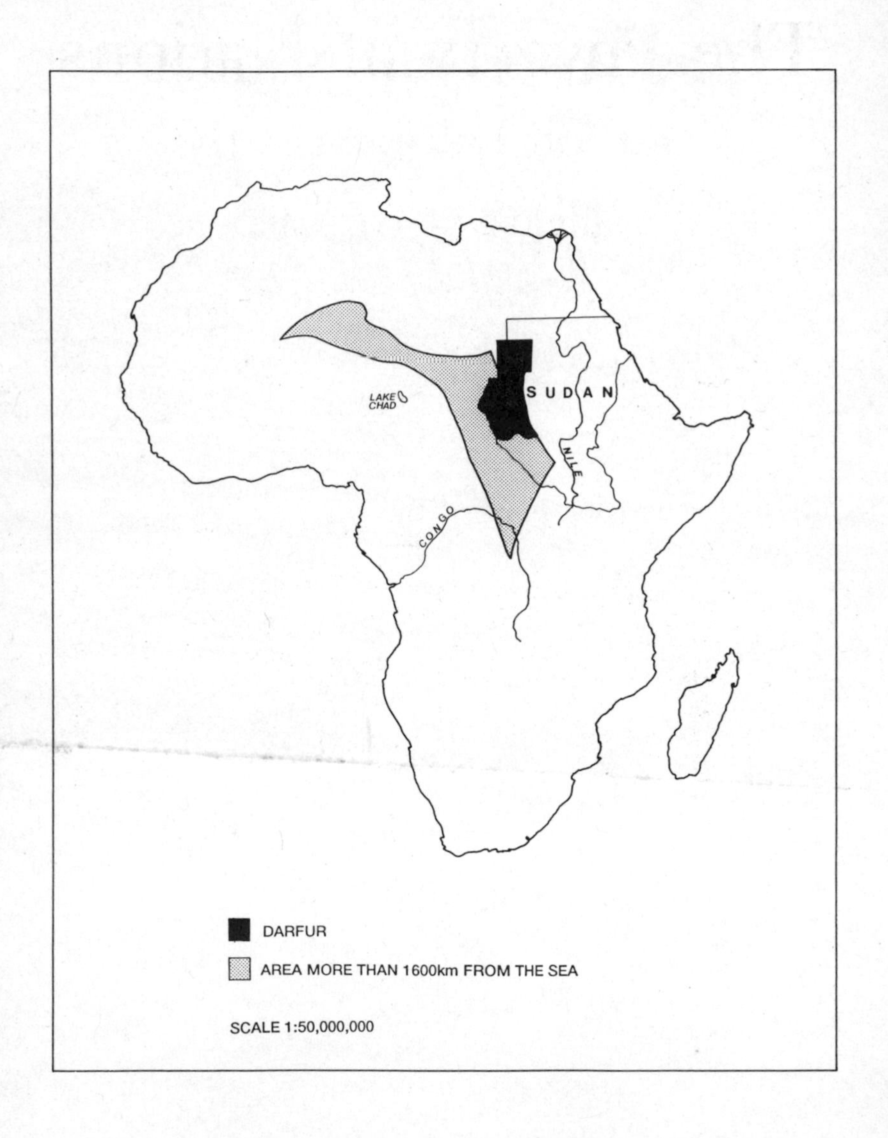
SUDAN
LAKE CHAD
NILE
CONGO
DARFUR
AREA MORE THAN 1600km FROM THE SEA
SCALE 1:50,000,000

The Poverty of Nations

The Aid Dilemma at the Heart of Africa

James Morton

I.B.TAURIS PUBLISHERS
LONDON · NEW YORK

This edition published in 1996 by
I.B.Tauris & Co. Ltd.
Victoria House
Bloomsbury Square
London WC1B 4DZ

In the United States of America
and Canada distributed by
St Martin's Press
175 Fifth Avenue
New York
NY 10010

A full CIP record for this book is available from the British Library

Library of Congress catalog card number 95–62319
A full CIP record is available from the Library of Congress

ISBN 1–86064–034–6

Phototypeset by Intype, London
Printed and bound in Great Britain by
WBC Ltd, Bridgend, Mid Glamorgan

CONTENTS

TABLES

FIGURES

ACKNOWLEDGEMENTS

This book has been many years in the making and many have contributed in one way or another. Perhaps the first foundation was laid when Sayyid Abdalla AbdulRahman, director-general of the Western Savannah Development Corporation, and Mr Stuart Marples of the World Bank agreed to allow me to spend some months in 1985 on a review of development in Darfur. If my conclusions now point in directions with which they would violently disagree, that does not mean I shall not always be grateful for that early encouragement. My thanks also go to Dr Babo Fadlallah and Sayyid Abdalla Yahya, director-general of the Western Savannah Development Corporation and of the Jebel Marra Rural Development Project respectively, for their permission to use data gathered while working for them.

I am especially grateful to all my colleagues in the Planning Monitoring and Evaluation Unit of the WSDC and the Monitoring and Evaluation Department of the JMRDP; above all to the enumerators, who worked long and hard collecting the data in circumstances that ranged from the difficult to the outright dangerous.

The work of my colleagues in Hunting Technical Services provides much of the background to my work and I must also thank them and the management of the company for their patience and encouragement.

Thanks go to Dr Paul Collier, Oxford University, Professor Alan Hoben, Boston University, Mr Peter Ayre, SOAS, and Mr Brian Kerr of the Commonwealth Secretariat, all of whom have provided guidance and information on important references. Brian Kerr, in particular, has supported this work for many years since its very inception and been a most patient friend and support.

Without the year spent at St Antony's College, Oxford, on a Mid-Career Fellowship, it is unlikely that the book would ever have been completed and I owe a considerable debt to the warden and members of the College as well as to the sponsors of the fellowship

The standard disclaimer of responsibility does not apply. All of the above share some of the blame, if only for not telling me that I was wasting my time. Professor Hoben is the honourable exception who did not spare his criticism of my excesses. The book is better where I have accepted his guidance and probably worse where I did not.

Last but far from least, my wife Áine has put up with the work through several long years. I know she will be heartily glad to see the back of it.

INTRODUCTION

> Experts are addicts. They solve nothing! They are servants of whatever system hires them. They perpetuate it ... When the world is destroyed it will be destroyed not by its madmen but by the sanity of its experts and the superior ignorance of its bureaucrats. (John Le Carré, *The Russia House*)

Despite three decades of ever-increasing aid, Africa is no better off now than it was at independence. Socially, economically and politically many nations have made little or no progress. The worst cases, Somalia, Liberia and Zaire to name but three, have gone backwards. There are many possible reasons for this. Africa has, perhaps, been unfortunate. There have been repeated droughts and the world economy has not been kind. Nevertheless, other parts of the developing world have suffered equally difficult times without being reduced to anything like the same degree.

This book is about the Darfur region of Sudan, but it is also about much more than that. It is about the way all parts of Africa have lost the economic momentum that they had at independence. It is about the way age-old problems of tribal and ethnic relations continue to dominate. And it is about the failure of western aid, western technology and western political ideas to provide answers to these questions. Above all, it is about the need to learn about an area, any area, in as many dimensions as possible before imposing the prescriptions of that modern, western world. Paradoxically, it is also about the fact that it will never be possible for outsiders to know enough and that it should not, in any case, be necessary to do so. Africans already know enough. What they are not getting are the opportunities to use their knowledge.

Darfur lies on the watershed between the Nile, the Congo and the Lake Chad basins. There is a small strip of Africa that is more than 1,600 kilometres from the sea in any direction. A large part of that strip runs through the west of Darfur. T-shirts in Khartoum describe Sudan as the heart of Africa but it is really Darfur which has the right to that title. The people of the region are typical of the many communities of small farmers and pastoralists throughout the continent, from the edges of the Sahara to the boundaries of South Africa. In this sense, too, they represent the heart of Africa. They are fighting to strike a balance between a difficult environment, a weak and increasingly unstable political framework and an economy that is inextricably linked to world markets even in an area as remote as this.

Sudan is so vast that even a region like Darfur is as big as France. It is home to some three and a half million people who make their living from farming and livestock. In 1985, as the scale and severity of the drought affecting western Sudan became apparent, there was a heightening of interest in this previously little-known area. This interest reached its peak in Band Aid and Live Aid, those great outpourings of western popular culture moved to offer assistance to peoples so much poorer than itself. Darfur, perhaps because it is the remotest and least known of all, received much of this attention. That interest has now slackened, just as the excitement generated by the Sahel drought of the late 1960s and early 1970s faded away. More recently, Darfur has been the scene of tribal fighting, complicated by the spillover of more serious conflicts from neighbouring Chad, and drought and famine seem never to be far away.

In the first half of the twentieth century, by contrast, Darfur saw relatively rapid economic growth and even limited political development. This book is an attempt to answer, for Darfur and by extension for Africa, the question: What went wrong?

'Aid' is the best shorthand for the international effort to transfer development from the First World to the Third. Aid is a political and cultural phenomenon. To justify its existence, it depends on a mythology, a cultural view of the world, at least as much as it does on a science which explains the way that world works. Nevertheless, aid is now one of the world's largest industries, so totally dominant that it sets the entire development agenda for the remotest regions. Even in Darfur, there is no longer any choice but to work within that agenda.

'Rural Development Tourism' has been a dirty word in the aid business for many years now. All those who hope to make a career in the Third World, be they from the First World or from the Third World themselves, know the importance of 'putting the last first'. But these well-sounding rules are just one example of a prevailing tendency to confuse process with product, to confuse knowledge with effect. The 'last' may well be more prominent in the intellectual debate than they used to be, but their ability to act and their material position remain unchanged. They may even be reduced because the more they are studied and discussed the more their lives become directed by external forces.

For all the money spent, the field studies carried out and the ink spilt on development, there remain many Third World countries which continue to make little or no progress. A significant proportion is clearly moving backwards. Why is this, if everybody knows the mistakes to avoid? Why is it, when the armoury of approved techniques grows ever larger: Social-Cost Benefit Analysis, Rapid Rural Appraisal, Bottom-up Approach, Structural Adjustment, Sustainability and so on and so on?

The conclusion is becoming inescapable that the problem lies not with the techniques of aid giving, not with the fact that individual practitioners do not do it properly, but rather with the concept of aid itself. This is why a comprehensive study of one region may throw light on the whole business of aid. Perhaps it is only from a full understanding of one particular area that it is, paradoxically, possible to see the world-wide view. It is only by following the aid network all the way down to its ultimate recipient that the irrelevance of much of what is done can be appreciated and the reasons for that irrelevance made clear. This approach risks the inevitable charge that Darfur and the Sudan are special cases. Those who dislike the message of this book will undoubtedly argue that its general conclusions are not valid for that reason. The benefits of seeing all sides of the question in the same context make the risk well worth taking.

Darfur, translated literally from the Arabic, means 'homeland of the Fur tribe'. The part of Sudan now known by this name includes more than that, although it covers areas which were all more or less subject to the 19th-century Fur sultanate. It ranges from the Sahara in the north to the dense savannah woodland of the south, where rainfall may reach 1,000 millimetres per annum. The 3.5 million people are ethnically diverse, of Hamitic, Arabic and Sudanic stock, and there are some 14 distinct languages; although only a few, apart from Arabic, are still widely spoken. Others have already disappeared.

As the sun and the Inter-Tropical Convergence Zone move north in the northern hemisphere summer they bring the rains to Darfur. There are three mains seasons. The *kharif*, or rainy season, starts sometimes as early as April and it extends through to October. Temperatures at first fall after the hot dry summer and then climb again as the rains taper off. Then comes the *Darat*, the time of the harvest. The cool dry winter season, *Shita*, lasts from December to February, after which temperatures climb to their peak in the summer, or *Sayf*.

Most rain falls in heavy storms with dry spells in between. This means that drainage is entirely different from that of more temperate areas. It is better to use the arabic word *wadi*, not the same as the word for river, to underline the fact that watercourses only flow for part of the year, in some cases for only a few days or even hours after rain. When they do flow, however, they are violent and the water carries a heavy load of silt. The violence and short duration of the wadi spates and their heavy silt loads, which can fill a dam in two years, mean that water storage for irrigation is rarely practical.

The wadis flow most strongly through the hilly areas. Once they reach the extensive flatlands they lose their force and spread out into ill-defined meanders. On both upland and lowland travel is very difficult during the rains. There are few roads, apart from a single stretch of tarmac between Nyala and Zalingei and a gravel road between Nyala and the capital El Fasher, but most areas can be reached by truck during the dry season. Nyala is the rail terminus of a line running to central Sudan but this line is weak and unreliable, especially during the rains.

Darfur's boundaries touch Libya in the north-west and Chad and the Central African Republic in the west. Historically, the region has tended to look northwards towards Egypt and westwards towards the states of the Saharan Sahel and the central African savannah rather than east to central Sudan. It was only after the Anglo-Egyptian conquest of the Sudan that the link with the east began to dominate and Darfur was the last region to be taken over, in 1916. 'Darfur as befits a child born as an afterthought to a large family has always had an identity very much her own' (Gillan, 1939).

The region forms a vast plain, between 2,000 and 3,000 feet above sea level, dominated by the Jebel Marra range of mountains in the west. This is the watershed between the Nile basin and the system draining towards Lake Chad. In the south, the boundary between Darfur and Bahr el Ghazal is marked by the Bahr el Arab, the most northerly watercourse draining into the White Nile. In the very south-west of the region the mountains containing the headwaters of the Bahr el Arab form the watershed between the Nile and Congo basins.

Darfur is, therefore, frontier territory. It lies on Sudan's boundaries with three other states. It also lies on the watershed between three of

Darfur

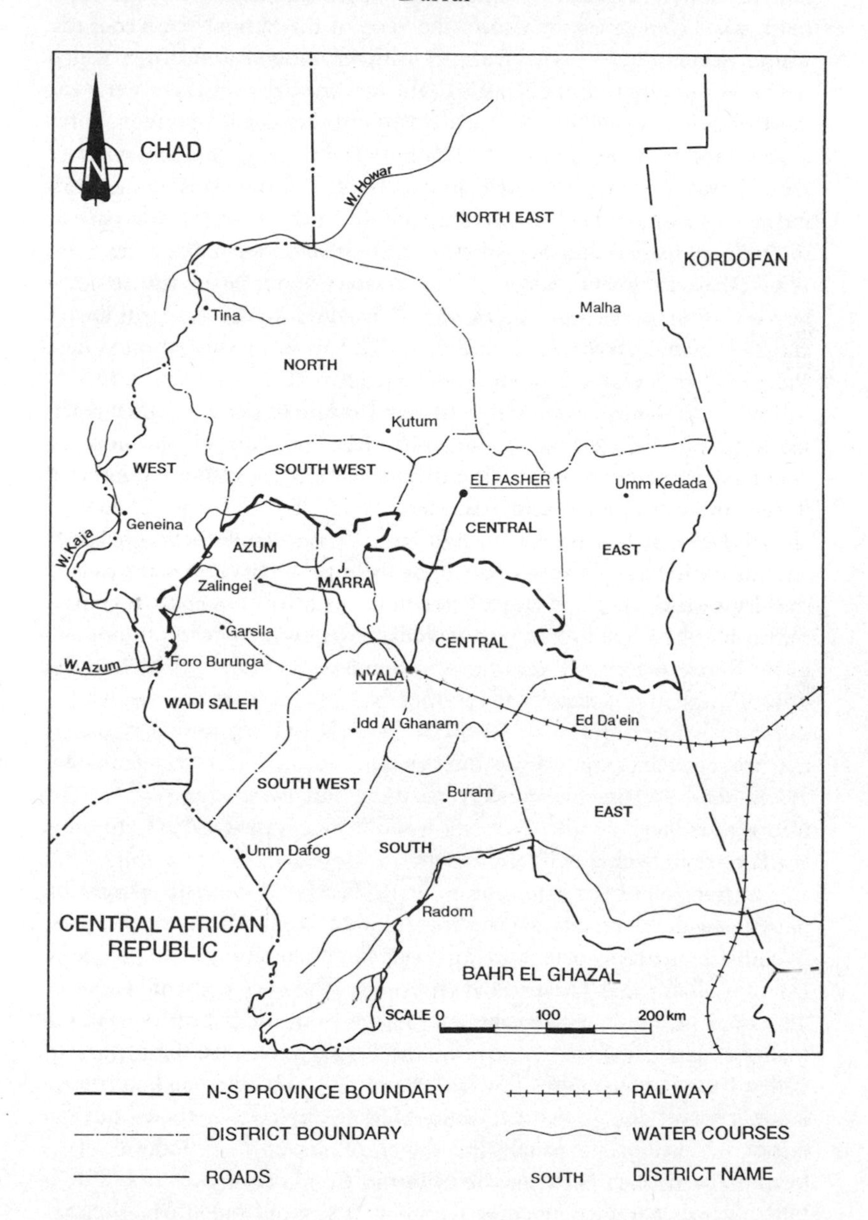

CHAD
N
W. Howar
NORTH EAST
KORDOFAN
Malha
Tina
NORTH
Kutum
WEST
SOUTH WEST
EL FASHER
Umm Kedada
Geneina
CENTRAL
W. Kaja
AZUM
EAST
J. MARRA
Zalingei
Garsila
CENTRAL
W. Azum
Foro Burunga
NYALA
WADI SALEH
Ed Da'ein
Idd Al Ghanam
SOUTH WEST
Buram
EAST
Umm Dafog
SOUTH
Radom
CENTRAL AFRICAN REPUBLIC
BAHR EL GHAZAL
SCALE 0 100 200 km
N-S PROVINCE BOUNDARY
RAILWAY
DISTRICT BOUNDARY
WATER COURSES
ROADS
SOUTH
DISTRICT NAME

Africa's largest drainage systems. The southern boundary of the region marks the divide between Muslim north Sudan and non-Muslim south. There is one other, special sense in which Darfur is frontier territory, the most important sense of all. It still lies on the frontier between the 'desert and the sown'; between the world of the nomad, who moves over a landscape with his animals and does not change it, and the world of the cultivator, whose activities inevitably lead to a permanent change in the shape of the land. Physically, this frontier lies at the edge of the furthest field which has been newly cleared from virgin forest.

In the Arab world, history is often seen in terms of the struggle between the desert and the sown. The sown is the land of towns, cultivators and, above all, civilization. The desert is just that: empty, barren and dangerous. The Sudanese word for the bush, the land outside the cultivated zone, is *khala*; literally emptiness or vacuum, which accurately reflects this feeling. It does not matter whether the *khala* is an arid sand waste or dense, uncleared bushland. It all counts as desert if it has not been brought under the hoe.

The fact that Darfur lies on this frontier has economic implications that are central to all development in the region. Because there is still bushland which could be cleared and cultivated, it is possible to increase production by extending the cultivated area. This is in contrast to much of the developing world, especially in South Asia, where production can only be raised by intensification: that is, by increasing the investment put into a fixed area of cultivated land. Of course, development by extension can only continue as long as there are unused reserves of land. When they are finished a shift to more intensive strategies will be essential. Following rapid population and income growth, there are some small signs of such a shift in Darfur.

The transition from extension to intensification is the central question of African development. According to what is known as the Boserup hypothesis, the transformation will happen automatically. The people of Darfur will adapt as circumstances change. The very roots of economic development, the hypothesis argues, spring from the population growth that stimulates this 'autonomous intensification'. The counter-argument is that 'autonomous intensification' cannot keep up with the high population growth rates of Africa. 'The relevant question in the context of Africa is whether the catalyzing factor of population is ahead of or behind the pace of farmer-based innovation' (Lele & Stone, 1989). If population is ahead, then farmers will be forced to push the extension process too far, or to intensify merely by reducing fallow periods. The consequences are soil exhaustion and poverty rather than intensification and development. The only solution, it is argued, is 'policy-led intensification'.

The whole justification of aid depends on which of these views is correct. If the farmers and livestock herders of Darfur are resourceful enough to help themselves, then aid may be able to offer them little. If, on the other hand, they cannot manage all the necessary technical, economic and social adjustments quickly enough, aid might have a major role to play in assisting them: to 'facilitate' the process, in the ugly jargon.

Superficially, the evidence from Darfur supports the latter view; drought, desertification and famine all seem to point to a failure of autonomous intensification. It is, nevertheless, incorrect. Where not constrained by external factors, the people have shown ample capacity to adapt rapidly to changing circumstances. Attempts at 'policy-led intensification' have been miserable failures by contrast and Darfur's current difficulties owe far more to misconceived and mismanaged policy than they do to an excess of population growth over the rate of intensification.

There are, however, two critical areas in which this laissez-faire conclusion does not hold, summed up in the words administration and supply. Much of the development seen by the Darfur economy in the mid-20th century depended on administrative improvements in security, public order and justice. Much of the decline in recent years has been accompanied by a deterioration in those same areas. While there are good grounds for believing that Darfur can make the most of its technical opportunities, there are few for believing that it can generate an internal solution to these problems. And some solution is essential to the Boserup transition, which can only happen if markets are free to operate, if different groups in the region can feel able to trust one another and if all are able to rely on the judiciary to resolve disputes promptly and evenhandedly.

Supply covers the provisions of necessary inputs for more intensive agriculture as well as consumer goods, in sufficient quantity and at attractive prices. It is those goods which will make it worth the farmer's while to grow cash crops more intensively. The whole range of price policies, export tax policies and so on can be summed up as a failure of supply. Transport and foreign exchange are two critical factors. Both administration and supply are inextricably linked with politics in Sudan. If 'autonomous intensification' has failed, it is because it has been blocked or stifled by a breakdown in the political arena, a breakdown that aid has spectacularly failed to tackle.

In a poor area there are hard decisions about what developments are affordable and sustainable. Long-term benefits such as soil conservation, reductions in desertification, income equality, sexual equality and even education may be beyond the capacity of the region to finance unless incomes rise. This conclusion need not be too pessimistic. Yes, there are dangers in intensified use of the land, for example, but the evidence that they have reached the scale of widespread desertification is extraordinarily thin, given the heat and emotion generated in discussion about it. Yes, more intensive use of capital increases the risks associated with market prices. On the other hand it may reduce the risks associated with erratic rainfall. Yes, more intensive use of capital may increase the risk of wealth inequalities, or of inequalities between the sexes. At present, however, Darfur society is in many ways both more open and more egalitarian than the societies of those who spend their efforts agonizing over these matters. Even with regard to education, it is far from self-evident that a lack of formally educated human capital has much to do with Darfur's problems. Sudan still has illiterate millionaires. More important, perhaps, is the fact that as much as two-thirds of the country's educated work-force has already emigrated. Education in Sudan runs a great risk of merely providing the key to the door marked Exit.

Technologies to increase production are essential to development and it is a short step to conclude that research is also essential. The widespread failure of research in Africa is usually assumed to mean that there is not enough of it or that it is being done wrong. Vast aid resources have been spent on this proposition. In Darfur, however, development is being blocked in the political and macro-economic arenas. The result is that there is no demand for the technologies research can produce, however much is spent on it and however well or badly it is done.

Even if the political barriers could be overcome, the capabilities of research should not be overestimated. A basic tenet of the aid myth is that western science can identify the perfect technology and that African farmers will not accept a technology that is less than perfect for their circumstances. Research has failed, it is argued, because it did not reach that perfection and just a little more fine-tuning will achieve it. This assumption is wholly wrong. Darfuris are capable managers of an extreme environment. Their agricultural techniques and their social organization are adapted to that environment. This adaptation retains a great deal of flexibility and there is no evidence whatsoever that 'tradition' forms an obstacle to development. Wherever a new technique, crop or market opportunity of genuine worth has appeared it has been adapted, mastered and exploited to the full. In other words, they can quickly perfect any reasonably strong technology for themselves.

Development work is hampered by preconceptions about what is 'appropriate', preconceptions that frequently lead to overhasty implementation. Mechanization without soils analysis, settlement without feasible crop rotations, credit schemes without knowledge of likely profitability, irrigation and animal traction without demonstrable economic feasibility, land conservation without attractive returns to the farmer are just some of the potential traps created by the pressure to implement a programme before a genuine opportunity has been identified. Aid is largely an attempt to buy time. Unfortunately, time is more important than money and research to gain a proper understanding of the technical side of crop and livestock production, let alone to generate improvements, is inevitably slow: especially so under erratic rainfed conditions. A caricature of a development project is one where the people are asked to make a substantial investment in protecting the environment for future generations by aid donors who at the same time demand demonstrable success and high rates of economic return in two to three years. All too many recent proposals for development in Darfur contain some elements of this caricature.

To make these points it will be necessary to range widely, from the technicalities of soil science to economic theory, from history to the current socio-economic situation. Every effort is made to make these comprehensible, but no apology is made for the fact that some work will be required of the reader. The myth is about finding the Holy Grail of instant, easy development: that grail to take the form of a global theory. This book is more about what Huxley defined as 'the great tragedy of science – the slaying of a beautiful hypothesis by an ugly fact.'

I should explain where I stand in the Aid Machine. For the last ten years I have been working as a consultant economist, principally as a member of technical assistance teams on integrated rural development projects. Prior to that I worked on a large rural resource survey in the Yemen Arab Republic. Six out of the ten years were spent in Darfur itself, but I have also worked in Bangladesh, Indonesia, Zimbabwe and the Gambia: enough to convince me that development projects and aid in general have many things in common, wherever they are and whatever is being attempted. All this means that I am one of a class that is currently least popular with the aid consensus: long-term expatriate technical assistance is widely regarded as both expensive and unproductive, a necessary evil at best.

I have worked both in line management and as adviser on projects that were being implemented by parastatal government bodies, My experience and, to a certain extent, my sympathies lie with another particularly unpopular group in the aid hierarchy of good and bad: lower-level government officials and the rural élite to which they are linked. Somewhat despairingly, I hope to persuade the reader that both these groups are more sinned against than sinning and, indeed, that allocation of blame is futile. There are far more fundamental problems. It is also futile to criticize many of the different development policies that have been proposed over the last 30 years. While some were undoubtedly flawed in one way or another, others that have since been discarded as failures were perfectly sound as far as they went. The cause of their failure lay elsewhere.

Using Robert Chambers's classification of the aid community between 'practitioners' and 'academics', I come on the low end of the 'practitioner' scale. At the top of that scale are the staff of the aid-giving organizations, whose primary concern is to 'move the money', in Tendler's phrase. Those like myself are required to make that money work on the ground. The gap between the aid-giving 'bureaucrats' and the field 'practitioner' is a chasm compared to that between the 'academics' and the 'bureaucrats'. Indeed, there are worrying signs that the bureaucrats have captured the academics, or possibly vice versa, to the exclusion of any field 'practice' at all.

A short speech from the accused. This book has a most presumptuous title. I mentioned it half in jest to my publisher and he has been embarrassing me with it ever since. But, on reflection, why not? It is also a presumptuous book that takes on a number of large, powerful targets. It might as well be hung for a sheep as a lamb; for there will almost certainly be a prosecution. The main charges will be that it is too damning, arrogant even, that a general case about aid cannot be based on the special case of Darfur, that inadequate credit is given to many others who have made the same points and that not enough attention is given to those who have refuted some of the arguments given here.

As for arrogant and damning, I have tried to tone it down but I cannot wholly eliminate the acid tone. If it conveys some of the frustration and disappointment that is part of the aid experience, then it is at least an honest reflection of that experience. It is undeniable that no general case can be wholly proven from the specific. But my own experience is considerably wider than just Darfur and through my colleagues' experience I know of similar patterns across a much greater area. I myself have no doubt that what I describe in Sudan is not significantly different from the general situation. I cannot prove it, but then it is not really susceptible to proof. Readers will have to make their own judgement.

There is, inevitably, a vast amount of work, both in support of my arguments and against, that I have not cited. Blame partly my publisher again, who still thinks this book is too long, and partly my lack of time to read it all. But is that really a valid criticism, anyway? If debate cannot progress until every single reference has been traced and cited, then it will never move at all. I nevertheless apologize to any I have unfairly ignored. They will no doubt let me know.

1· THE ROAD TO HELL

. . . Knowledge is as food, and needs no less,
Her Temperance over Appetite, to know
In measure what the mind may well contain,
Oppresses else with Surfeit, and soon turns
Wisdom to Folly, as Nourishment to Wind.

(Milton, *Paradise Lost*)

In the past critics of aid have rallied around such slogans as 'Aid as Imperialism'. They have revelled in the expense of the luxurious menus enjoyed by World Bank officials and in the moral inappropriateness of their flying first class. They have recounted every horror story of inefficiency. The aim here is quite different. It is to analyse why aid fails, in its own terms and despite the best of intentions. The analysis uses the same tools of standard neo-classical economics as the aid orthodoxy itself uses. It subscribes to broadly the same western liberal views as aid itself embodies. Analysis from this standpoint proves far more devastating and radical than attempts to seek a hidden agenda behind aid, to attribute its failures to its motives, or to pin its general failure on a multitude of specific inefficiencies. Aid is run by human beings who are no more and no less honest or competent than the general run. If they fail, it is time to consider whether it might not be because they are being asked to achieve the impossible.

There are four fundamental propositions to aid: that additional capital is a sufficient if not a necessary condition for accelerated development; that what I shall term control is not required; that research will identify a general answer to the problems of under-development; and lastly, that aid can act in two directions simultaneously, promoting equity as well as economic growth.

Capital

Aid's strategy for the 1990s is set out in the World Bank report *Sub-Saharan Africa: From Crisis to Sustainable Growth* (1989). Simplifying greatly, the report lays stress on investment in improving institutions and human capabilities in African nations. Where in the past funds were mainly directed to the productive sectors, it is now suggested that these are best financed by private investment while governments should, with the support of aid, concentrate on providing an 'enabling environment' and on 'investing in people'. What is termed 'Human Resource Development', principally health and education, should receive twice as much investment as any other sector of the economy. Since productive sector investment is to be mainly financed out of private funds, this means that the Human Resource Sector will get an even larger share of aid.

For aid, 'Intersectoral allocations are dominated by prior decisions about which sectors have especially urgent investment needs' (Toye in Emmerij, 1987: 30). In the beginning there was the industrialization and modernization approach. That was believed to have failed because insufficient attention was given to agriculture. So we moved on to the agriculture/integrated rural development approach. But that failed because macro-economic policy was bad. The cure for this was going to be Structural Adjustment. Which is now failing for lack of institutional and human capabilities. So now we are to have education, health and infrastructure. One wonders where the focus will shift next: back to industry? Although this summary is a caricature of a much more complex process, it helps to identify the idea that aid has only to find the right sector of the developing economy and, latterly, of the developing country's society as a whole, in order to pour resources into it and bring about development. It might be called the Key Sector Fallacy.

It is too soon to judge whether or not the human development sector will at last prove to be the right button for aid to push. It is not, however, too early to see what caused the failure of attempts in the sectors that were fashionable earlier. Was it because the work was being done in the wrong sector and because it was being done in the wrong way? In which case better directed and better managed efforts in the new, correct sector can be expected to succeed. Or was it because there is a problem with aid itself? In which case experience in the new key sector is likely to be drearily familiar.

It was Lord Bauer who first pointed out the tendency to see the developing countries' need for foreign capital aid as axiomatic, as a generally accepted truth which did not have to be discussed or analysed. Bauer argued that the experience of the First World, which had by definition developed without foreign aid, demonstrated that this axiom was false: that foreign aid was neither a necessary nor a sufficient condition for development (Bauer, 1976). This unpopular point of view was widely derided. It was argued, validly enough, that if development had occurred in the past without aid that merely demonstrated that it was not a necessary condition. It might still be a sufficient condition or even if not a sufficient it might be 'useful in facilitating' development.

Whatever the intellectual merits of the argument, aid clearly won it in the political arena and the volume of money has increased with every passing decade. Which means that there should now be ample evidence on which to settle the matter one way or another. Attempts to do so have been made. Books with titles like *Does Aid Work?* have made the 'basic finding that the majority of aid is successful in terms of its own objectives' (Cassen, 1986: 294). The more sceptical reader finds, however, that the evidence presented answers a rather different question, namely 'Can Aid Work?' Which, of course, it can, given all the right circumstances.

At the macro-economic level there have been many attempts to show, by comparing one country with another, that more aid generates better performance. These have rarely done more than establish an absence of unimpeachable negative data, which is frequently taken as proof of the positive case. It would be just as valid to argue the negative case from an equal lack of unimpeachable positive data. The strongest possible positive statement seems to be that 'although one would be happier if international statistical analyses did show a stronger relationship between aid and growth, one should not conclude from the absence of a strong statistical relationship that aid is not contributing to growth' (Cassen, 1986: 298).

An equally large body of evidence is that provided by the detailed evaluations which the aid donors carry out on their own projects. There is a conflict of interest in the fact that the donors are to some extent evaluating their own performance. Nevertheless, a great deal of effort produces reports that are far from uncritical. From those reports the World Bank, for example, judges that 70 per cent of its projects in Africa, which performs far below the rest of the world, are 'satisfactory'. Even the unsatisfactory ones are not necessarily outright failures. On the other hand, only 32 per cent are classified as 'likely' to be sustainable (World Bank, 1990). This might be considered quite a reasonable performance. Africa will never be an easy place to work in, after all. There remains, however, one major difficulty. All those apparently successful projects should add up to a considerable boost to the economies of the African nations. Why has the sum of all projects proved so negative when the majority are individually positive?

Another, quite ubiquitous, approach is to argue that aid is a learning process: 'We must resist the tendency to say we have tried everything and almost everything has failed. The slogan must be turned into "We have tried everything and almost nothing has failed completely." There is something to be learned from all experiences not excluding those based on socialism' (Emmerij, 1987). What these Panglossian statements do not address is the question of when some useful judgement will be allowed. Clearly, if we are always to focus on the far horizon of possibility, then a solid factual conclusion will never be drawn. Given that the current strategy for Africa does not see a significant reduction in aid requirements until AD 2010 at the earliest, one might be forgiven for feeling that the horizon is disappearing into the future.

The last approach is to argue that some successful countries have received aid and that their success is therefore attributable to aid. Korea is a favourite example. The dangers of comparisons between Korea and Africa are obvious, however. 'S. Korea is not a model that can be emulated by other nations but it has been a model user of foreign assistance' (Cassen, 1986: 357).

And yet there is one piece of evidence, evidence that does not seem open to the slightest doubt, that clearly shows that aid does not work; or at the very least has not worked in one very large area over a considerable period: 'Africans are almost as poor today as they were 30 years ago' (World Bank, 1989: Introduction). This means that some Africans are far poorer than they were 30 years ago, despite per capita aid receipts substantially greater than anywhere else in the world: $13.7 per capita in 1980 compared with $9.6 for all Less Developed Countries (World Bank, 1981: 121).

None of these attempts to measure whether aid is working addresses a central problem: the 'inescapable though largely unrecognised dilemma. If all conditions for development other than capital are present, capital will soon be generated locally, or will be available from abroad commercially' (Bauer, 1976: 97). In other words, aid will only be needed when it is likely to be useless because of other constraints. What this means is that there is a very narrow window between those countries whose strengths are such that aid is unlikely to make more than a marginal improvement in their performance, which would have been good anyway, and those countries which are too weak to make any effective use of aid. If anything that window is growing narrower as the Newly Industrializing Countries graduate beyond the 'need for aid' and the sub-Saharan African countries make equally rapid progress in the reverse direction.

Yet the volume of aid just grows and grows without regard for its chances of being put to productive use. Because it is impossible to be certain where countries stand in relation to this window, attempts to determine whether aid is working at the general level are almost bound to fail. Hence this book and its attempt to work from the particular.

The World Bank is the dominant intellectual force in the aid arena. It presents by far the best case for what is being done. In the text of its 1989 report, the Bank gives a detailed and frank account of the problems of development in Africa. It is, for example, admitted for the first time that 'half of the completed rural development projects financed by the World Bank in Africa had failed' (World Bank, 1989: Ch 1). That frankness does not however extend to a discussion of the fundamental justification of aid or the problems of such a justification. As a result the prescription for a cure is not nearly so thorough as the diagnosis. To continue the metaphor, the basic medicine remains unchanged. That medicine is capital, for which the dosage is determined not by any detailed knowledge of the likely actual effect but only by rough estimates derived by taking the desired effect as axiomatic: by the use of ' "global target rates of growth in GNP" from which the assistance required is deduced' (Tendler, 1975: 91).

The World Bank report presents the case for continued massive aid flows to Africa lasting until AD 2010. It calls for Official Development Assistance (ODA) to grow at 4 per cent per annum throughout the 1990s to a target of $22 billion in the year 2000 (World Bank, 1989: Ch 8). The rich countries can find these sums quite easily. They are, however, quite overwhelming in the context that matters, in relation to the economies of the poor countries that get the money. They would be equal to 9 per cent of Gross National Product for those recipient countries. This means that aid is sometimes equivalent to or even greater than both total government expenditure and domestic investment. For many sub-Saharan African countries, aid in the early 1980s ran at 20 per cent of GNP (Cassen, 1986: 23). In 1991, rumour had it that aid was over 50 per cent of the Gambia's GNP, but then the Gambia is a small country. In 1982, net ODA was greater than 100 per cent of gross domestic investment in 5 out of 38 sub-Saharan African countries and greater than 50 per cent of government expenditure in 7 out of the 28 for which figures were available (World Bank, 1984: Statistical Annex).

The new emphasis is on policy reform and institution building: Human Resource Development. The 1989 report admits, 'These activities are not resource intensive, but neither can generate a supply response without costly supportive infrastructure – social and physical.' That afterthought of a 'but' is the only logical link provided to explain the apparent inconsistency between a strategy that is 'not resource intensive' and a recommendation that vastly greater resources be supplied. No attempt is made to cost the new strategy directly. Instead the volume of funds required is calculated using extremely simple assumptions, with a model which is determined by its target: an economic growth rate of 4 to 5 per cent per annum. This growth rate is determined in its turn by the high African rate of population growth and an assumed minimum requirement for per capita income growth of 1.5 per cent per annum.

Once the target has been set in this way the aid requirement is calculated using two factors: the level of domestic savings and the Incremental Capital Output Ratio (ICOR). The ICOR measures how much capital is needed to generate one extra unit of output. It therefore determines how much investment is needed to generate the target increase in output. Once that is decided, aid is used to finance the difference between that target investment and the investment that domestic savings can finance. The ICOR is itself decided by the efficiency of use of capital. If efficiency is low then growth will be low even when investment is high.

The figures on which the World Bank based their 'Strategy for the 1990s' are as follows. The 'Net Transfers' figure is what determines the requirement for foreign capital. Not all of this has to be aid. Some could be commercial loans, but it may be assumed that for Africa the bulk will be aid in some shape or form.

Table 1.1: Modelling Africa's aid requirements

	Actual		Projected	
	1975–80	1986–87	1990	2000
GDP GROWTH				
Per cent p.a.	2.8	0.8	2.5	5.0
INVESTMENT				
Percentage of GDP	21.4	15.1	17.0	25.0
of which				
Domestic saving	19.6	11.8	12.0	18.0
Adjustment	–3.0	–2.9	–3.0	–2.0
Net transfers	4.8	6.2	8.0	9.0
EFFICIENCY				
Return on investment (%)	13.0	5.0	15.0	20.0

Source: World Bank, 1989: Ch 8

Some would argue that these global calculations should not be taken too seriously: they are only budget figures, after all. That is naïve. As any bureaucrat knows, once a budget is agreed there is only one imperative, to make sure it is spent. What started life as 'merely a global estimate', soon becomes a hard, dominant political fact.

These figures highlight a general feature of aid economics; one that is repeated at every level from the smallest project up to this continental analysis. And that is a determined refusal to face up to the realities of what the data is saying; because to do so would mean acknowledging that the desired goals are not achievable. Assumptions are therefore determined by requirements, not by evidence. Incremental output in Africa dropped from 31 per cent of investment in the 1960s to below 5 per cent in the 1980s. 'The low return on investment is the main reason for Africa's recent decline' (World Bank, 1989: Introduction). A glance at the figures for Efficiency of Investment in the model shows that these facts have been completely ignored. Instead it is assumed that a measure that has been in free-fall decline between 1980 and 1987 can be reversed so rapidly between 1987 and 1990 that it will not merely return to its 1980 level but even exceed it. Is this likely? Surely not, but it is necessary to assume it to make the model work at all.

Investment, by definition, represents additional capital. The concepts of return on investment and ICOR say nothing about what happens to returns on existing capital stocks, that is to say on capital that has been built up by investment in the past. Although it does not affect the argument here, it is very important to note that problems in Africa are so severe that declining returns to existing capital are probably far more significant than low returns to new capital, to investment. Sudan, where major national assets such as the Gezira irrigation scheme have been decaying rapidly, is a particularly clear example of this.

The World Bank approach addresses the question of efficiency more by implication than as a clear strategy. Policy reform and institutions, research and human resource development are, all of them, measures designed to raise efficiency and hence returns to capital. The new strategy may therefore be seen as a redirection of aid from the productive sectors to the supporting sectors, to what may be termed a 'technical-change sector'. It is argued, in effect, that low returns on investments in the productive sectors are the result of inadequate investment in research, human development and infrastructure.

The fact is, however, that these new sectors have been far from neglected in the past. The previous World Bank strategy document, with its equally ringing title, *Accelerated Development in Sub-Saharan*

Africa – An Agenda for Action (1981), devoted a whole chapter to Human Resources and even then acknowledged that education was already receiving between 25 and 35 per cent of total recurrent expenditure in Africa, more than any other single item. How much more priority can be given?

The economics of health and education are complex, but there is supposed to be much technical evidence that education in particular has a high rate of return. This evidence is difficult to match with the general picture. There has, for one thing, already been considerable progress since independence in health, education and infrastructure, at least as far as coverage is concerned. Primary school enrolment in 1978 was 'only 63% for the region as a whole'. Life expectancy rose from 39 to 47 between independence and the late 1970s. As far as infrastructure is concerned, 'post independence Africa was "opened up" with extraordinary speed' (World Bank, 1981: 14ff). Despite that 'only' on primary school enrolments, it is quite clear that all the elements of the latest World Bank strategy received very considerable investment in earlier years, however acute their more recent decline. If African economies failed to grow despite these earlier investments in Human Resource Development, one can hardly feel confident that a new wave of health, education and infrastructure programmes will meet their expectations.

The widespread existence of 'open unemployment, especially of educated youth', and the fact that tens of thousands of well-educated Nigerians, Sudanese and many other nationalities are already employed overseas and unlikely to return for the foreseeable future cast further doubt on the likely benefits of yet more education (World Bank, 1989: Ch 2). Some argue that this is just because there has been too much secondary and, especially, university education and not enough primary. That certainly appears to be the pattern in Sudan (ILO, 1987). However, this observation is misleading. Secondary and university education are both of them licences to emigrate to the Arab oil states, which makes them highly profitable to the individual graduate and even to the Sudanese economy as a whole. The economic benefits of primary education in the highly constrained domestic economy are minute by comparison. Here for the first time is a theme that will return again and again; that it is the constraints on the domestic economy as a whole that matter, not the correctness of any particular sectoral allocation or any particular management technique.

It is, of course, argued that the problem with previous attempts to strengthen the human development sector was quality. Now, 'the pursuit of excellence must be ruthless.' Greater recurrent funds are also to be provided because poor quality is believed to have arisen from the lack of adequate materials. And, just as investment is being redirected from the productive sectors to the human resource sector, so it is to be redirected within that sector: from higher education to primary and from sophisticated medicine to primary health care. Nevertheless, the strategy remains the same in one crucial sense for all the various 'reorientations'. It involves the injection of additional resources, either as capital or as recurrent expenditure that is 'capital-like in its effect' (World Bank, 1989: Ch 8). Similar arguments apply to infrastructure. The very fact that the bulk of the recommended new funding for infrastructure is destined for maintenance and rehabilitation highlights the fact that infrastructural problems cannot be attributed to inadequate investment in earlier years, but rather to poor returns on earlier investments. The new strategy depends therefore on a hope that greater recurrent cost funding will improve performance instead of merely subsidizing continued poor performance; a hope that is not backed by any logical mechanism to explain how it will be realized.

A brief, over-simplified discussion of development theory provides a framework. It has long been established that economic growth is not just a matter of capital investment, 'scarcely half of the increase in America's productivity per capita and in real wages can be accounted for by the increase in capital itself. More than half of the increase in productivity is a 'residual' that seems to be attributable to technical change – to scientific and engineering advance, to industrial improvements, and to 'know-how' of management methods and educational training of labor' (Solow, quoted in Samuelson, 1976). Almost from the day Solow first identified it, economists have been locked in debate about whether the residual exists and, if it does, what it really is and what causes it. Continuing to simplify brutally, some say that it does not exist but merely represents the secondary effects of capital investment. One man's investment provides a market for the next and so on (Scott, 1989). Many others lay emphasis, much as Solow does, on research and education, in essence investment in human capital.

Liebenstein took a different line, drawing a distinction between Allocative Efficiency and what he termed X-Efficiency. Allocative efficiency meant the ideal situation of neo-classical economics, the result of perfect competition in an undistorted market. Liebenstein discovered that the effect of market distortions was quite small and sought an alternative explanation for why some countries experienced economic growth and some did not. He found the answer in motivation: 'people and organizations normally work neither as hard nor as effectively as they could' . . . 'responses to [competitive pressure and other motivational factors], whether in the nature of effort, search, or the utilization of new information is a significant part of the residual in economic growth' (Liebenstein, 1966). Perhaps it should be emphasized, lest any should doubt it, that he was referring to the most developed parts of the First World, to a common feature of all human nature, not to some special problem of the Third World.

X-efficiency is the potential for doing the job better that human idleness normally ignores but which can be called forth fairly readily if the incentives are there. It is particularly important to note that new ideas or technologies, developed by research or transferred by teaching, are not the issue. 'The knowledge may have been there already and a change in circumstances induced the change in technique. Motivational aspects are involved *entirely apart from additional knowledge*.' (My italics.) And even research is a matter of motivation, of that 'external motivational efficiency' which competition for markets provides. Up to two-thirds of all research work done by commercial firms in the USA was shown to be 'passive, forced on firms for defensive purposes'. In other words, two-thirds of innovations would not occur without competitive pressure. Management is another key component in X-efficiency. Standard microeconomics assumes that individual firms are rational and efficient and this is why free, competitive markets lead to the best situation through allocative efficiency. In fact firms are only as rational and efficient as their managers and that in turn depends largely on how much they are paid, their motivation (Liebenstein, 1966).

Aid rejects the idea of X-efficiency. When African economies are recommended by their western mentors to adopt free market policies, the emphasis is on allocative efficiency and on the distortions in the market. Resources are poured into research and education because 'external motivational efficiency' is not expected to be forthcoming. Most importantly of all, however, the need to motivate a managerial class is never accepted because of aid's deep ambivalence about the élite. On the one hand the strategy depends on such people: to improve standards in the political and bureaucratic arenas, to generate the new small firms in the commercial sector and so on. On the other hand the same class is to take the full burden of generating the domestic savings needed to support the strategy. As far as possible, aid is to be targeted at the poorest groups and to bypass the élite. If X-efficiency is the major source of technical and institutional change and if management is the greatest part of X-efficiency, which is likely, then the deeply disincentive effect aid has on the élite may be the largest single factor behind the poor performance of the heavily aid-dependent countries. This disincentive combines a lack of both competitive and other disciplines with an absence of attractive rewards.

There are three ways to explain what has gone wrong. One is the key sector fallacy, which says simply that aid has been directed at the wrong targets: first at industry and then at agriculture, instead of at the technical-change sector. Another idea, given much attention in the literature, is that aid is applied in the wrong way: top-down instead of bottom-up is a typical diagnosis of this type. The third possibility is rarely considered: that the sheer volume of capital aid causes its own failure. This possibility looks very real in the Sudan.

'Asymmetry' is a frequent feature; what aid prescribes for the developing countries is very different from the practice of developed countries. 'Asymmetric liberalism' over trade is the most obvious case; the fact that developing country exports are $512 billion (1980 figures) while aid is only $38 billion means that a relatively minor reduction in First World protectionism would almost certainly give more to developing countries than the total value of aid (Cassen, 1986: 257). And yet the aid prescription consists of more money and liberalization for the Third World with little more than promises of liberalization in the First World.

More insidious, however, are the myriad other asymmetries that appear, especially in theoretical areas. Despite, for example, the evident strengthening of the case for liberal, market-led economics in the First World, especially following the collapse of the communist economies, there remain strong elements of central planning and control in the aid prescription. The literature is littered with appeals for less *dirigisme*, for a grass-roots approach, but these are at least balanced by demands for greater co-ordination, for 'policy dialogue' and so on.

As far as capital is concerned the asymmetry lies in a failure to recognize that changes in the way economists understand First World economies have enormous implications for the Third World as well. This is partly because of the tendency to look for a separate economics of developing countries, but it is also because it weakens the whole concept of aid. If there is one simple theme to be drawn from modern First World economics it is the recognition that governments' power to move economies is quite strongly limited. The early post-war belief that Keynesian economics could control unemployment using fiscal and monetary tools is the most obvious example. Nowadays it is widely accepted that this is not true, beyond narrow limits, because there is such a thing as the Non-Accelerating Inflation Rate of Unemployment, or NAIRU. In other words, attempts to stimulate the economy lead to inflation, not employment.

Development economics has so far ignored what this may mean in the Third World, despite the fact that aid is no more than an attempt to stimulate developing economies. Given the severe problems in many major aid-recipient economies, the possibility of relatively rigid limits to what can be achieved, analogous to the NAIRU, seems strong. I would propose a simple paraphrase: the Non-Accelerating Inefficiency Rate of Investment, or NAIRI.

If correct, this concept offers enormous problems because it implies that accelerated growth, the fundamental goal of aid, cannot be achieved outside narrow limits. Yet the evidence that some such mechanism is at work in Africa seems quite compelling. Growth has not occurred and, by all accounts, inefficiency is now a widespread and deep-rooted problem. If there is such a thing as a NAIRI, then the possibility that failure springs from the sheer volume of funds supplied becomes a reality. Too much aid leads directly to inefficiency and not to growth.

Is there any more direct evidence that excessive volumes of aid are a problem? There is, in fact, rather a lot, although it is rarely interpreted as such. Tendler, writing in 1975, identified what she called the Abundance of Development Assistance: 'It appears to anyone who has spent much time in a development assistance organisation as if aid funds were abundant.' However, her explanation is that this reflects not a lack of worthwhile uses for development assistance, but rather the weakness of recipient governments who are 'not institutionally equipped to produce the kind of bureaucratic output required' to generate worthwhile projects. The result has been that the aid donors have been sucked in to generating projects for themselves.

Tendler was also one of the first to identify the fact that aid abundance led aid bureaucracies to give priority to 'moving money', instead of making sure that it was only spent on worthwhile projects. Many have commented on how damaging this 'fund channelling effect' is to the quality of the projects that are funded (Cassen, 1986: 309). 'I believe that the integrity of the World Bank's project analysis suffered as a result of Mr MacNamara's drive to increase the volume of lending' (Little in Emmerij, 1987: 47). If there was one single factor behind my determination to write this book it is personal experience of the way project proposals are rated as good or bad solely by their size, of the way the scale of investment in a given project is determined in advance of any economic analysis and of the way projects themselves are rated good or bad, depending on whether or not they spend the money. Last, but far from least, there is the way project staff become overwhelmed by demands not merely to spend the money originally allocated but to expand and take up more and more new activities, in order to use extra funds that donors have been unable to dispose of as they had originally planned. Throughout the developing world there are good little projects, some of them begun without any donor assistance at all, that have been kidnapped by aid and inflated into bad large projects by the pressure to expand at a pace far beyond any reasonable expectation. In the words of an old joke, 'never mind the quality, feel the width' is a guiding rule of aid.

Even outside aid, capital may be abundant. There is strong evidence from Sudan that a country which is, on official statistics, desperately in need of capital aid and which has run up massive public debts as a result, has an 'underground economy' of such strength that the private sector has saved more than the total of that debt. That underground economy was driven by remittances from the Gulf states. Because of the disincentive effect of grossly distorted policies the majority of that private saving has disappeared in capital flight. The outflow of private capital is so great that the Sudanese pound is under constant pressure to devalue. In other words, capital is so abundant, relative to the likely chances of profitable investment, that the private sector is not merely failing to invest but it is actually disinvesting so fast that large quantities of aid-financed capital imports cannot balance it and sustain the currency. The reasons for this extraordinary situation are discussed in Chapter 5.

Another strong indication that capital is abundant is the fact that African banking systems are typically highly liquid. That is to say that African banks hold liquid assets far above the levels required by statute or by banking prudence. In some countries this may be as much as 60 per cent of bank liabilities. Since the return on these liquid assets is low this means that the banks cannot pay their depositors well and, indeed, that they are not interested in attracting deposits. In the Gambia, commercial banks actually ration deposits. At times they even refuse to accept deposits into any interest-bearing accounts. The result is a system where the banks borrow short and lend short. Growth in the banking system is slow or non-existent. Just as Tendler had to put forward a rather complicated theory of 'organizational dynamics' to explain why development agencies were 'capital abundant' when developing economies are, by the aid definition, capital poor, so studies of the African banking system, working to the same definition, have to find complicated reasons to explain this excess liquidity. Riskiness in commodity-based economies is one such idea.

If, on the other hand, the aid axiom is abandoned and it is accepted that capital is, in fact, genuinely abundant, then all of the features that seem anomalous are simply and logically explained. Since capital abundance in this sense merely means that too much money is chasing too few profitable projects, something that seems all too evident to a fieldworker, this should not be so difficult to accept. Occam's Razor, which states that a simple theory is better than a complicated one, would certainly give it the edge.

The conclusion, that the sheer volume of aid is the problem not the cure, strikes at the very basis of aid. Yet the strength of the push to ever greater volumes of aid is extremely strong. Almost every report or study concludes that more aid is required. If unrealistic assumptions are necessary, for example, they will always fall on the side of more aid, not less. Look back at the World Bank model, and notice that the assumptions about Domestic Saving are as unambitious as those for Efficiency of Investment are unrealistic. Savings are assumed not to change at all between 1987 and 1990. A relatively minor assumed improvement in savings, say only one-sixth, would reduce the aid requirement by a quarter. This seems far more likely than the assumed 200 per cent increase in Efficiency of Investment, especially in the light of the evidence from Sudan. It is also more logical, since improvements in the Efficiency of Investment and in the return to capital should stimulate greater savings. Given the difficulties that aid has in making good investments, it also seems far more likely that domestically-financed investments will be efficient and help to raise the overall efficiency. Since, however, these arguments do not help the case for more aid, they are not explored. Further proof of Bauer's theorem: that the need for as much aid as possible is taken as axiomatic. Alternatives are not considered.

Control

No nation, however materially wealthy, would consider itself developed while it remained subject to outside direction. This is especially true for the many developing countries which owe their existence to their escape from colonialism. The result is the second axiom of aid; that it is not appropriate for donors to control how aid funds are used. If projects are to be implemented or policies are to be reformed and institutions created, control must remain in the local government's hands. If research is to be carried out or education strengthened, it must be done by local researchers and teachers, and so on. Foreign involvement beyond a preliminary stage is not acceptable. There are strong pressures to reduce the length of any such preliminary stages. National sovereignty is the battlecry of control

In many ways aid has been formed by the tug-of-war over control that has resulted. As each wave of aid has failed, so the donors have added more 'conditions' in the attempt to improve the next. What they cannot do is take direct control to ensure that the conditions are met. On the other side, national governments apply increasing political pressure for greater independence by, for example, demanding the removal of expatriate technical assistants, part of whose function, as they quite correctly perceive, is to monitor their performance on behalf of the donors.

Many of the normal, straightforward mechanisms for maintaining discipline and promoting efficiency in the use of aid – management for lack of a better word – are abdicated. The most important of these are profit-and-loss accounting and incentives. Aid projects are mostly carried on government budgets and financial targets are not set. Staff are paid on government pay scales. They are frequently given incentives to join an aid project, but there are neither rewards for good performance nor sanctions for poor once they have joined. In the absence of management accounting criteria, performance can only be measured subjectively anyway. Instead of these more simple forms of management, aid has had to develop its own elaborate apparatus of monitoring and evaluation techniques based around Social-Cost Benefit Analysis.

Ostensibly these techniques are better because they measure the true welfare value of a project, not just the simple financial worth. In reality, they represent a politically acceptable compromise over control. For donors to insist on direct supervision of management and accounts would not be acceptable, but their right to an interest in the welfare impact of the money they give cannot be denied. In any case, there is far less loss of face in allowing expatriate involvement in an obscure and complex topic like Social-Cost Benefit Analysis than there would be in management and accounts. The struggle between donor and recipient over these issues is continuous. In some cases donors gain considerable control, in others they are lucky even to know where the money has gone.

The dilemma this compromise creates is well illustrated in the history of Structural Adjustment lending to Africa. This approach, which came to the fore in the early 1980s, involved a decision on the part of the donors that aid was bound to fail until serious policy problems were resolved. Those problems lay at the root of the widespread inefficiency and it was only by a process of policy dialogue between donors and recipients, with more or less open recognition that the latter would have to make policy adjustments, that progress could be made. 'Conditionality', whereby aid was made explicitly dependent on recipient reforms, became such a central plank of the strategy that it was sometimes argued that the primary benefit of aid lay not in its financial value but in its ability to persuade governments to reform, in effect as a bribe: 'the resource transfer role of the Bank becomes the vehicle for institutional strengthening' was the polite way of putting it (Cassen, 1986: 202).

The 1989 World Bank document shows the reaction to the early phases of Structural Adjustment, when donors were felt to have overstepped the mark in imposing conditions on recipient governments. It also recognizes the possibility of aid having 'negative, as well as positive, effects, not the least of which is enabling hard decisions to be postponed'. What the Bank is unable to do is propose an alternative to conditionality, beyond some unconvincing calls to 'set a good example' and such-like. The basic problem remains. Aid does not appear to be working, but direct control that would allow First World representatives to try and do better is politically unacceptable.

The resulting strategy is deeply inconsistent. On the one hand it states that 'Africa's future can only be decided by Africans. External agencies can play at most a supportive role.' On the other hand, remarks like 'the willingness of the donor community to tolerate impropriety aggravates the malaise of corruption' can only imply that donors have the right to intervene at some level. Similarly, calls for early and rapid reductions in expatriate technical assistance are not consistent with the requirement that recipient governments become more actively involved in policy dialogue, in planning and co-ordination, in economic analysis and in many other technical areas. It is not explained how an area of evident weakness is suddenly to become strong when the only apparent means of creating strength, the provision of technical assistance, is to be dispensed with.

The level at which donors may intervene is crucial, as is the mechanism by which they are to do so. How, for example, is a donor to know when impropriety has occurred? It is only by maintaining a parallel accounting system that it can be sure to know and that is rarely permitted. And if impropriety is identified, what sanction does the donor have? There is only one and that is to cut off the money. Most donors are incapable of such an action because it would mean that all aid stops. Aid cannot defend itself except by destroying itself, which is not acceptable to the donors' own First World constituency except in the most extreme circumstances.

Furthermore, corruption and outright impropriety are only a small part of the efficiency problem. Sheer waste and failure to achieve the targets set are far more widespread and still less amenable to politically acceptable donor control. Most important of all is the lack of pressure towards X-efficiency. There are many well-run projects which fail for perfectly honourable reasons. Almost all aid project plans call for performance above the norm: they are bound to since the aim of the exercise is an improvement. Nevertheless, the donor can hardly impose sanctions on a management that fails to perform above that norm.

The strength of the pressure against control may be seen in a tendency to move aid away from areas where simple financial management tools might be used to promote efficiency. What is called programme aid, where large sums are allocated to broad sectors of the economy rather than to planned projects, is increasingly popular as is the Human Resource sector. Performance under programme aid and in health, education and infrastructure is not nearly so easy to measure as on projects in the productive sectors. It would be too cynical to suggest that such a shift reflects a conscious policy. Nevertheless, the need to prevent embarrassment and maintain a consensus can have the same result; an avoidance of areas where failure is easy to see and a preference for others, not because they are any more productive but because they are less simple to evaluate and hence less likely to present obvious failure.

What then are the aid donors to do? Recipient governments are not capable of generating enough worthwhile projects to use all the money the donors want to provide. Those projects that do get started do not produce satisfactory results. Yet direct donor involvement is by definition forbidden. The only sanction available, to stop the flow of aid funds, is severely undermined by the difficulties donor agencies would have in winning approval for such action at home. It is virtually useless as a result. Aid has never been cut off for reasons of even the most abject inefficiency. Decisions to cut the flow of funds are almost always taken for overtly political reasons, never because the funds themselves are being misused.

This dilemma has led the aid community into ever more complex attempts at indirect control. Using Tendler's terms, many of the changes in the way donor organizations act reflect attempts to 'gain control of uncertain task environments' (Tendler, 1975: 103). For example, donors originally did not wish to be involved in project preparation because that would bias their judgement over whether to finance a project or not. In the end, however, they had to undertake preparation, otherwise there were simply never enough projects. 'Another contingency-reducing action was the IBRD's strong emphasis on autonomous agencies.' For many years the World Bank insisted on the establishment of corporations to implement its projects. The idea was that the corporation would be able to operate more efficiently with a degree of autonomy from the rest of a weak government service, but it was not incidental that this gave the Bank a separate, smaller institution with which it could negotiate more directly and more forcefully and so retain a greater degree of control. The implications of this policy became most obvious when Bank representatives were seen negotiating with national governments on behalf of corporations that belonged to that same government.

Even with autonomous corporations project aid remained bedevilled by complexity and failure, hence the shift to the simpler form of programme aid. This greatly eased the control problem for the donors. Targets were largely reduced to the spending of money. It was no longer necessary to worry about performance at all. Another recent donor fashion, for support to and through Non-Governmental Organizations (NGOs), also allows a control that bypasses the national government. In this sense the NGOs are no different from the corporations. The widespread and increasing resentment felt towards NGOs reflects the national governments' awareness of what this implies. In his recent promise of massive aid to Russia, President Clinton called for it to be 'not government to government but people to people'. These were not just fine words, they were the first sighting shot in the battle for control of the aid that is just beginning.

If, however, we think back to the conclusion of the previous section, that there may be too much aid, very different implications arise concerning efficiency and control. It would mean, for example, that recipient governments' inability to generate enough worthwhile projects or to implement them successfully reflected not their incapability but simply an absolute lack of such projects. If this were the case, increasing donor involvement would not change anything and nor, indeed, would the whole range of indirect control mechanisms.

And this, surely, is what has happened. Donors have been directly involved in project preparation for nearly twenty years now and results have not improved, except in the sense that much more money has been moved. Autonomous agencies with strong support from technical assistance advisers have been in operation for nearly as long with similar disappointing results. Vast sums of money and unbelievable levels of technical complexity have been expended to try to make Monitoring and Evaluation, which is little more than an indirect substitute for good management, into a functional tool. Yet it is still possible for one of my colleagues to report that 'World Bank representatives did *not quite* admit that they had spent $40 million, of money lent to the Nigerian government for Monitoring and Evaluation, to very little effect.'

Even Structural Adjustment, where the donors made the most explicit and forceful attempts to impose conditions on recipient governments, very significantly in breach of the principle that African governments should maintain their own sovereignty, does not appear to be working. As for all the other failures of aid, the tendency has been to seek technical reasons for this failure: Structural Adjustment is too much of a 'universal prescription' and inadequately sensitive to variations from one country to another; or it is too insensitive to the 'human side of Structural Adjustment'; or recipient countries lack the capacity to participate effectively in the policy dialogue of Structural Adjustment. 'With few exceptions it seems that the initiative in Structural Adjustment Lending programme formulation lies with the World Bank' (Cassen, 1986: 85).

There is a simpler, alternative analysis. Because direct donor control is still out of consideration, donors need an incentive with which to encourage governments to undertake the reforms they see as necessary. The only weapon to hand is money. 'The degree of leverage is related to the volume of aid offered' (Cassen, 1986: 96). But money is precisely the wrong thing to offer as an inducement. It eases the only pressure inside the domestic economy that might bring about necessary policy changes. It provides foreign exchange, undermining the effect of the devaluation which is usually a key component of the policy reforms that are being proposed. Lastly, like all aid which must pass through government hands, it strengthens the government's position and so undermines the pressure to make government more accountable, which is the second key component of reform. The disastrous history of IMF relations with the Sudan is the clearest possible illustration of how this process works, or rather fails to work. Conditionality did not work in Sudan because the conditions were simply not met. The 'bribe' was both too small, because policy was not reformed, and too much, because it was actually used to help postpone reform, not to implement it.

These risks are recognized. 'There can be too much external assistance in some instances, thereby undermining the domestic commitment to the program as well as too little' (World Bank, 1989: Ch 8). What is not acknowledged is that there are pressures that ensure that it will always be too much rather than too little. The first is the fact that the money offered is not related to need but rather to the degree of political resistance that has to be bought out. The second pressure comes from the commitment the donors have made to their constituency in the First World that they will provide aid to the Third World. Performance against that commitment is measured by the volume of 'money moved', not by the efficiency with which it is used.

The final sections of the World Bank report illustrate the difficulties. The need for African self-reliance is repeatedly stressed. 'Africa's decline can and must be reversed. The alternative is too awful to contemplate. But it must happen from within Africa. Like trees, countries cannot be made to grow by being pulled upward from the outside; they must grow from within, from their own roots.' (It is surprising that the writers resisted the temptation to draw an analogy between aid and fertilizer placed on those 'growing roots'.) The other side of the coin is much less boldly stated, but it is clear nevertheless: 'Donor support would vary according to performance in implementing the target programs. Countries with weak performance should receive much less assistance' (Ch 9). The critical question is, therefore, whether or not the donors will, when the crunch comes, reduce the aid given to poor performers. It is a very safe prediction, that, at the least, a fifth of African countries will 'perform weakly'. But the World Bank has made a commitment in its strategy to use a volume of funds that would only be needed if 100 per cent performed especially strongly. It is, therefore, also safe to predict that the political pressures on donor agencies to avoid declaring 'weak performance' against any country, which would require them to reduce aid, will be overpowering. Especially strong will be the argument that it would be morally wrong to punish the poor people of a weakly performing country by reducing aid. The fact that agencies have already committed themselves to higher aid expenditures in order to persuade First World governments to promise the money also means that they will face acute political difficulties if they then have to turn round and admit that they cannot spend it.

To conclude, one of the most fundamental weaknesses at the very foundations of aid is the fact that it must – because the intention is to bolster not reduce African independence – violate the old rule that 'he who pays the piper, calls the tune'. First World aid is paying, but it cannot call the tune beyond quite strict self-imposed limits. Struggles over control are endemic as a result and the net result is a severe lack of true control, in the sense of clearly conceived and consistent direction that is capable of working steadily towards realistic goals as well as in the sense of straightforward incentives to efficient use of resources.

Paradoxically, the breach of the link between payer and spender is seen at its clearest in the lending of the World Bank, the most financially sound and by reputation economically orthodox of the donors. Because World Bank money is a loan (albeit on very cheap terms) to a sovereign government, the Bank does not have any financial interest in the projects it finances. Its loan is guaranteed by government regardless of the performance of the project. This is in spite of the fact that that the project surveys were funded at Bank instigation, the project itself was appraised by Bank staff and the design was heavily influenced by whatever was the current Bank development fashion. Without the Bank, the project would not have happened. Yet the Bank takes no financial risk whatsoever. Which means that its political and bureaucratic motivations to move the money are allowed free play. If the disciplines of profit-and-loss are lacking, it is among the donors as much as among the recipients.

The fate of Structural Adjustment shows the power of the control axiom. It says much about the political strength of the recipient countries and the weakness of the donors, that even the World Bank puts more emphasis on the donors' having overstepped the mark in trying to impose policy reform and on the possibility that the policy was not wholly correct, than it does on the recipients' failure to implement the reforms even when the most forceful 'conditionality' was applied. Nevertheless, the problem of control is secondary to that of the volume of capital. At every level, discipline is undermined not by ill will on either side or by incapability. Instead, it is the pressure to spend which ensures that one of the most basic rules of management is broken: that achievable targets be set. Unrealistic targets, which staff know or soon realize are beyond their reach, are the most powerful demotivating factor in the Third World today, and aid is the primary cause of their imposition.

Knowledge

The idea that research and more generally knowledge will enable aid to reach its goals is a relative newcomer. Early attempts to transfer development involved naïve applications of unadapted First World technology in Third World conditions. At the extreme, a lack of knowledge was even made a virtue, most notably in Hirschman's theory of the Hiding Hand. This proposed that 'since we necessarily underestimate our creativity, it is desirable that we underestimate to a roughly similar extent the difficulties of the tasks we face so as to be tricked into understanding tasks that we can, but otherwise would not dare, tackle' (Hirschman, 1967). Hirschman himself acknowledged that the Hiding Hand which carried out this trick was only of temporary benefit: 'A more effective cure would come with improved knowledge.' Nevertheless, the theory of the Hiding Hand was so suited to the aid community's wish to push ahead, to be able to spend vast quantities of money without the necessary assurance that it could be used, that the qualifications were forgotten.

The Hiding Hand was never formally abandoned, but the increasing evidence of failure soon meant that the knowledge business became the most rapidly expanding sector of aid. There must now be tens of thousands of researchers working on the problems of development. Hundreds of thousands of books, studies, articles and reports have been written. Hundreds of universities offer courses in 'Development'. Major donors allocate more and more of their aid funds to research on increasingly esoteric issues such as the use of 'microcomputers in three small Caribbean islands' or studies of 'substitute care policies and provision for young children in Colombia'. It is not unusual nowadays for academic research projects on relatively restricted development issues to cost $500,000.

And yet only a minute proportion of all this knowledge is read and used, even by those who plan aid policies, let alone those who are required to implement aid programmes in the field. Academic critics of this book will undoubtedly list hundreds of different studies that I should have read, and they will be right. But they will also prove my point. As an aid practitioner I am lucky in having had a whole year with nothing to do but read, yet I could not possibly have read any more. When I go back to the field to work I shall never have the time to read even a hundredth of what is published that might be relevant.

Of course, there is a long and respectable tradition of academic research for its own sake: for the general improvement of human understanding and refinement of truth. And it is certainly true that much of human progress has sprung from the results of such 'pure research'. Nevertheless, the academic value of knowledge as its own justification is explicitly rejected in most aid thinking: 'With rural deprivation, where the questions concern the life, suffering and death of hundreds of millions of poor people, that view cannot be sustained. Instead tough thinking is called for about priorities and choices in the deployment of [research] resources' (Chambers, 1983: 62).

Just like the roundabout of aid allocation policies, so there has been a steady progression in the knowledge business. When simple transfers of First World technology failed, intensive and wide-ranging surveys of quite large individual areas were instituted to provide an understanding of what was needed. Typically, these would cover as much as 50,000 square kilometres and involve aerial photography, mapping, soil-survey, agriculture, livestock, forestry and economics. However, a perception developed that these studies were expensive and that the reports generated were rarely read and more rarely implemented. In reaction, the modern formula involves a combination of single-issue academic studies, which frequently cover more than one country, of techniques like Rapid Rural Appraisal, which purport to offer a more cost effective way of identifying good development opportunities, and of increasingly sophisticated approaches to research on the ground, such as Farming Systems Research.

Bauer's dilemma of capital aid, that it is only needed where it cannot be used, is paralleled by a dilemma of knowledge: 'It is very unlikely that domestic policy makers will be able to implement policies which they are not competent to design.' In other words, the current strategy of policy dialogue is failing not because of a lack of knowledge but because the recipient partner in the dialogue cannot use that knowledge effectively. Just as the capital dilemma is ducked in many different ways, using many different partial arguments or no arguments at all, we are asked to believe that the knowledge dilemma can be solved by outsiders more or less as a matter of faith: 'Someone should be finding ways to empower the weaker party to the policy dialogue' (Toye in Emmerij, 1987: 32).

If it is simpler to believe that there is just too much capital aid, so it may be that there is just too much knowledge about developing countries. However desperate the 'rural deprivation', however dire the crisis of African countries, the answer is not to be found in more information or analysis. And if most of the knowledge collected is not used, it is not because it is the wrong knowledge or because it is being collected in the wrong way but because there is no way of putting even a reasonable proportion of it into action.

There is, unfortunately, an additional problem. Knowledge can be too much not merely in that it overwhelms the capacity to absorb it. It can also be 'too much' in the sense that it creates more difficulties than it solves. Almost inevitably, greater understanding of a developing area tends to lead to reduced expectations. Such reductions are very unwelcome to governments who are eager to see rapid and visible developments and even more so to donor agencies, awash with abundant funds and desperate for projects to put them into. In aid too much knowledge is a dangerous thing, because it might undermine the whole exercise.

The first field survey I worked on was in the Yemen Arab Republic. Some twenty professionals worked for two years and concluded that the scope for accelerated investment was extremely limited. Cautious proposals costing about $1.3 million, if memory serves me, were put forward for one area, the Wadi Rima. They were rejected out of hand because neither the donor nor the government was willing to think that small. The reason for putting forward such limited proposals was simple enough: a recognition of the efficiency of what the people of the area were already doing. The existing system, which had developed over centuries, was already capturing 60 per cent of the available water. That system was enshrined in a fairly equitable arrangement of customary rights with written documents dating back 300 years. What water did escape went down into the ground where it could be economically recovered using pumps downstream. In the face of this advice the World Bank and the Dutch government financed major irrigation works which cost, in the end, $26.6 million plus 100 million Yemen riyals in local expenditure. The only beneficiaries were the upstream farmers who were able to get the lion's share of reliable water and expand the area of bananas grown for cash. In exchange, cropped areas downstream were greatly reduced: from around 10,000 *ma'add* (3,600 hectares) to 400 *ma'add* at one large village. Up to two-thirds of sharecroppers were driven off the land and those who did get control of the water were able to charge others for it. Even technically the scheme was a failure, because it was little more effective than the traditional system at capturing the water. It was built in the early 1980s and by 1987 downstream users were trying to rebuild the old intakes and canals.

This story leads to much the same conclusion, in miniature, as the whole of this book; that full knowledge of developing areas suggests that ambitions must be cut back. It also underlines the central point; that lack of knowledge is not the problem. What creates disaster is the pressure to reject negative knowledge that might, by reducing expectations, stand in the way of efforts to 'move the money'.

Avoidance of unwelcome conclusions affects knowledge itself. It is difficult, for example, not to believe that it was precisely because they led to 'over-realistic' conclusions that intensive and comprehensive studies of developing areas became unpopular and were replaced by the more 'modern and cost-effective' combination of academic studies, of rapid appraisal techniques and of single-topic research. It is also difficult not to conclude that the widespread denigration and unpopularity of long-term technical assistance is principally because the expatriate TA advisers are in the best position to point out the practical limitations to what can be achieved. They are a block to moving the money.

Much of what is presented in the chapters that follow is derived from the 'intensive and comprehensive' type of study and from long-term experience as a TA adviser in Darfur on projects designed using the very detailed reports that resulted. It demonstrates two completely contradictory points. First, that this rather old-fashioned approach to research can provide a good understanding of an area where the more modern, arm's-length approaches cannot. Second, that even a good understanding does not offer much hope that knowledge will make a significant contribution to development; at least in the sense that it is not going to identify ways in which the vast sums of money available for development aid can be usefully spent.

The 1970s were the heyday of the 'intensive and comprehensive' approach, when some donors, most notably the UK ODA, commissioned a number of integrated rural resource surveys. By chance, south Darfur was a centre of this activity and major studies were carried out in three separate sections of the province. Typically, these studies began with aerial photography to generate maps. There followed a two- to three-year period of ground survey which included all the major disciplines: soils, hydrology/hydrogeology, agriculture, livestock, ecology and economics. Shorter studies of other subjects were commissioned where necessary. Professionals in the core subjects spent at the least two years in the field. This was not Rural Development Tourism, whatever else it was.

Because the various specialists were living and working as a team, the degree of interdisciplinary pluralism was as great as it feasibly can be. These exercises were expensive and, as already described, they frequently came up with the 'wrong answer'. Nevertheless, they offered a coherent and systematic description of relatively large populations and areas. The final reports included full-length studies of all the core topics together with a complete set of detailed thematic maps on everything from water availability to wildlife. With hindsight, one suspects that these studies were not nearly so expensive as believed at the time, especially when put on a per capita or per square kilometre basis and compared with the costs of studies of social issues covering, say, ten Bangladeshi villages, to quote but one example of the approach that is more fashionable today.

The day of 'intensive and comprehensive' passed and the later 1980s saw a move to smaller-scale approaches, heralded by Robert Chambers's book, *Rural Development – Putting the Last First* (1983). This is a brilliant analysis of the sociology of aid and how it affects the generation of knowledge. His call for 'A balanced pluralist approach, empirically based and with a wide span in both political economy and physical ecology, [that] is more likely to fit the reality and reveal what best to do', must be correct. One aim of this book is to show what can be done in this direction by presenting a pluralist and balanced description of Darfur.

Chambers's analysis of the underlying biases and disjunctions that often prevent the achievement of such an approach is also compelling. His elaborate framework of biases can, in fact, be reduced to one: a bias towards the short-term. They almost all spring from a refusal to spend enough time in an area, a refusal to acknowledge the value of experience. Obviously if a visitor is short of time he will stay on the road, see only the good projects that people want to show him, talk only to the men, who are more forthcoming, and see only the better-off, for the same reason. And so you have the Tarmac, Project, Male and Elite biases. 'Knowing what they want to know and short of time to find out, professionals become narrowly single-minded' and this gives the Professional bias. Yet Chambers's own recommendation does not anywhere include the suggestion that more time is needed – far from it. Instead he concentrates on a range of tools to increase the efficiency with which knowledge is generated; attributing the failure of research to the range of 'biases' and to the fact that knowledge and research techniques are divided between three cultures that do not communicate: the 'academic', the aid 'practitioner' and 'rural people'.

The failure of capital aid was the stimulus to the burgeoning knowledge business, but it has taken its shape from the control dilemma: from the difficulty, even possibility of reconciling substantial foreign involvement with African self-reliance. This is why the conclusion that the problem is a lack of time, not a failure of technique, is always avoided.

This is why all the individual biases to the way knowledge is acquired can be seen very clearly, but the underlying short-term bias remains obscured. Because the only way out of a short-term bias is for foreigners to spend more time in an area. This can only result in a greater likelihood that they would get to understand and even get involved in no-go areas like politics and society, directly infringing on the control axiom.

One result is that modern high-technology methods, which avoid the need for direct interference, have a particularly strong attraction; let us call this the Remote Bias, because the modern technology of Remote Sensing from satellites is a perfect example. Recently, the concept of the Early Warning System against drought and famine in Africa has become very fashionable. The use of satellites to monitor vegetation at early stages in the crop season is seen as a vital tool in the technique. These exercises are hugely expensive. Yet there can be no earlier warning of how rainfed crops are doing than to record the actual rainfall on the ground. Satellites measure the green growth that happens after the rain, or at best the clouds that come just before the rain. Rain gauges are a very old, very simple technology and most African states had, at independence, extensive networks of such gauges managed by official meteorological services. To restore those services would cost a minute proportion of the satellite technology, would provide just as early warning and would be more accurate. However, the collapse of those services is entirely a problem of local management. Outsiders would have to get involved in a sensitive domestic issue to bring about such a restoration. This is not attractive when compared with the glamour of the satellite technique; not attractive to outsiders, who would have to deal with the tricky problems of control, nor to insiders, who would have to acknowledge a failure in a simple and boring piece of work.

There are many other examples of the remote bias. Macro-economic studies, making complicated comparisons between a number of different African countries, require only a minimum period of data collection in a country. The analysis can be done safely at a distance. Satellites are used to monitor deforestation, cropped areas and so on, jobs that used to be done by agricultural inspectors and forest rangers on horseback. To repeat, the aid community is forced to seek these indirect methods to control, or at least monitor, what is happening because direct control is not acceptable and the national system does not, or cannot, put the same priority on control anyway. At least a portion of the work being done on development research is, in fact, aimed not at development but at indirect methods to control development.

Because of the pressure to minimize foreign involvement, research done by 'outsiders', to use Chambers's term, must at some stage be transferred to 'insiders' for use in action. To do otherwise would violate the principle that Africans must be in charge of their own destiny. This throws up another of the great inconsistencies of aid: that knowledge about Third World countries has first to be extracted by 'outsiders', who then transform it in some unspecified way before it can be handed back to the people of those countries who are to put it to productive use.

It is increasingly common but still somehow illogical to see First World researchers doing intensive field work at the grass-roots level in developing countries, in order to return and convey what they learn to Third World professionals studying 'development' at European and American universities. It is as though knowledge is now only valid when it has been brought into the international aid community's domain. Once it has been validated in this way, then it can be returned to the Third World for application.

One difficulty concerns second-round knowledge, by which I mean feedback, the process whereby an idea is implemented, results are evaluated and future implementations adjusted accordingly. Does this feedback not have to be 'transformed' by outsiders too? If not, why not? What is the difference between the first round and the second round that allows an outsider role in the one but not the other? Here again the reason lies in the question of control. For outsiders to have a role to play in the feedback and adjustment process they must, inevitably, become closely involved in day-to-day matters over relatively long periods, in other words in management. There is no way this can be prevented from breaking the principle of unalloyed local control. This explains the social and political pressures that make outsider involvement in second-round knowledge generation so unwelcome. It does not offer any logical, technical reason why their advantages in the first round are not needed in the second. Indeed, there does not seem to be any logical, technical reason.

Two modern techniques illustrate these contradictory pressures. Both Rapid Rural Appraisal and Farming Systems Research are widely advocated as ways to overcome the various biases and the barriers between the different 'knowledge cultures'. Yet they are both attempts to substitute technique for experience. 'Collinson pioneered an approach which sought to condense a wealth of insight and experience into a replicable field method' (Chambers, 1983: 67). This begs the question as to why insight and experience should not be sought directly rather than being replaced by a 'condensed method'. But we already know the answer, which is that long-term presence of outside researchers needed to generate insight and experience is, by definition, not acceptable.

The pattern is most clearly seen in the concept of Rural People's Knowledge. It is now accepted by all that the people of Africa are rational and knowledgeable. To the extent that is possible, they are in control of their environment and they also have considerable ability to change when faced by changes in that environment. The new paradigm is, therefore, that 'Rural people's knowledge and modern scientific knowledge are complementary' but 'outsider professionals have to step down off their pedestals and sit down, listen and learn' (Chambers, 1983: 75). But why is the initiative with outsiders? Why do they have to learn from rural people? Would a sensible division of labour not be for outsiders to concentrate on what they are good at, modern-style research, and leave rural people to maintain what knowledge they need for themselves?

There are a number of reasons. One is the short-term bias itself. 'Outsiders' do not have the time to learn by doing and to gain some local experience and insight. Instead, they have to try to gain it indirectly, by drawing on local insight and experience, on Rural People's Knowledge, in some organized manner. Another is an implicit belief that some local people know better than others. 'Outsiders' hope to extract such information in one place and offer it to the less knowledgeable rural people elsewhere. Mixed cropping is a good example. 'It took organised agricultural research decades to realise that what appeared primitive and unprogressive was complex and sophisticated' (Chambers, 1983: 87). (The complexity and sophistication was mostly in the 'outsiders' perception. For the rural people it was simple to do and to understand: it worked.) Nowadays, mixed cropping has been 'validated' in the modern knowledge sector and is widely promoted in areas of Africa where it is not common, regardless of the implied inconsistency: that Rural People's Knowledge in the mixed crop areas is good, but Rural People's Knowledge in the single crop areas is bad. An extreme example, but it illustrates the problem with Rural People's Knowledge; that discussion about it is principally aimed at justifying an 'outsider role' in the process, not in devising ways in which the rural people can extend the ways they can use their own knowledge. Yemeni farmers have, in the last couple of decades, succeeded in learning how to use both tractors and diesel driven pumpsets for irrigation. Although they made a lot of mistakes in the process, they quickly learned how to exploit the new machinery to the full. As far as tractors are concerned, the number in use in one area went from 5 to 75 in about 5 years (Morton, 1981). To do this they had little advice beyond limited support offered by the commercial Yemeni companies importing the machinery and a few local people who had worked in Aden and elsewhere. In other words Rural People's Knowledge worked extremely effectively without any outsider involvement whatsoever. This experience may be compared with the numerous aid-financed projects which endeavour in Chambers's words to 'involve rural people themselves as partners in research'. The contrast lies between a rural community exploiting 'outsiders' knowledge' as and when it suits them, on their initiative, and attempts to marry Rural People's Knowledge and outsiders' knowledge, at the outsiders' initiative.

Consider, for example, the statement that 'small farmers' expertise represents "the single largest knowledge resource not yet mobilized in the development enterprise . . . We simply cannot afford to ignore it any longer" ' (Chambers, 1983: 92). Surely the people who have that knowledge are neither ignoring it nor failing to mobilize it. By implication, however, true mobilization can only be provided by aid 'outsiders' and small farmers' knowledge is not actually 'known' until those aid outsiders know it. Chambers states that 'the initiative lies with outsiders but the aim is to transfer more and more power and control to the poor.' Three things remain unexplained. Why should the initiative be with the outsiders in the first place and what prevents the insiders taking it for themselves? How are the outsiders to avoid their initiative being an imposition of their own ideas? And how is this curious transfer of initiative from outside to insider to be managed? The obvious danger is that once the outsiders have arrogated the initiative to themselves it will prove impossible to return it.

Chambers acknowledges that the outsider will always be 'an outsider seeking to change things . . . From this paternal trap there is no complete escape.' However, his only answer is to say that 'Respect for the poor and what they want offsets paternalism.' As so often with aid, the difficult central point is skated over with pious hope instead of analysis. Is it too strong to suggest that the way to show true respect for rural people, and the people of developing countries as a whole, is not to involve them in some condescending and patronizing 'partnership' but merely to leave them alone, in the confidence that they do have the necessary strengths and abilities to make their own choices? Would the more appropriate outsider role not be to spread the wares of outsider knowledge and allow rural people to choose for themselves what they think would be useful? If this were to reduce the outsiders to nothing more than salesmen, that might well be more honourable than a so-called partnership, from which the principal gain is often the senior partner's advancement in his own separate academic or bureaucratic community.

The evidence from Darfur is not that the people are short of knowledge or incapable of acquiring it. The factor that has done most to stifle their ability to use and extend their knowledge is the absence of imported technology in the market. There is massive repressed demand for all kinds of agricultural and other technologies, even for those that farmers have not seen before. The desire to experiment is strong but the materials to do so are totally unavailable, partly because of the acute economic crisis but also because the knowledge community tends to insist on detailed research and the avoidance of all risk. Relaxation of the rules for licensing new classes of agricultural inputs and foreign exchange to put them in the market would do far more for Rural People's Knowledge than any amount of 'participation'.

The position is no different at higher levels in developing societies, where the élite are nowadays required to go to European universities to learn about their own problems: to attend courses in development, rural management and the myriad other topics identified by outsiders as relevant to development. What they do not learn about is the way the First World works, the way modern rich economies and societies reached this position. In other words they are kept back from the path of imitation, so successfully exploited by Japan and many others, and condemned instead to cut their own entirely new path. Like the rural people, they too are required to join a partnership, 'a compact that does not diminish the Africans' right to determine what happens on their continent, but that at the same time responds to the concerns and insights of the external development community' (World Bank, 1989: Ch 9). The manner in which the Africans' role is to remain undiminished is far from clear.

At bottom, a vast amount of modern development research takes a simplistic and futile form: what may be called argument by transference. This suggests, for example, that a particular strategy has worked in say, Bangladesh and therefore 'deserves serious consideration' in sub-Saharan Africa. The idea, is not, for some reason, seen as inconsistent with the repeated identification of 'inattention to local circumstances' as a general fault (Cassen, 1986: 15). Argument by analogy is an allied and very popular line of thought. Chambers presents a complicated analogy with the geneticists' 'tools for thought', which involves attempting to locate 'soft spots' or 'points of competence in an "epigenetic landscape" ' (Chambers, 1983: 158). Hirschman prefers an analogy with the way the aerospace industry approaches Research and Development while Tendler uses models derived from the sociology of large organizations in the First World (Hirschman, 1967; Tendler, 1975). The resort to these arguments illustrates the constraints on aid knowledge. Useful knowledge is best sought by working continuously over long periods in one area learning and applying simultaneously so that what is learnt is constantly refined by second, third, fourth and so on rounds of experience: in other words, to grow the knowledge where it is to be used. The opportunity to do so is denied the 'outsider' by the need not to trespass on local control and the short-term bias. There is little left for him to do, therefore, except to seek lessons in one area and hope that they can be applied elsewhere: an attempt far more likely to fail than otherwise.

To sum up, a contrast needs to be drawn between knowledge that has been validated by the aid community and what may be called Knowledge in Place. Knowledge in Place is to be found in the hands of people who actually live and work in a developing area: farmers, shopkeepers, bureaucrats and so on. At any one time they have a stock of knowledge and an ability to add to that stock according to changing circumstances. The basic failure of aid knowledge is that it adds neither to the stock nor to the ability to increase it. Instead it simply transfers the stock into the international domain where it may well be intellectually stimulating but is otherwise largely sterile.

The result is that the modern aid professional is burdened with a vast array of academically validated research techniques. What he is not allowed is time: time to read generally about a country, time to learn the language, time merely to become acquainted with the country he is working in and time to test which of the approved techniques actually work and which do not. Instead, those techniques are assumed to be universally valid and capable of generating the knowledge that is needed in one pass, at the first round. Where, for example, it is decided that expatriate technical assistance staff are too insensitive to local people's feelings, the recommendation is to introduce 'mandatory training for experts in the art of cross-cultural communication and techniques for effective personal relations with local counterparts' (Cassen, 1986: 215). The possibility that much more would be achieved by allowing the expert a longer period in-country to learn the language and do the job in a more relaxed manner is not considered. The pressure of unreasonable targets on tight time-scales does far more to destroy relations between expert and counterpart than anything else. Also not considered is the fact that such experts are already considered to be too expensive and yet more training will only raise the cost. Aid tries to substitute techniques derived from First World commerce like 'training in interpersonal relationships' for a commodity that conflicts with the given attitudes of aid, even though it is more likely to raise efficiency, namely a longer expatriate presence.

One large question has not, so far, been raised. Why are the 'outsiders' needed at all? Why they want to be needed is obvious. After all it is clear that the First World wants to help the Third with money and reasonable enough, therefore, that First World people, the outsiders, would want to help by offering their intellectual and other abilities as well. It is also clear that the natural desire of Third World people to retain control of their affairs poses certain limits on that outsider involvement. What is not clear is where there is a gap in Third World capacities that will allow the outsider to play a useful role without breaching those limits. It is now recognized, after all, that much of what seemed irrational in the Third World reflects perfectly sound strategies in the face of difficult conditions: hence all the emphasis now laid on Rural People's Knowledge. Nor is it very convincing to argue that the rural people have these strengths but that the middle and upper classes that have sprung from those rural people do not.

One explanation is that there is a barrier which prevents the insider from being able to generate knowledge as effectively as the outsider. This barrier might simply be education, although the problems with this have already been mentioned. The fact that education has not been terribly successful in the past, the tendency for the educated either to leave or to end up unemployed, even the steady decline in educational standards itself, all imply that the demand for the abilities which education can provide is not as great as believed. It is difficult, for example, to believe that the answer lies in such a simple educational change as a reorientation away from passive absorption towards 'active personal search and problem solving in relatively unstructured situations' (Toye in Emmerij, 1987: 34). Here we have yet another example of a prescription derived from unproven First World theories and proffered whole, without thought or revision, as a panacea for Third World problems; as they are perceived through First World eyes, that is.

Perhaps the central moment in the expatriate development professional's experience is the moment when he becomes convinced that his national staff counterpart understands very clearly the advice being given but does not intend to take it, for reasons that can only be guessed at. This experience is common to the IMF negotiator, who sees high government officials ignore what seem inescapable economic realities, and to the agriculturalist, whose counterparts insist on ignoring the farmers' main concerns. One thing that is evident is that the problem does not lie in any lack of education and it is difficult not to arrive back at some inbuilt weakness, some X-factor that explains the inertia. A formula that is popular, because the critical implications are somewhat disguised, is that the missing factor is a 'willingness to search' for solutions, for new developments or for improvements. This involves the idea that development springs from a combination of agreed social objectives combined with the willingness to search which enables society to achieve them. Underdevelopment is the expression of a failure in the willingness to search (Bruton, quoted in Emmerij, 1987). Put in these terms, the whole apparatus of aid knowledge may be seen as an attempt to stimulate that willingness or to substitute for it. The difficulty lies in stimulating a willingness to search without actually stifling it with assistance, producing a mere 'imitation ethic'.

To identify a lack of 'search' as the problem and to place its roots firmly in society is not enough. It is still necessary to explain why society takes the shape it does and why that shape is translated in its turn into 'search' or, in the developing countries, into a lack of search. It is very tempting to resort to the factors that distinguish one group of human beings from another, principally race and religion, as the determinants of the willingness to search. This book will draw a different conclusion. Two straightforward concepts are crucial: economic incentives and political development. For incentives, a return to Liebenstein's X-efficiency provides an answer that does not depend on any lack of search ethic or excess of 'imitation ethic' but, more happily, on a simple belief in the commonality of human nature; the fact that human beings are capable of great things if given an incentive or motivation, but that they also like their leisure and will not sacrifice it for no reward. If the Darfuri or the Sudanese people as a whole seem unwilling to search for new opportunities it is because they judge, largely correctly, that the rewards will not match the risks. Furthermore, if foreign aid reduces the willingness to search, it is not because it dampens any ethics but because it destroys the material incentives and competitive motivations to 'search'.

In the promotion of economic efficiency it is the use of knowledge that is important, not its generation. 'Such new knowledge involves knowledge dissemination not invention' and motivation of one form or another is critical to that dissemination (Liebenstein, 1966). If 'outsiders' seem so frequently to have to take the initiative at every level in aid, especially in aid knowledge, it is because the rewards to them are adequate where those to the 'insiders' are not. At the extreme, an elegant piece of research on a development topic that is useless in practice may still secure academic advancement for the outsider. (Even this book has some elements of that!) The insiders' lack of interest in either carrying out such research, or in using the results when transferred to them is understandable, however.

Clearly, research can work and has worked many times in the past. This discussion is not to deny that. Instead, it is to show that knowledge, and by extension research, can only play a role when the time is ripe and when it is not distorted by the pressures of volume and control that underly the aid process. The acknowledged poor performance of African research institutions lies, like so much else, in the fact that the framework in which they are required to operate is not practical.

Society

It can no longer be believed that it was the 'puritan ethic' alone that led to the development of European capitalism and, by implication, created the 'willingness to search' that underpinned that capitalism. There are too many examples of Catholic, Buddhist and Shintoist societies which have outdone the puritan capitalists. Nevertheless, the point stands that some ethical consensus has always been critical to development. Such a consensus must, however, be at least as much a result as a cause. In an era in which the technical and market conditions were not favourable for rapid capital accumulation, for example, it is unlikely that the puritan ethic would have made much headway. Even more importantly, the very shape of the consensus itself depends on the motivations of all parties. Those motivations depend, in turn, on the physical resources of a nation, on the market opportunities on offer and the technology available. In Africa, for example, the rather loose, individualistic social forms of tribalism reflect the relative abundance of land and the advantages of flexibility and mobility in an uncertain environment.

There is much evidence of the fact that such social forms are flexible and responsive to the needs and circumstances of the people they serve. This kind of flexibility is central to the processes of development. Conversely, 'traditions and values are not subject to direct manipulation; instead they change under the impact of new opportunities and new pressures' (Hayami & Ruttan, 1971). In all too many cases, however, aid has found little in the way of new opportunities to offer. To apply new pressures or even to allow them to develop is even more difficult. The conflict with aid's humanitarian goals is too great. For these reasons, there have been frequent attempts at direct manipulation. Much of the development work done in Darfur, for example, has depended on a mistaken belief that social attitudes to communal land and pasture management were the cause of the problem, when they were, in fact, merely reflections of the strategies used to deal with a given set of circumstances.

The same is true at the national level, where aid puts increasing emphasis on aspects that are essentially political or social, on 'good governance'. As always, the sensitivity of control means that aid can only approach these issues indirectly. It is, for example, hoped that education will not merely enhance the government's capacity to rule properly but that it will also raise the population's consciousness, people's ability to monitor and discipline the performance of their rulers. Similarly, the institutions of liberal democracy – such as a free press and multi-party politics – are expected to make governments more accountable to their people. Various ways in which aid money can be used to stimulate such changes are canvassed, from the direct pressures and bribes of 'policy dialogue' to education and training. At both national and local levels aid attempts to manipulate attitudes; an attempt that is only necessary because it cannot provide the new opportunities or apply the new pressures which might stimulate a more natural process of change and development.

Aid that goes wrong can either leak away to nothing or it can actually distort the society it affects. The evidence of leakage is clear. Accelerated education leaks away into the brain drain or to unemployment. Increased investment is wasted or lost to overseas bank accounts. Distortion is more subtle but even more damaging. It happens partly because aid is such a powerful motivating factor in itself and partly because it breaks important links that bind society together. The failures of government are so widespread that even the major aid donors can no longer ignore them: 'Because countervailing power has been lacking, state officials in many countries have served their own interests without fear of being called to account. In self-defense individuals have built up personal networks of influence rather than hold the all-powerful state accountable for its systematic failures. In this way politics becomes personalized and patronage becomes essential to maintain power' (World Bank, 1989: Ch 2). What these analyses never do, however, is acknowledge the strength of aid's own contribution. Sudan is a typical, perhaps the classic, example. 'The availability of the substantial external financial flows no doubt allowed Nimeiry to engage in what seemed to be an astute political juggling act for longer than would otherwise have been possible' (Brown, 1990: Ch 5).

This awkward conclusion is avoided by placing the emphasis on power, by implication a factor not affected by aid, although even that is arguable. It is suggested that the problem lies in the 'all-powerful state' and the lack of 'countervailing powers' which can act as the weapon of accountability against that state. The truth is rather different. An increasing number of African governments are far from all-powerful and many of them do not have the strength to overcome prolonged resistance, usually by separate ethnic groups. The recent history of administration in Darfur and in the Sudan as a whole illustrates how the state is also powerless at a lower, more day-to-day level. These simpler limits to power are rarely recognized, because they are so ordinary, but they are even more widespread than open civil war.

The real reason why African states are so unaccountable is not power but the almost total dissolution of taxation as the means by which the contract between a state and its people is regulated. It is taxation that is the missing weapon of accountability, not power nor democracy. And aid is the major factor. In the weaker developing countries aid now outweighs government's own, locally generated resources very substantially. One extreme example was in Darfur during the 1984–5 famine, when Save the Children Fund, a foreign NGO involved only in famine relief, had a budget for transport only, not counting the value of the food relief itself nor of the expatriate staff involved, in excess of the regional government's budget. Two large aid-funded projects also commanded greater resources than regional government. A very large part of the regional government's budget was, in any case, financed from central funds, which meant that the contribution of local resources to local government was close to zero. For Sudan and for many other countries the situation at the national level is little different. Even the revenues from taxes on export crops reflect large volumes of aid-financed inputs used to grow those crops while revenues from import duties depend on aid funds used for balance of payments support.

One result is that the relation between government and people no longer depends on an exchange of services for taxes. Instead, the more democratic governments trade aid-funded services for rather less active support or for passive acquiescence. The other result is that most of the managerial talent at government's disposal is absorbed into aid related activities: negotiations with donors and with the people over the distribution of benefits and, subsequently, the management of the expenditure itself. Instead of the traditional skill of taxation – Colbert's 'plucking the goose so as to obtain the largest possible amount of feathers with the smallest possible amount of hissing' – governments are now practising the joint skills of raising the maximum aid with the minimum surrender of sovereignty and providing the minimum service consistent with popular acquiescence.

Because the funds spent are not provided by the people, their perception of the cost is small and reactions to corruption are considerably muted. At the same time, popular demand for services becomes more or less infinite and for the same reason; the people do not perceive the cost. On the other hand, they lose their one weapon against government: a refusal to pay tax. The net result is a severe weakening of the basic contract between governor and governed. Because tax is no longer so important to the state it actually needs less power, not more; less power in the sense that it no longer needs the ability to contact each individual member of society, however indirectly, in order to ensure his social contribution, which is tax, and to police the defaulters.

Taxation, specifically resistance to taxation, has played a central role at virtually every major turning point in the development of modern First World political systems. If the British parliament is the mother of parliaments then the very Eve was that 'Mad Parliament' held at Oxford in 1258, where the English monarchy first began to concede the principle of taxation by the consent of a formal assembly. The so-called English revolution of the 17th century was started, symbolically at least, by the refusal of John Hampden to pay an ancient and forgotten tax called Ship Money. This was the revolution which saw 'ideas whose fruits still influence the modern world – tolerance, anti-slavery, feminism and pacifism – [that] had for the first time won a hearing' (Larousse, 1964). Last, but far from least, it was the slogan 'no taxation without representation' that became the rallying cry for the American people during their War of Independence.

The fact that there were many other factors at work in all these events should not hide the critical role of taxation in articulating the struggle: in defining the social contract between ruler and ruled and in enabling a redefinition to come about. In the words of Cicero, 'Vectigalia nervi sunt reipublicae': Taxes are the sinews of the commonwealth. (To mistranslate *nervi* as 'nerves' makes the quotation even more apt by underlining the role of taxation as a means of communication between the people and the state.)

Some suggest that there is little evidence that aid affects taxation, in the sense that 'One cannot argue that aid is systematically substituted for public savings by government' (Cassen, 1986: 25). This statement is a little difficult to accept for anyone who has seen the way governments of developing countries manipulate the exchange rate against aid donors. By paying the donor a rate below even their own official commercial rates, the government gains the maximum amount of hard currency for the minimum local currency, a straight substitution of aid for public savings. Nevertheless, that is not really the issue. It is far more important that the aid funds, which government controls, are vast relative to what is raised by local taxation. Government's ability to act unfettered by the discipline of resentful taxpayers is correspondingly vast. Far from taxation without representation, most Africans now have representation without taxation.

This is the explanation for the otherwise incomprehensible behaviour of African ruling parties. Their uninterest in economic affairs, shown equally by elected governments and dictatorships, reflects the fact that those affairs are no longer of importance to their interests as a governing group. This is why they are sometimes surprisingly willing to surrender economic policy to organizations dominated by the World Bank and other donors, such as the Paris Club, despite the evident infringement of sovereignty. When donors complain of weakness of 'recipient government' participation in 'policy dialogue', it has far more to do with the fact that those governments are not actually interested than with any lack of capability. For the same reason, persistent donor recommendations for stronger central planning functions and support for greater economic analysis capabilities meet with equally persistent failure. Most donor staff would testify to a surprising degree of unconcern among recipient country politicians when policy reform is discussed.

There is, however, one sector of government that has been almost forbidden territory for aid: law and order. There has been some politically motivated aid to support security services, but that is in the interests of the state. What receives almost no support is the provision of law and order to the citizen. It is worth remembering that the basic Hobbesian contract between ruler and ruled consisted of 'the indispensable need that human beings have to surrender some of their natural rights to liberty in order to secure their lives against death and their property from plunder' (Gamble, 1981). This view of the world may seem too crude to western eyes but would seem highly relevant to many citizens of African countries. (Current events from Liberia to Somalia and also outside Africa, in Cambodia and Yugoslavia, have seen a sudden breach of the rule that outsiders must not become involved in law and order matters: a breach justified as a temporary, emergency-only measure. The results of this *ad hoc* approach have not been encouraging.)

This is where the nexus of capital aid and control of sovereignty has had its most pernicious effects. Capital aid has released governments from accountability to their people as taxpayers and it has diverted most of governments' attention to development matters, by definition exclusive of law and order. There has been some, ineffective, substitution of accountability to outsiders in the development areas, but this is not acceptable in such a sensitive area as justice and policing. The result has been that the duties of the state that are the most central to the development of a stable society have been the most neglected. The recent turbulent history of Darfur reveals all these patterns. Because the collapse is not as total as in Somalia, for example, it is in fact rather easier to discern what has been happening.

The modern aid prescription explicitly recognizes the scale of these problems. Great emphasis is laid on the need for 'good governance – a public service that is efficient, a judicial system that is reliable and an administration that is accountable to its public.' Even the possibility that aid might have contributed to the problem is occasionally hinted at. However, a detailed discussion of what the implications would be, if aid is in itself a major factor, is avoided, for the very good reason that it would lead to only two possible conclusions: the need for a reduction in the volume of aid or greater infringement on local control.

Instead the modern recommendation throws up the usual flurry of partial solutions that seem to offer a way to bypass the central problem. One is to stress simple economic and administrative aspects: calls for 'rural legal departments', for 'price inspectorates', for land registration (Chambers, 1983: 152), for legally enforceable contract and property rights and for dispute arbitration to release the entrepreneurial spirit (World Bank, 1989: Ch 6). At the national level, where it is acknowledged that 'foreign aid has greatly expanded the opportunities for malfeasance' and led to a 'profound demoralization of society at large', the recommendation is for 'prompt and scrupulous accounting' which the aid donors 'have a right to insist on' (World Bank, 1989: Ch 2).

These prescriptions ignore one fact; that they have all been tried and failed. Almost without exception, the colonial powers left active and effective rural legal systems and even price control arrangements in place. It is not enough to call for what will be nothing more than a re-institution of these mechanisms without finding out why they died in the first place. Similarly, for decades every major aid donor has demanded the most complex paperwork to ensure honest procurement and accountancy. Project documents have explicitly committed recipient governments to meet donor audit requirements. These provisions are rarely enforced or enforceable. If there was one critical difference between the two major aid projects in Darfur during the 1980s, it lay in the willingness of one donor to enforce his accounting requirements and in the willingness of project management to accept it with good grace. Such a combination is rare indeed; and the aid community needs to address the problem of why it is rare, if it is ever to progress beyond repeated calls to discipline that are never answered.

The second part of aid's social prescription involves a belated recognition of the strengths of African social traditions. 'Customary institutions are not stagnant, but rather constantly evolving in response to the changing environment. To be successful, development programs need to take fuller account of a country's social context and cultural dynamics' (World Bank, 1989: Ch 2). This is a considerable advance on previous ideas about society, but customary institutions always embody local values. These never place the same value on equity, in terms of wealth and especially between the sexes, as the First World donors would wish. This is one of the few areas where donors are willing to make explicit requirements in breach of the principle of local control, and it leads to some difficult inconsistencies. The universal difficulty of aid also recurs: If the potential is there why has it not been realized? How can aid by itself bring about such a realization if the potential is not there? In other words, why have these institutions not evolved naturally to take up the role aid is now prescribing for them and what is the magic aid-financed ingredient that will enable them to do so now, all of a sudden? Lastly, what is to be the relation between the state and these institutions? Will the strengthening of substate institutions not merely delay the development of a healthy universal state?

In the past there were many examples in Africa of what has been termed 'the moral economy' where the 'redistributive élites', such as the Sokoto caliphate of Nigeria, maintained stocks of grain as insurance for all against bad years. At a lower level, strong kinship mechanisms and associated systems of communal ownership such as the concept of *Doudal* among the West African Fulfulde were designed to offer security in very uncertain circumstances. Since this meant, for example, that those who survived a drought period best were obliged to assist those who had done worse, the result was egalitarian at least in tendency if not absolutely. The very strong obligations to hospitality and generosity in Islam, at least as strong as in Christianity and considerably stronger than in modern capitalist humanism, reflect similar attitudes to the moral economy.

It is argued, however, that these moral economies are in retreat: 'the traditional responsibilities of the rich, or less poor, for those who are poorer, have been fading' (Chambers, 1983: 137). This is because of economic growth and a shift to the 'acquisitiveness of the smaller family'. The most common criticism of the social impact of aid is that it 'reinforces the political and social status-quo which engenders poverty' (Cassen, 1986: 63) and that rural élites set up 'nets' that 'intercept benefits intended for the poor' (Chambers, 1983: 104). A contrast is drawn with earlier, more optimistic 'trickle-down' theories that predicted that if the élite made progress they would pull the poor along in their wake. The result has been that social equity has become one of only two areas where the aid community is willing to override the axiom of local control and make quite explicit requirements about the goals of aid. The target is not just economic growth but 'equitable growth' (World Bank, 1989: Ch 2). Equity is required not merely at the national level but even at the 'intra-family' level where, for example, special feeding programmes for women and children are advocated (Cassen, 1986: 62).

Even for equity, however, economic and developmental justifications are presented to disguise the extent to which First World mores are being imposed in breach of that sovereignty of control. Perhaps the commonest and certainly the strongest argument is that long-term political stability is impossible without equity and that growth is not possible without stability. A second common argument is that inequity implies that the capacities of the poor are not being fully put to use. Women, 'given the right opportunities, can have a greater impact on the development of the continent than in the past' (World Bank, 1989: Ch 3). The problem arises, as so many times before, with motivation. Relations between classes and between the sexes are part of a complete society. If it is accepted that society and its structures reflect the pressures and incentives that motivate it, then attempts to change those relations without changing the motivations are unlikely to succeed.

This drive for western standards of equity, standards to which the west itself has only recently come and which it is still arguably imperfect in meeting, conflicts directly with the stated new policy of relying on local customary institutions, which are almost always quite strongly hierarchical. Any 'grass-roots' policy makes an arbitrary decision as to who or what is the grass-root. If it is to be the poorest of the poor, or women, who are to be 'empowered to grass-roots action', then the opinions of the grass-stem, that is to say the slightly less poor and the husbands, will have to be overridden. Yet how can the grass be any healthier with a broken stem? If, however, the whole rural farming community is taken as the grass-root, then that community's own decisions about equity will have to be accepted as given. But this merely pushes the problem higher up the social scale. The ethics and aspirations of the merchant, bureaucratic and other classes have to be overridden in their turn.

Reduction to absurdity, perhaps. Yet anyone who has witnessed attempts to bypass the rural middle class, typically by the young, First World, middle-class representatives of NGOs who insist on addressing only the poorest, rainfed farmers, will appreciate that this absurdity is not imaginary. It is happening. And anyone who has taken the time to listen to the slightly better-off – who will never in their lifetime see one tenth of the wealth of the NGO staff – will soon get the measure of the resentment that it creates.

Much has been made of the so-called 'missing middle' in Africa, the fact that Africans do not seem to use the various intermediate technologies that are recommended as 'appropriate'. Here, it is mentioned merely by way of contrast with what can only be termed the 'uprooted middle' in society. It is aid that is largely doing the digging. The drain of the more talented local people into the aid-financed bureaucracy, into ever-extended periods of training and ultimately to high-paid work overseas is only part of the problem. The training itself, which contains a high element of imposed western social ideas and attitudes, further deracinates the educated middle-class. Lastly, aid has diminished the role of the middle directly. In earlier years, aid financed centrally controlled public services, which were based on western models offering services on an individual basis. By doing this they bypassed one of the traditional middle-class roles, as mediators of state services. That approach continues, but lack of resources and management has meant that it never really succeeded. Latterly, therefore, it has been replaced by attempts to promote services through direct support to 'grass-roots' groups: NGOs, co-operatives and so on. Once again the aim is to bypass the middle class.

Obviously, the middle class fights back in its own interest, usually by capturing the flow of aid. This may be done in many ways, positive as well as negative. The presence of lead farmers in control of aid-financed co-operatives may reflect the élite carrying out its well-established, distributive and socially responsible role in a new format, just as much as it does a new acquisitive, exploitative élite 'capturing the benefits of aid'. Managing a co-operative is one of the most thankless tasks going and may well lead to substantial costs. On the whole, however, it seems likely that the effects will be negative and that aid at these lower social levels will operate in exactly the same way as it does at the national level. There it undermines the force of taxation as a link between ruler and ruled. Here it removes the similar link between élite and supporters because the aid money comes free. The élite member no longer needs a subscription from his supporters and they will no longer greatly resent his corruption. After all, it is not their money. Even if the rural élite does not succeed in capturing the benefits of a programme of support to the poor, it can only be human for them to resent such a programme, to cut off any support they might have given to the poor themselves and to resent also the role of the new élite that has taken their place: typically an alliance of the better educated urban élite and foreigners.

Economics does not usually grant success to policies that aim at two targets with one weapon. Yet project after project has been designed to provide high internal rates of return and improve the lot of the poorest simultaneously. Programme after programme has been aimed at helping the poorest and generating growth, often flying in the face of social realities. Much of the sophisticated apparatus of Social-Cost Benefit Analysis is designed to allow projects to work to these two targets at once. Only those who are condemned to try and fit the ragged edges of Third World data to the elegant models it produces and, even harder, to try and meet the targets it sets up, can appreciate how unreal this is. Hitting the single target of higher production is far from easy. To try for equity as well makes it many times more than doubly difficult.

The idea that it is necessary to offer a certain level of incentive to the better-off has been becoming much more widely accepted in the First World, even in the Second World of the socialist European countries. The rule of asymmetry has meant that the Third World is given different advice. The World Bank continues to prescribe that the top 5 per cent of the population in the modern sector will 'contribute most to the reduction of public dissavings' (World Bank, 1989: Ch 8). In other words the élites are not to benefit from the next few years of development. They will merely be required to make the greatest effort. Almost without exception, the latest prescription calls for greater efforts in areas that can only be met by the relatively well-educated middle classes: greater accountability, more sensitivity to local customs, more cost recovery without excessive demands on the poor, more local consultants, higher-quality education, better-managed parastatals and so on and so on.

Current aid strategies call for a reduced and better focused role for the state, which should concentrate on providing an enabling environment. This would allow the people to manage their own development, partly through the market and partly through grass-roots organizations of one kind or another. It is well to acknowledge that this is a backward step, however necessary at present, for it will reverse the processes of political development, that balanced shift of both rights and obligations to the state and away from sub-state organizations such as religious or ethnic groups or tribes. Such a reversal is, probably, inevitable, at least partly because aid itself has upset the balance of obligations. Nevertheless, to go back to a more pluralist society will inevitably require that some social goals have to be delayed. Higher levels of equity will be the first of these because some groups will advance more quickly than others. Anyone who has worked with rural communities must recognize that personality and a lot of other special factors will mean that some grass-roots organizations will take off and others will not, for no apparent reason or difference between them. If the call for more grass-roots initiative is genuine it must leave room for this to happen, however unwelcome the inequality that may result.

Relations with the state will present a practical problem as well. If lower level institutions are to receive foreign aid and yet remain independent of the state, there would have to be a direct link between donor and institution, with minimum state mediation. There will be a very fine line to be trod between creating institutions that are, in effect, clients of foreign agencies and creating units that are merely new arms of the state itself.

The Pressures in the Machine

Aid is a colossus of unimaginable size: a machine, a bureaucratic-academic complex which may not rival the military-industrial complex at the global level but which is even more overpowering for the sub-Saharan African countries that have become its especial concern. (Recent developments in Eastern Europe may well see the aid machine overtake the military machine on a world-wide basis.) The forms aid takes are many and wonderful. This attempt to simplify it is bound to give an unjust picture of the sheer scale of a very largely sincere effort to transfer development to countries that have yet to enjoy much of its benefits. In particular, the constant reference to the World Bank is not because it deserves to be pilloried more than other donors. Instead, it reflects the fact that the Bank tries harder than most to understand what it is doing and to explain it to outside observers. It is because the Bank's documents make the most coherent and thorough statement of what aid is trying to do that it receives most attention here. Nevertheless, 'the road to hell is paved with good intentions' and the injustice must be risked if a way off that road is to be found.

Taken singly or as a group, all four of the aid axioms seem deeply problematic. The question is, therefore, why do they remain so strong, so impervious to the doubts that the evidence is bound to raise? Why is it that aid donors still accept that 'the momentum of aid generated in the past few years will have to be maintained during the 1990s' despite the evident failure to make good use of aid, despite the extreme unlikelihood of the assumptions used to justify the expenditure, and despite the underlying inconsistency with the calls for greater discipline? Why is it that donors still do not feel morally justified in insisting on standards of financial reporting that they themselves claim to be their right? Why is it that funds allocated to arm's-length research on diminishingly small topics far outweigh those devoted to the management of aid expenditure? Why do donors feel able to advocate social equity in the strongest possible terms while being quite unable to enforce their disapproval for thoroughly inequitable regimes?

One reason is that aid is now, quite clearly, a First World consumption good. The volume of aid is not related in any way to the capacity of Third World economies to use it or to the return on the investment it finances: it is determined by what the people of the First World want to spend. This is not quite so clear for official government aid, which is controlled by political processes and to some extent by the pressure to subsidize First World industry and agriculture, but the Live Aid and Band Aid events made it absolutely evident; aid is a popular event for the citizens of the First World. This is not to question the sincerity of the desire among those citizens to help those poorer than themselves, to acknowledge how lucky they are and to share their good fortune; it is to underline the fact that aid is a unique economic act because the giver exchanges his money for the act of giving and nothing else. Because it is a First World consumption good, the volume of aid is determined by incomes in the First World and will grow rapidly as the developed economies grow, at a pace that far outstrips the lagging economies of the less developed countries which have to absorb it. On the other hand, aid must be compatible with the giver's own ideas of social justice. This is where the inconsistent combination of a desire for social equity with a wish to respect local sovereignty and avoid the taint of neo-colonialism comes from. So too does the more recent emphasis on environmental matters. There is also a strong wish to see aid as a force for development, not as charity, in keeping with western ideas of equality of opportunity rather than equality of material wellbeing. Pure charity is acceptable in emergencies like famine, but not as a never-ending dole to people who may be less rich but are not actually starving.

Because the giver's interest in aid comes from the act of giving, his interest in what happens to it is relatively small. He expects no further personal return beyond the act of benefaction. His interest in the results is not zero, in that clear evidence of the misuse of aid would destroy the act of giving as a benefaction, but he certainly is not sufficiently interested to undertake the considerable costs of supervising it directly. This means that the general level of interest in accounting for aid is low. The major donor agencies are among the least accountable organizations in the world, not because some efforts are not made to measure their performance but because it is impossible to make a definitive measurement and because such an assessment is not necessary to their continued existence. The spiralling levels of academic debate on aid testify to the difficulties of definitive measurement. Provided that debate continues without a clear outcome, the giver is normally willing to give aid the benefit of the doubt on the basis that it costs him so little and that even if it is only marginally useful it is still worth while.

Donor agencies, like all organizations, develop a natural desire to grow, to do better, and this means that they have a strong interest in maintaining the volume of aid. Since the ultimate givers of aid are driven by a wish to be generous, overestimates of the aid requirement are, in some ways, more welcome than underestimates, so both First World partners in the aid business conspire to maintain high levels of aid.

The political motives for aid should not be forgotten. Some African nations have made considerable use of their geo-political position to secure aid. Sudan has been able to exploit its position between Libya, Egypt and the Red Sea, for example. Even this represents the working out of First World concerns on African territory rather than any genuine community of interest between First World and Third World countries, but that is the way it has always been since the dawn of imperialism. If the end of the Cold War reduces this factor it will be the first time since Europe first discovered Africa.

Should there be doubts about the nature of aid as a First World consumption good, the First World's behaviour over trade will dispel them. Despite the near-certainty that trade liberalization would meet all the goals of aid at less cost and without the undeniably undignified aspects of aid for both donors and recipients, the political costs of such a move remain prohibitive. It would affect direct First World economic and political interests, whereas cash aid is actually beneficial to the First World giver. It makes him feel good.

The World Bank Strategy for Africa, which may be flawed but remains an honest account of what is happening and which acknowledges most of the problems, is prefaced by the statement that 'this is a study by the staff of the World Bank and the judgements in it do not necessarily reflect the views of the board of directors or the governments they represent.' Fair warning that aid is a political not a technical issue, and it will remain so. Fair warning that the more difficult parts of the prescription, that donors should not give aid to those who demonstrably fail to put it to good use, will not be taken up.

2· ECONOMIC DEVELOPMENT IN THE PAST

> 'Merchants are the cause of the prosperity of the lands.' From an 18th-century *laissez-passer* of Wadai Sultan to a group of Darfuri merchants. (O'Fahey, 1980)

The recent past is given undue weight in unfamiliar areas. Visitors describe the people they meet and what they do as 'traditional', as though it had been that way since Noah's flood. Then they talk to the people themselves, who are naturally most concerned with recent events. The visitor concludes that what has happened in the last ten years is the first change in centuries to affect a 'traditional society'. Inevitably that first change seems overpoweringly important when seen from this perspective: disastrous, revolutionary, the collapse of a golden age and so on. In Darfur this twisted view of events is very strong. Coming to wider attention as it did in the 1970s, after the Sahel drought, that drought was seen as the epochal change that explained everything that is happening in the region. The subsequent droughts of the 1980s only seemed to confirm this. There has been a series of gloomy analyses marked by apocalyptic interpretations of what happened and correspondingly radical predictions about what would have to be done if disaster were to be averted.

A typical comment: 'Darfur has far to go. It is almost at the bottom rung of the development ladder. If the people's possession of material goods is any indication they are among the poorest in the Northern provinces. Other indices such as levels of adult literacy, crude birth rates and life expectancy tell the same story.

'Rapid expansion of human and livestock numbers has severely reduced the carrying capacity of the land and the subsistence pastoral economy has been replaced by an agricultural one. Present social and political institutions are inherited from the subsistence economy, especially the systems of land and water rights. In the presence of a stagnant primitive technology, rapidly expanding population and declining rainfall the destruction of the environment is accelerating at an alarming rate' (HTS, 1974).

This line of thinking provided much of the rationale behind development projects established in the 1970s. It is still widely accepted and it parallels similar analyses in many African countries. To a large degree it is typical of the aid view of what is happening in Africa as a whole.

It is, however, based on several false concepts summed up in the word 'stagnant': the implication being that Darfur is stuck in a primitive social and technical framework, out of which it cannot break of its own accord. This is quite the opposite of the truth. The Darfur economy has been expanding quickly for most of the 20th century. Any technical changes that were practical were absorbed with great rapidity. The social and commercial framework shows every sign of adapting effectively to circumstances, given the chance. Even the unsophisticated political institutions 'inherited from the subsistence economy' have proved more robust and more useful than the variety of more modern forms offered since independence.

Darfur is a classic example of the economic process called 'vent for surplus'. By generating demand for goods, trade opens the door for and mobilizes 'surplus labour and land in underpopulated areas with a smallholder production system. It is presumed to be a costless type of growth which could be largely self-financed by small farmers and local traders' (Eicher & Baker, 1982: 31). In Darfur the extensive savannahs provide the surplus land and the labour has been either available locally or drawn in from countries to the west. However, there are two crucial constraints: transport and water. The region developed through increasing production for export markets, as and when those markets opened up and as and when the key technologies to break those two constraints became available.

Many see development through trade as a sudden event linked to the introduction of a cash economy: 'monetization', in the jargon. The vent for surplus has a much longer history than that and agricultural expansion through labour mobilization on a free land resource started long before the development of a full cash economy in Darfur. What may be called quasi-currencies had been in circulation for a very long time. Salt, thread and cloth were common examples and standard exchange rates with grain and livestock were formally established. There were even mechanisms for adjusting those exchange rates (Kapteijns, 1985).

There was considerable trade in the era of cloth and other quasi-currencies. This trade was controlled by the Fur Sultans, who claimed export goods like ivory by right and sold them through traders. In this way imports could be generated without any domestic currency exchange at all (Kapteijns in Manger, 1984). Indirectly, however, those exports were still used to finance agricultural expansion. The sultanate of the 18th and 19th centuries mobilized labour through the Hakura, or estate system. Some estates were worked by slaves and others by tribal communities, but they were managed by an élite whose reward came in the form of imported prestige items bought with the state's exports.

It is commonly suggested that trade breaks down traditional social forms such the communal work party called *nafir* in Darfur. In point of fact there is some evidence that market demand for crops may even have strengthened the *nafir* well into the monetary era. Links to the market economy 'enforce the cohesion of the nafeir group which becomes the main referent to achieve all the labour intensive activities' (Salih in Manger, 1984). A similar pattern may be seen in the Jebel Marra area, where the *nafir* work group is most commonly found on the upper parts of the Jebel Marra mountain itself, by far the richest section of the district thanks to cash crops of potatoes and oranges (JMRDP Wet Season Survey, 1987). In short, it is not currency or monetization that is crucial to a vent-for-surplus development. It is the opportunity to exchange surplus production for imported goods, by whatever means, that matters.

Governor-generals' reports from the period of the Second World War illustrate how crucial imported goods were in stimulating production in Darfur: the classic vent for surplus process. In order to supply the armies in Egypt and the Middle East, the government had an urgent need for sheep and cattle from Darfur. The area also exported considerable quantities of grain. The result was that 'the large amount of cash circulating among the people seriously interferes with the Darfur economy, for the proceeds of exports . . . cannot be absorbed by the present volume of imports. Consequently there is little inducement to the countryman to sell large quantities of his grain, to offer his services on the labour market or turn his attention to such laborious tasks as improving the quality of his hides or butter. The countryman has perforce remained largely self-supporting' (Sudan Government, 1945). Nothing could be done about this situation because during the war imports were very tightly rationed.

Six Commodities

Darfur's history centres on six export commodities: slaves, ivory, ostrich feathers, gum arabic, groundnuts and livestock. Each in turn has led the way in stimulating the economy and strengthening its links with the outside world. The slave trade dated well back into the 18th century. Situated as it was on the frontier between Muslim and pagan and with a direct link to Egypt via the Forty Days Road, Darfur was an ideal base for raiding the Negro tribes and sending them north. Napoleon, when in Egypt, wrote to the Sultan Abdal Rahman asking for '2,000 esclaves noirs ayant plus de 16 ans, forts et vigoureux' to be sent to him. History does not record whether he got them (O'Fahey, 1980).

Internally, slavery also contributed labour for the expansion of cultivation. Even the development of the Fur Sultanate during the 18th century was attributable to 'the employment by the sultans of slaves as soldiers, labourers and bureaucrats' (O'Fahey & Abu Salim, 1983). The close links between trade and the development of the state are perhaps best revealed in the import of paper: a vital commodity for the establishment of justice and administration. Imports of European-made paper from Egypt date back as early as the Keira Sultanate of the 17th century. By the mid-19th century, the French Consul in Cairo estimated that up to 2,400 reams a year went to Darfur, 5 per cent of all Egypt's imports (Daly, 1985).

Slaves had one important feature as an export: they could walk; they were a self-transporting commodity. With the region's enormously long lines of communication this was of paramount importance and transportability remains critical to this day. Ivory and ostrich feathers are almost as portable as slaves, giving high value for a low weight. Although they may seem rather trivial items in the context of economic history, the fact remains that the Victorian era in Europe, that time of ivory billiard balls and ostrich plumes, was in this way reflected all the way to Darfur. In 1905, Gleichen listed the principal exports of Darfur as 'feathers, ivory, pepper, rhino horns, tobacco, camels and cattle from Wadai'. The importance of the ivory and the feathers was shown by the fact that they alone bore a royalty of 20 per cent.

In the end, however, it was the slave trade that drew the Egyptian traders into competition with the sultanate and led to its fall. Zubayr Pasha, the greatest slaver of them all, defeated the Sultan Ibrahim Qarad at the battle of Menawashei in 1874. From that time on Darfur was ruled from Khartoum, apart from a late flowering under the last Fur

Sultan, Ali Dinar, between 1898 and the conquest by British-led forces in 1916.

In the early 20th century, gum arabic, a product of Darfur and neighbouring Kordofan, was 'The main stimulus to an economy that was recovering from utter stagnation [in the Mahdia].' Gum contributed 54 per cent of the country's export earnings in 1903 (Beshai, 1976). In 1923 it was 39 per cent and even in 1983 it was 7.5 per cent. The relative importance of gum fell because other sectors, especially cotton, were expanding even faster, not because the gum arabic trade did not continue to grow rapidly, at a rate which up to the 1960s can only be described as spectacular. Neither the First World War nor the great depression halted an expansion that averaged 2.9 per cent per annum for the 60 years between 1907 and 1967.

Gum arabic has a very long history. It is found in pharaonic mummies, for example. In the modern era it is used in foodstuffs, confectionery and pharmaceuticals as well as inks and paints. No other producer has been able to match Sudan for either quantity or quality. One reason for the growth in demand in the 20th century has been a shift in European tastes away from boiled sweets to gums in the 1920s and 1930s, another illustration of how the remote west of Sudan has long been integrated into the world economy and sensitive to European fashions.

As Figure 2.1 shows, the collapse of the gum trade in the early 1970s was as spectacular as the earlier growth. Labour emigration, declining rainfall and increasing interest in crop production all contributed to the collapse, but the major problem was a sharp price rise which drove users in the industrial world to find substitutes in synthetics and in gum made from the guar bean. These problems were compounded by government interference. Gum arabic had always been subject to high government royalties and other controls since the days of the Mahdi and before. Nevertheless, the government's attempt to squeeze the last drop out of high export prices in the 1970s undoubtedly helped to drive consumers to seek alternatives.

Darfur started as a small gum producer compared to Kordofan: 1,231 tons of Darfur gum was sold in 1941 compared with 10,211 tons of Kordofan gum. In later years Darfur's share of the gum market rose and by the early 1970s the region produced around 20 per cent of Sudan's total exports. This late expansion indicates that the reason that Darfur was less important earlier was that the capacity to trade was restricted, the vent for surplus was not open, rather than that the area was not capable of producing the crop in quantity.

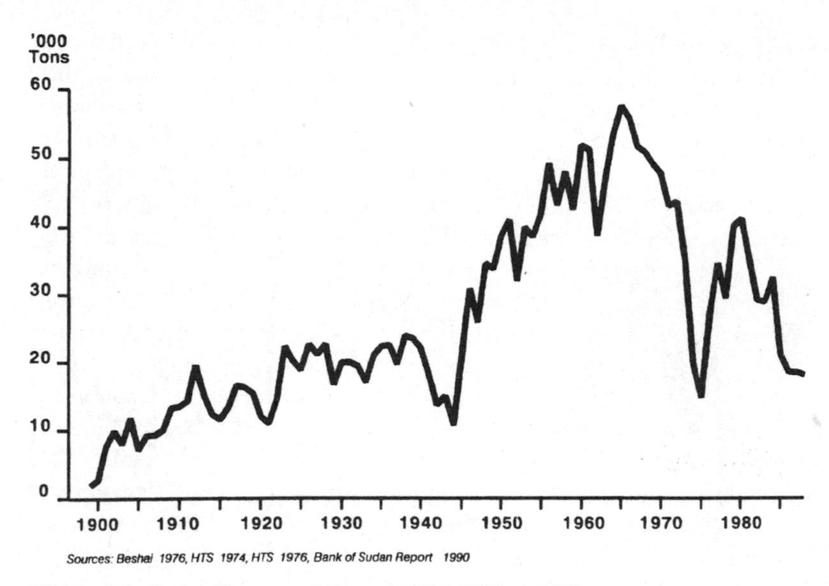

Figure 2.1 Sudan Exports of Gum Arabic, 1899 to 1989

While Darfur took second place for gum, it was always the dominant producer of cattle. Between 1939 and 1941, recorded sales in south Darfur alone were between 94 and 136 per cent of the whole country's exports (Sudan Government, 1939–41). Sales in Darfur still exceeded the nation's exports even in the early 1980s, and they probably still do. In 1980/81 more than 31,000 head were sold in Nyala market alone, the vast majority adult bulls. In 1981, Sudan only exported a little over 18,000 head.

Sudanese cattle exports have been erratic, with two extraordinary boom periods divided by equally sharp depressions. In both world wars the normally restricted demand for live cattle became virtually limitless, as the British tried to maintain their armies in Egypt and the Middle East. Even the recent strong demand from Saudi Arabia and other Middle Eastern countries has failed to raise exports much above half the level achieved in 1942. Figure 2.2 illustrates Sudanese cattle exports since 1907.

Groundnuts, the third great export commodity from western Sudan,

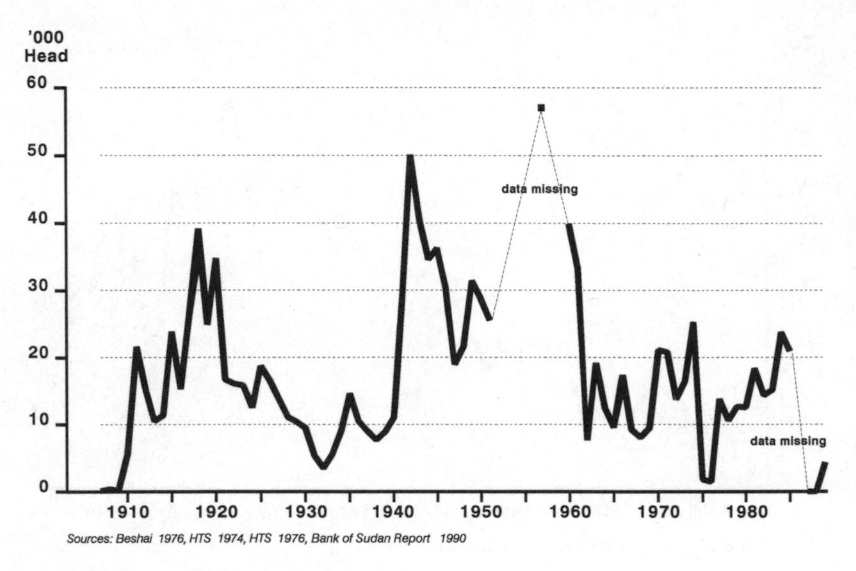

Figure 2.2 Sudan Exports of Cattle, 1907 to 1989

was the last to achieve importance. After the Second World War demand in Europe rose rapidly at a time when India, which had been the major exporter with 44 per cent of world exports in 1929, dropped out of the market. India had no exports by 1965. Nigeria was the first to take over, followed by Senegal and Sudan (Beshai, 1976).

Sudanese exports began to expand rapidly in the early 1950s and this rise continued up to 1965, when it had 11.8 per cent of the world's trade. Extension of the railway to Nyala in 1959 enabled Darfur to participate in the second half of this period and it was estimated that by 1964/5 Darfur produced 36 per cent of the national crop, ahead of Kordofan which had 29 per cent (Low, 1967). There followed a setback to 1970 and then a second even more explosive rise to 1976. From then until now there has been a disastrous slump. All these movements are illustrated in Figure 2.3.

The evidence of the three major export goods, gum arabic, cattle and groundnuts, is that Darfur has been through a number of periods of boom and bust but that there has been strong underlying growth through

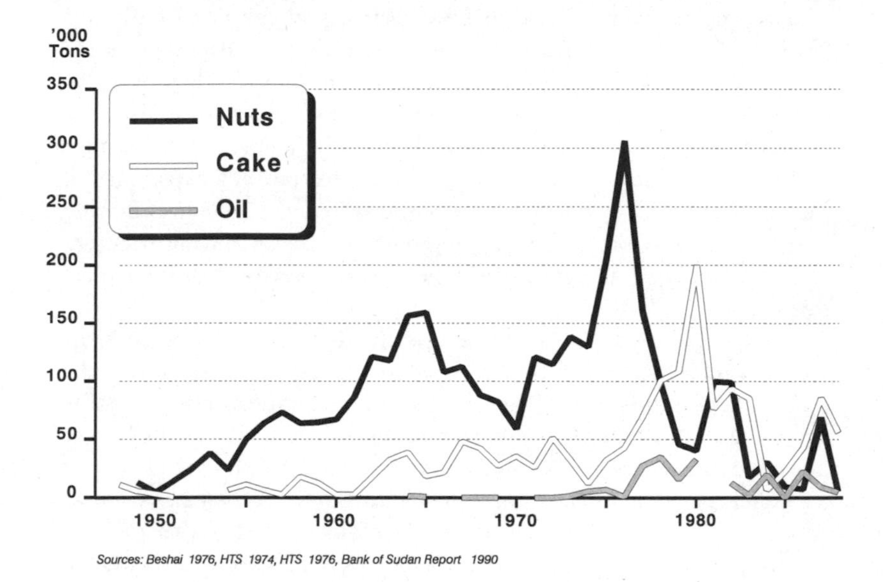

Figure 2.3 Sudan Exports of Groundnuts, 1948 to 1989

the first 75 years of this century. The strongest and most prolonged boom came after the Second World War, when gum arabic exports entered their period of most rapid growth up to 1965, the wartime cattle boom lasted through to 1960 and the early phase of expansion in groundnut exports lasted to 1965 as well.

Exports do not, however, tell the entire story as far as cattle and groundnuts are concerned. As the great irrigation schemes of the Gezira and elsewhere became established and the Khartoum metropolis expanded, rising urban and irrigated sector incomes have meant that domestic Sudanese consumption of both meat and groundnut oil has been rising steadily. This has cushioned the impact of export problems for the Darfur producer.

To sum up, the farmers and livestock herders of Darfur make the most of what market opportunities are within their grasp. Production can be raised extraordinarily rapidly during boom periods. Groundnuts developed from virtually nothing in the late 1950s, before the railway reached Nyala, to a crop second in importance only to millet by the mid-1960s. The fact that Sudanese cattle owners, the Darfuris predominant among them, were able to raise their export surplus from 8,000 head in 1938 to 50,000 in 1942 is equally striking. The Darfuris are also capable of maintaining production during slumps. They have the resources and the tenacity to see them through short-term setbacks. Nevertheless, if markets turn against them in the longer term they may be forced to withdraw. The Condominium government's experience of the 1940s showed how the people of Darfur were quite capable of moving into the cash economy when it was profitable and of moving back out again if there were no consumer imports worth buying with the money they earned.

One last point cannot be emphasized too heavily: all these developments were almost entirely the result of private initiative. Even the crucial introduction of the Barberton groundnut variety, now grown by almost all, is credited to one merchant's initiative. Until well after independence, government's role was restricted to building railways and introducing auction markets for crops and livestock. This changed almost entirely in 1970, after the accession of the Numeiri regime with a largely left-wing programme. Then the Gum Arabic Company and Sudan Oilseeds Corporation were created with monopolies in the export of their respective crops. Despite the relatively rapid removal of the Sudan Communist Party from government and a turn back to more right-wing policies, trade in western Sudanese produce has never again been completely free of government intervention. Cattle exports never fully recovered from a ban on livestock exports in 1975, in response to consumer pressure over high prices. Gum arabic was severely damaged by the mismanagement of prices during the 1970s boom. Groundnuts have suffered from repeated changes in the status of the Sudan Oilseeds Corporation, which sometimes had a monopoly and was sometimes required to compete with private traders. Lack of a clear policy over producer prices compounded the problem.

Migration to the newly rich OPEC states of the Gulf accelerated sharply in the early 1970s. Some decline in export production from western Sudan was probably inevitable, given the loss of labour to the Gulf and rising remittance incomes leading to increased domestic consumption. It seems clear, nevertheless, that it was direct government intervention combined with the gross macro-economic distortions discussed later that turned a decline into a slump. By the end, as many migrants were being pushed out of Darfur by the depression there as were being pulled by the attraction of higher wages elsewhere.

A Shifting Balance

Many parts of Darfur are of little or no agricultural use: especially but not solely the deserts of the far north. Agro-ecological zones which cover only 64 per cent of the region contain 96 per cent of the rainfed cropped area and 100 per cent of the irrigated area. The remaining areas are of virtually no farming interest. Even within the 64 per cent only some 6 per cent of the land area is cropped. For farming the region can be divided into two: the north and west and the south and east, referred to as north/west and south/east from now on. In the first area, alluvial soils along the wadis of the basement zone are the most important source of crop land. The volcanic soils of the Jebel Marra massif are also important. In the second, south/east, area, most of the crop land is on the large areas of windblown sandsheet, called *goz*. The *athmur*, sandy dunes which are found in the middle of the alluvial areas, are also farmed.

Ease of cultivation, soil fertility and access to water are the critical factors. Ease of cultivation matters because farmers who only have hand tools cannot manage heavy or hard soils. The light *goz* sands are infertile, but the yield difference between light and heavy soils is not as great as might be expected and ease of cultivation more than compensates. The importance of water is self-evident; areas without drinking water cannot be farmed, however good the soil. Both pre-season work and, especially, harvesting have to be done well outside the rainy season, so cropping is impossible if there is no way to store water near the fields for these periods.

The division between north/west and south/east reflects the influence of all three factors. The north/west group is more varied but fertile soils are available. Some are too heavy to work but others are well suited to traditional hand cultivation, especially along the wadi valleys. By contrast, the soils in the south/east are either light but infertile sands (*goz* and *athmur*) or so hard and compacted they are impossible to cultivate without tractors. Water is relatively well provided in the north/west group, where shallow wells along the many wadi courses can last through the dry season. The best land is also found along the wadis, so there is a good match between water supply and crop land.

In the sandy south/east there is no such match. Until the introduction of deep boreholes, dry season water was only available along the lines of wadis or buried watercourses, where wells can be dug by hand, or in depressions where ponds of standing water can last. Most of these water sources were in the alluvial areas, where the soils are too hard or sometimes too wet to be usable. Farming was largely confined to the boundaries of the cultivable *goz*, where it was in reach of water sources in the alluvium, and to sandy *athmur* ridges within the alluvium. Much of the history of agricultural development in Darfur over the last century reflects the way in which the water problem on the *goz* was solved, so that it now provides the largest single area of cropped land: 41 per cent.

The heartland of the Fur state, based around Jebel Marra, was well suited to a subsistence economy, growing grain on the heavier wadi soils and on the volcanic soils of the mountain itself. The export products – gum, cattle and groundnuts – are all better adapted to the south and east of the region. There the *hashab*, the gum arabic tree, has its natural habitat, there groundnuts do best on the light sandy soils and there the largest cattle herds traverse the broad lowlands. One result of expanding exports has been a significant shift in the centre of gravity in the region. Perhaps the first step in this process was the establishment of the capital of the later Fur sultans at El Fasher, on the plain to the north-east of Jebel Marra. This set the seal on the sultanate's move down from the mountains to the wider crop lands of the savannahs. The establishment of Nyala and the extension of the railway to that town confirmed a second shift of emphasis, to the *goz* crop lands and the cattle herding areas of south Darfur.

The arrival of motor vehicles undermined one of the great strengths of the north, its vast camel herds for transport. The inclusion of Darfur in Sudan conclusively turned its attention eastwards to the Nile. Before it had also faced north, along the Darb al 'Arba'īn to Egypt, and west to Wada'i and West Africa. 'All the early towns of the region have now disappeared with the exception of El Fasher and Kabkabiya. All were directly associated with caravan traffic (in the north) and most could not survive the era of road and rail transport. The southern parts of Darfur had no caravan routes and hence no towns' (Abu Sin in Pons, 1980). The largest and most rapidly growing towns are now all in the south.

In keeping with the gloomy, 'stagnant' view of what is happening, the drift of people from north to south Darfur has been blamed solely on drought and desertification. In fact the drift to the south contains a strong positive element: the exploitation of export opportunities. That has been a factor for much longer than drought: 'The persistent migration from north to south has been checked by good rains over the northern areas. Lack of water in the north and easy living in the south, combined with increased public security everywhere encourages this southward drift, a natural and inevitable movement' (Sudan Government, 1945).

Population estimates from before the first census, in 1955, are little more than guesses. Even the census figures for 1955, 1973 and 1983 are open to question. Nevertheless, it is certain that population in Darfur has been growing at a rapid rate for most of the 20th century, since before the great advances in health to which such high rates are usually attributed. Immigration, especially from West Africa, has been important, but natural increase was the major factor. In the 1955 census the excess of births over deaths was already 28.8 per thousand, greater in fact than the annual population increase over the next 15 years. If there was immigration, it seems to have been balanced by emigration. In 1955 there were more Darfuris resident elsewhere in Sudan than there were outsiders resident in Darfur.

The most striking measure of development in Darfur was the rate of urbanization, especially in the south.

Table 2.1: Urban population growth rates, per cent per annum

	Total	N. Darfur	S. Darfur
1955–64	6.0	4.9	8.6
1964–73	5.2	4.3	9.5
1973–83	5.3	4.7	6.0

Source: WSDC, 1985

Even between the towns, the balance between north and south was shifting. In 1955 El Fasher, which had been the capital since the Fur sultanate, had a population of 26,000: twice as large as Nyala to the south or El Geneina to the south-west. By 1983, Nyala had 115,000 inhabitants, a third larger than El Fasher, and even El Geneina was catching up on it. Some smaller towns, notably Ed Da'ein and Umm Kedada in the groundnut growing areas, had also grown rapidly. In earlier years, the towns had served principally as administrative centres, El Fasher in the lead. As trade and production boomed, commerce, transport and even industry took over as the main engines of urbanization. With a less significant commercial hinterland, El Fasher began to lag.

Nyala was exceptional, not just in Darfur but also in the Sudan. Of all the Sudanese towns, only Juba grew faster over the whole period between 1955 and 1983. Before the annexation of Darfur in 1916, Nyala had not even existed, beyond a 'mere nomadic camp'. In the 1920s and 1930s it became a 'small service village' as the administrative centre for southern Darfur (Abu Sin in Pons, 1980). Zalingei, Kutum and El Geneina were all more important. The decision to extend the railway from El Obeid to Nyala indicated that its importance was increasingly recognized and the arrival of the railway in 1959 opened the way for its explosive growth.

The origins of the new urban populations show that urbanization was the result of increasing opportunities, not of rural unemployment. In the 1955–6 census, there were more urban-born Darfuris living in the rural settled sector than the other way around. There were even more urban-born among the nomads than there were nomad-born in the towns. In other words the drift was, if anything, actually from the towns to the country. This did not mean that the towns were not growing as well, partly through natural growth, but also through immigration from outside Darfur (Dept of Statistics, 1956).

Immigration from outside Darfur continued to be a leading factor in urban growth. From central Sudan there came 'traders, investors, crop dealers and government officials'. These introduced the urban lifestyles of the Nile valley. They activated the urban economy and gave an 'impetus to the diffusion of the urban economy into the rural hinterland'. Most importantly, they mobilized capital from both inside and outside Darfur for investment in Nyala. The other flow came from the west. West Africans have made the hajj pilgrimage to Mecca since the King of Takrur did so in the 11th century. For almost as long, they have sought work along their route to pay their way in a journey that can take years or even never reach its end. The slow march from west to east was 'inextricably interwoven with economic factors in the form of a search for jobs'. Many West Africans ended up in Darfur and especially Nyala (Abu Sin in Pons, 1980).

The Darfuris themselves were probably the last to join the flow into the towns, although they became the largest element in the higher urban growth rates of later years. It is impossible to judge how much of this was the result of bad rainfall in north Darfur and how much the response to the continued attraction of towns showing rapid economic growth. Either way, groups like the Zaghawa of the far north-west became important in trade and many others sought urban employment alongside the western immigrants.

Large as Nyala was, it remained a country town. A lot of the work, in the groundnut mills and the brick kilns, was seasonal and almost everyone continued to farm. In 1973, it was estimated that 73 per cent of the Nyala population 'remained wholly or partially dependent on agriculture'. Even among railway employees, in the most modern sector of the economy, 45 per cent had cultivation plots near town (Abu Sin in Pons, 1980).

The Development of Goz Agriculture

In the production of surplus grain to support other sectors and of groundnuts for export, agriculture on the sandy *goz* lands of the south and east was the driving force for development for several decades. Without new technology to raise yields or labour productivity there was limited potential for increased production in the Fur heartland to the north and west. On the *goz*, on the other hand, there were extensive lands on which cropping was, and is, very profitable. The poor fertility of the sandy soils is more than offset by the low cost of cultivating them.

The development of techniques to farm these waterless *goz* regions was crucial. Four circumstances have contributed: strong markets for millet, the introduction of a new crop, groundnuts, improved water supply and the widespread availability of cheap steel hand tools, for clearing as well as for cultivation. Increasing population has been the main reason for the demand for millet, but a strong local preference for millet over sorghum, combined with the fact that the people of Darfur could afford to pay for that preference thanks to rising incomes, was also important.

It is frequently argued that cash cropping makes peasant farmers more vulnerable to unstable commodity markets and contributes directly to famine. This is not the case in Darfur. Millet and groundnuts are a good crop combination in the sense of security just as much as profitability. The subsistence crop, millet, is in any case just as much a cash crop as groundnuts and it is frequently the poorer farmers who have to sell grain in order to buy other necessities or small luxuries. (Even the poor have a wish for small luxuries.) Because it is almost entirely directed at the local market millet sellers cannot avoid the farmer's inescapable problem: good harvests bring poor prices and vice versa. Prices for an export crop may be variable, but at least they do not vary with the local rainfall and farmers are, therefore, able to reap the full benefit of good harvests. This means that farmers are able to build up their capital more quickly with groundnuts and that good years provide a decent bank balance to protect against the bad. It also means that even the poorer farmer has a chance of getting cash for his consumption without being forced to sell so much of his grain crop in a good year that he would risk running short in the next bad year.

None of this would have mattered if it had not been possible to develop ways to support life on the waterless *goz*. Even during the rainy season, the sandy soils drain the water away so quickly that drinking water can be a problem. During the dry season there is no water at all. Before the introduction of deep boreholes, *goz* cropping was only possible using baobab trees and watermelons.

'The main stems of these trees are hollow by nature and the cavities they contain can be substantially enlarged. During the rainy season water was collected in excavations made at the base of the trees from which it was hauled up in leather buckets and poured into the hollow stems through a hole cut in the top. As soon as the main stem of the tree was filled it was sealed up . . . They grow to a great age and in some cases have been known to hold as much as 3,000 gallons of water' (Sarsfield-Hall, 1975). From this account the intense effort required to gain the water to support life on the *goz* can be imagined. Once filled and properly sealed water stored in the baobabs remains sweet to the end of the hot weather and good trees are a valuable form of property, to be let or sold with or without the adjacent land.

It is difficult for outsiders to believe that watermelons can play a significant role in water supply. Nevertheless, whole villages, including the horses, cattle and other stock, used to depend on them. They were gathered up and stored in heaps; the skins were saved and given to the goats when the grass dried up (Gleichen, 1905). Even today it is normal for the traveller in the *goz* during the early dry season to be offered melon rather than drinking water and young calves can be seen eating chopped-up melon out of galvanized iron bowls.

Even with full baobabs and a large crop of watermelons it was not possible for everyone to spend the whole year on the *goz*. The important thing was to be able to stay long enough to complete the harvest and gum tapping. After that the grain would be buried in pits before the bulk of the household left with the livestock for the alluvial areas, where they could pass the dry season near the wells. A few old men would stay behind to guard the grain. By the end of the dry season they would be reduced to digging up succulent roots for water.

There are only so many baobab trees and a tree can only be filled once a year. Deep boreholes have changed the situation from one where at best a large baobab held 3,000 gallons for a whole dry season to one where a 12,000-gallon steel tank is filled, without effort, twice a day.

There are now no limits to farming the *goz*. The first boreholes in the *goz* were sunk in the late 1940s but the major expansion came in the late 1960s when several hundred were drilled.

It would be impossibly expensive to sink boreholes so close together as to put all the land within walking distance of water. For this reason, one further development has made a considerable difference, a development to delight the soul of the most ardent intermediate technologist. For it is a combination of old truck axles and empty 44-gallon fuel drums that has brought vast areas of the *goz* within range of the hoe. With a Bedford truck axle, complete with wheels and old tyres, it is possible to make a flat one-horse cart on which to put oil drums full of water and take them to farms up to 20 kilometres from a borehole. This is the ubiquitous *Karu*, also used for carting all kinds of goods around the towns of Darfur. On the flat sandy grassland of the *goz* the big truck tyres travel easily and the small Darfur horses seem to have no trouble pulling water considerable distances.

Lastly, the two necessary inputs for *goz* farming, aside from seed and sweat that is, have become much more widely and cheaply available than before: the axe and the flat steel hoe or *hashasha*. Without reasonable steel axes (and it should be emphasized that the Darfuri axe is still a very light and feeble instrument compared to a European felling axe), the effort of clearing would have been a major obstacle to expansion. Similarly, although the soils are light and easily hoed the essence of *goz* farming is speed in operation. Wooden hoes are just not adapted to the rapid sweep action suited to the sands. The cost of steel implements is therefore a critical factor.

These steel implements have become much cheaper in the last few decades. Once again the reason is a low-level technology which depends on the scrap of a more advanced imported technology: old car springs. Local blacksmiths are probably the most widespread and active of all local craftsmen and they now forge nearly every tool used in Darfur out of scrap: from arrow heads to gin traps large enough to catch a buffalo. Before this development hoes and axes were a major import for Sudan: 'metal goods such as axes, hoes and Fasses' (Gleichen, 1905).

It takes two years to clear new land, even with axes, and then, for some reason, the yield the first year after clearing is often poor. So it may take several years to reach full production and there is always the risk of a bad season, which may further delay the time when a full return is received for the effort invested. Farming households can finance this kind of investment provided they work slowly, perhaps not clearing all the land at once and maintaining their old farm until the new one is in full production. However, this is only possible if the new land is merely an extension of an old area or close to it. To develop an entirely new site, it is essential that a relatively large area is cleared at once. This is because the uncleared bush harbours birds and other pests and cropping is impossible if they are not driven far enough back. For these reasons, it seems certain that credit mainly from family sources but also from traders has played a role in the development of the *goz*. There are various ways in which farming households can finance their subsistence needs while waiting for their farm to come into full production: credit from small traders, labouring for established farmers or in the towns during the dry season, advance crop sales, and *sharaka*. The last may be translated as 'sharecropping', but understood slightly differently. Instead of the sharecropper paying the owner of the land part of his crop as rent, it is not unusual for farmer with his own land to contract a share of his crop to someone else in return for food and expenses during the cropping season: in essence sharecropping capital rather than land.

Entrepreneurs have also been investing in *goz* agriculture, principally for groundnut farming. They pay for clearing and farming larger tracts on a commercial basis. Up to 100 hectares is not uncommon and gangs of labourers are hired from the towns to do the farm work.

Development for the Domestic Market

Although cattle, groundnuts and gum arabic, the major exports, are also grown in the Fur heartland around Jebel Marra, this area benefited more from the production of crops to meet rising internal demand in the region; a demand that grew rapidly as exports led to higher incomes. A number of relatively new crops rapidly became staples in the Darfuri diet. The earliest examples were tobacco, introduced in the 1820s, and tomatoes, which were first grown in the 1870s. A number of other crops have been introduced since, foremost among them potatoes, citrus fruit and mangoes. Demand for other, older crops also grew: especially okra, chilli and onions. To take one example, there were just 17 hectares of citrus in all Darfur in 1943. By 1977 there were 913 hectares in the west of Jebel Marra alone. There were at least as many elsewhere. Most of these horticultural crops were grown for the urban communities of Nyala, El Fasher and even Khartoum: especially oranges and potatoes from the upper slopes of Jebel Marra. Others have become staples of the rural Darfuri dict: dried tomatoes, dried okra and onions in particular. The result is that while export crops finance imports, other crops are expanding to support the growing urban communities and to add variety to the diet of a rural community seeking a higher standard of living.

New techniques, or rather very old techniques introduced from elsewhere, were important. 'Onions, the chief annual crop grown under irrigation, appears to have expanded rapidly', stimulated by the introduction of the *shaduf* 'which was unknown in earlier studies and appears to have been introduced only in the last five years' (HTS, 1977). The *shaduf* is a centuries-old technique in Egypt and elsewhere that uses a bucket hanging from one end of a beam with a counterweight at the other end to assist in raising water short distances.

Increasing incomes have also generated demand for services. Probably the biggest single advance for the household economy in Darfur in the 20th century is the diesel-driven hammer mill, first introduced in the 1950s. The saving in labour, especially women's labour, offered by these machines is quite incalculable. Previously grain was ground with a stone roller on a stone slab laid on the ground: stooped labour at its worst. The mills are so popular that there are few market villages left in Darfur which do not have one, despite the endless difficulties over spares and fuel. Farmers will travel considerable distances and pay high rates to have their grain milled. Grain milling is the most frequent single cash expenditure for the rural household. In 1984, 94 per cent of rural people interviewed in one survey took their grain to a commercial mill and milling was the most frequent single cash expenditure (WSDC Farmer Survey, 1984).

The hessian sack is another relatively new input in the region whose importance it is easy to underestimate. Before sacks, Darfur produce had to be packed in matting made from dom palm leaves or wicker baskets. Both of these are laborious to make and far from ideal for transporting large quantities of heavy goods like grain and groundnuts. Without sacks trade would be considerably restricted. In 1984 sacks sold for more than £S2 each, some 5 per cent of the crop's total value (WSDC Farmer Survey, 1984). The high value put on all forms of empty containers, bottles, tins, plastic cans, however secondhand, helps to emphasize how revolutionary a ready supply of containers can be in a remote and developing economy like Darfur. In recognition of this a Nyala merchant established a factory to make plastic jerrycans in 1986. Even so, most of the groundnut oil sold in the region has to be packed in reused containers and a common sight on the major lorry routes is a load of empty plastic cans returning to Nyala to be refilled.

Transport is naturally based in the towns. Before the Second World War there were fewer than 100 vehicles in Darfur, government and private. There were 66 in 1938. By 1970 there were 786 and by 1987, 2,334. Maintaining and otherwise servicing this fleet is a major urban activity.

Apart from flour milling, groundnut processing is the most important industry. Up to 1961 almost all the groundnuts sold through Nyala market had been hand-shelled by the farmers themselves. Soon after the railway reached Nyala in 1959, merchants began to establish mechanical decorticating plants, so rapidly indeed that by 1972 virtually no hand-shelled nuts were sold. After shelling comes oil pressing. While the best quality of nut is reserved for export whole, much of the rest is pressed for oil in Nyala and other towns.

The groundnut oil industry has had as great an effect on consumption in Darfur as on production. Cooking oil is one of the three or four most regular items on the Darfuri household's shopping list. Local demand for oil is so strong that when the drought of 1984 destroyed the local crop, some millers were importing groundnuts from Khartoum to keep their machinery working. This industry, which was entirely unaffected by government until after independence, has put cooking oil within the reach of almost all the people of the region as well as expanding the income opportunities of the majority of farmers. On the other hand, cheap groundnut oil has greatly reduced the market for animal ghee. The Baggara tribes used to pay much of their tribute to the Fur Sultans in the form of ghee and even in 1948 'a national surplus of several hundred tons is annually available for export' from the Sudan (Tothill, 1948). In the modern era ghee has become a costly luxury, used only on special occasions. The linkages go further, because the declining market for ghee also means that cattle herders can leave more milk for their calves, so strengthening export beef production at the expense of dairy.

Since the 1970s, the groundnut industry has been subjected to relatively continuous government interference. The Sudan Oilseeds Corporation, a parastatal, has repeatedly been given a monopoly and had it taken away. Support prices have been raised high one year only to collapse the next, after it had been found impossible to pay for or to transport a large crop. Transport has been particularly critical. In 1976, the crop had to be stored in the schools for more than a year because Sudan Railways could not move it. In 1990, the same thing was happening once again. If these barriers could be removed, the potential for further development would seem very strong.

Many other industries have developed, ranging from modern, government-sponsored tanneries and weaving mills, through soap factories to traditional craft operations. Among the latter, the most important are tanneries and metal work, both directly linked to agriculture. The tanneries process hides and skins produced in the region, which are used in turn to make shoes, saddles, bags and many other articles. The metal workers produce axes, hoes and other tools from scrap steel, suitcases from old oil drums and cooking pots cast from scrap aluminium. Even though much of their material is scrap, metal workers face constant difficulties getting enough. The growth of the towns has created a lively construction industry, supported by brick kilns, lime burning and carpentry. The impact has spread well beyond the major towns and there are few villages now without one or two brick-built houses.

Catering is perhaps the last major sector. Most towns, small and large, have bakeries producing wheat bread from imported flour for the bureaucrats and traders and for the restaurants which serve the large travelling population. Every small market, on the other hand, has a number of tea stalls as well as sellers of roast meat and *merissa* (the local beer). There is also an active cottage industry producing roast peanuts, ground peanut butter, sesame cakes and the like.

The 1970s saw a particularly rapid expansion in industrial activity. In 1970–71 there were only three industrial establishments with more than 25 employees, all oil mills, in the region. By 1980 there were 38 of these larger units. There was an equally rapid expansion among the smaller units: from 41 to 345. These were predominantly in the food processing sector: smaller oil mills, flour mills and bakeries. Small metal workshops rose from 4 to 23, principally involved in the production of hand tools but two making metal furniture (Dept of Statistics, Industrial Survey, 1972 & 1983).

The industrial and commercial sectors in Darfur also serve communities and markets outside the region, especially Chad and the Central African Republic. Darfur is partly a staging-post in the export of central Sudanese produce, such as onions, and even imports to countries further west. Significant quantities of Darfur-made soap and groundnut oil go west as well. The onion growers of the Jebel Marra region have also found good markets in that direction. Grain and cattle are traded in both directions across the borders, depending on harvests in the different countries. Regrettably, this trade, which is potentially very beneficial to

Darfur, has been affected by political considerations. At times trade to CAR has been exempt by treaty from the heavier export taxes. However, outright tax avoidance is also easier on this relatively unpoliced frontier. For that very reason, there have been a number of rapid changes in policy over licensing trade to the west which have severely disrupted the markets. Rumours that important export crops like gum arabic or sensitive rationed goods like sugar were being smuggled westwards have resulted in absolute bans on the trade from time to time.

However, the biggest constraint of all on industrial development is the supply of inputs. This is true at every level, from the larger government-sponsored factories that operate intermittently at best to the blacksmiths and other scrap-processing workshops who have to make special trips to Khartoum to arrange supplies (Hansohm, 1989). By 1990, fuel shortages were so acute that even groundnut oil, a staple of the Darfuri diet grown in Darfur was rationed, because the oil pressing plants could not run full-time. The widespread impact of this persistent lack of inputs may be seen in every country town in Darfur: in the daily queues outside the bakeries when flour runs out and outside the grain mills when the diesel runs out, in the sudden disappearance of sesame seed cakes, a favourite snack, when the sugar runs out and in the closure of the small cafés when the tea runs out. It is very small compensation that one or two local craft products, such as the clay *ibriq* or ablutions pot, reappear when the cheap Khartoum-made plastic version goes off the market because the plastic has run out.

Markets and Traders

Darfur is covered by a network of markets ranging from the smallest of country *suqs*, where little is sold beyond roast meat and beer – '*minsas* and *merissa*' in the local phrase – once a week, to the vast and vibrant markets of Nyala that are busy every day of the year. The latter is as large as any market in Sudan, even including Omdurman. 'He is a barefooted, poorly dressed Fur or Masalit (or Arab or any other) man who regularly walks one of his goats to the weekly market to sell it. With the proceeds he buys a blue tob for his wife [and] a few yards of damuriyya, cotton cloth for his children. Carefully saving the last pound note for some beef, tea and sugar to take home, the rest of the money will be spent on celebratory merissa and roast meat, to be consumed during the afternoon with his co-villagers in the market' (Doornbos in Manger, 1984). Sometimes the farmer may be selling crops rather than livestock. If he or she is poor, there may only be a little stored grain to sell. During the season, however, there are traders buying large quantities of grain, groundnuts and other crops, even in quite small country markets.

The typical market will consist of a number of groups of stalls with a grass *rakuba* or shelter for shade. Each group will have similar commodities on sale: cloth in one area, such things as tea, sugar and spices in another, and so on. There will be an area for teashops, usually next to the hitching-place for donkeys and camels, and another for the butchers and the roast meat. The farmers lay their crops out for sale in another corner while the livestock market is a little further away.

The country markets fall into informal circuits, each one with its own day in the week, and traders travel from one to the next. The smaller ones work the smaller circuits with a donkey or camel load of goods, while the larger travel by lorry. 'An increasingly popular weekday tour lasts from early Tuesday to Thursday night or Friday morning: the lorries leave Foro Boranga in the early morning to attend the weekly market at Bindissi. In the late afternoon they will leave for the five hour trip to Am Dukhn, whose Wednesday market is attended by thousands of people offering livestock, dried fish and meat, guinea fowl and honey from Dar Fongoro. On Thursday morning the lorries begin their return trip and will unload their human cargo, trade goods and sewing machines once more in the open air market of Muraddaf, 20 kilometres north of Am Dukhn . . . The lorries will return to Foro Boranga on Thursday night or early in the morning on Friday, in time for the market [there]' (Doornbos in Manger, 1984). Trading activity is ceaseless on these gruelling lorry trips throughout Darfur. During the rains, traders and lorry owners take considerable risks. If the lorry gets stuck, as it often does, it has to be completely unloaded and the goods portered, one sack at a time to the other side of the obstacle. Sometimes a whole lorry and its load is lost in one of the larger wadis.

Trade liberalization is a central tenet of the modern aid prescription, which appears to believe that state intervention in trade is a new phenomenon. Things are more complex than that. The African state has always had a close interest in trade, which has been the engine not merely of economic growth but also, to a large extent, of state development. In Muslim Africa trade and traders have also been a major driving force in the spread of Islam and of the more sophisticated values of metropolitan Sudan. Even the colonial state, for all its lip-service to laissez-faire, took a close interest in trade. Merchants were licensed and licences were not issued to groups that British officials mistrusted or to those who could not show what they considered to be adequate capital.

Sudanese merchants are universally known as *Jallaba*. These are people from the tribes of the stretches of the Nile between Khartoum and the Egyptian frontier who have dominated the lower levels of trade in Sudan since the mid-19th century. Darfuri attitudes to traders are very ambivalent. On the one hand they mistrust them, as all customers do their suppliers and all producers their customers. This mistrust is compounded by a dislike of the *Jallaba* as outsiders. On the other hand, they look up to them as representatives of a more modern world. Paradoxically, they also trust them more than they do their own people. 'A Masalit informant commented on this as follows: "Masalit don't like to buy from other Masalit, they think they will be eaten and the traders get rich. So we buy from *Jallaba*. If you are a few piasters short, they don't mind, sometimes they give you small things. Masalit never do that. The *Jallaba* are strangers, they are here to trade and become rich. That is the only reason why they are here. We don't like them but they are straight, they don't eat us" ' (Doornbos in Manger, 1984). To 'eat' someone or something is the evocative Sudanese metaphor for corruption and exploitation. If the people somehow prefer to deal with strangers, so the trader often prefers to trade away from his own home. This is because it is only by isolation from the kinship and other group pressures of Sudanese society that a trader can avoid dissipating his carefully amassed capital on social obligations.

It is this mix of historical and social patterns that has determined Sudanese attitudes to trade and traders, not any shortlived political change such as the influence of the Sudan Communist Party under Numeiri's 'left-turn' of 1970. The Sudanese will not, therefore, be easily persuaded of the case for market liberalization. Like so many other of the seemingly simple prescriptions of the aid treatment, they are unlikely to do more than pay lip-service to it. The existing pattern whereby the state attempts to control trade in order to satisfy popular mistrust of traders, while state officials and even the state itself collude in the exploitation of those same controls, is deeply rooted.

There have been many studies of trade in Sudan, with as many conclusions. Some, influenced by the prevalent mistrust and by the fact that trade has been dominated first by large European companies and later by a rather small number of large Khartoum merchants, have found great inefficiencies in the market. It is also claimed, frequently but inconsistently, that the large number of participants in the lower levels of the trading system also indicates inefficiency, especially with respect to the purchase of export crops. Most serious studies have found little evidence to support either proposition. 'Given the very low level of infrastructural development in Sudan, the existing livestock marketing system works very well. It finances and organises the movement of livestock from the West to the urban centres and for export using a chain of traders, agents and merchants who are linked together in a complex but flexible informal network of financial and trust relationships . . . On average the pastoralists have maintained a reasonable share of the final market price for meat . . . Inevitably, merchants are able to make windfall profits occasionally but generally, the active demand situation and competition among independent traders limit the opportunities for exploiting the producer' (HTS, 1976).

'The *jallaba* are faced with a situation of numerous small sellers and buyers scattered over a vast area, producing a variety of goods for potential sale and demanding consumption goods like sugar, tea, salt, cloth, shoes and household equipment . . . The *jallaba*, therefore, delegate the buying function to agents, *wakils*, out in the local areas . . . Producers are reluctant to make a fast agreement, in consequence of which the transaction may be dragged out over hours. This provides an opportunity for the so-called *sibaba*, or middlemen: They make a profit out of buying a few animals at a time and then selling the lot to the merchants . . . Given the constraints, these different units perform essential functions of negotiating supply from the scattered producers' (Haaland in Manger, 1984).

The Role of Capital

Despite its importance to development capital, especially trade capital, is almost always regarded with suspicion, something the Sudanese ambivalence to traders merely reinforces. The suspicion compounds a tendency to muddled thinking, for there are three concerns which are easily confused. One is that traders, and capitalists more generally, are in a position of economic power which they can exploit. Another is that capital, for one reason or another, is incorrectly allocated. It is frequently suggested, for example, that over-investment in cattle leads to overgrazing and damage to the range land. The last is that capital is just not available, either generally or to particular groups. The latter view is, of course, central to aid.

There is little hard evidence to support the widely-held view that all rural credit is charged at extortionate rates. One small survey of two settlements in the WSDC area revealed a wide range of different arrangements. The two settlements were in different areas but with broadly similar circumstances. Despite this there was a considerable difference in indebtedness: 53 per cent indebted at Umm Rakuba and only 7 per cent at Al Amud al Akhdar. At Umm Rakuba, there were a number of different arrangements with widely differing implicit interest rates. Some borrowed grain and paid cash, some borrowed cash and paid grain, some borrowed one quality of grain and paid with another and so on. 'The average rate of interest on cash loans where interest was paid was very high: 50 percent. On the other hand, many more loans were made without any overt interest' (WSDC Settlement Survey, 1983).

Much is made in the literature about the Sudanese loan system called *sheil*: the cash loan at the beginning of the crop season which is repaid in kind after the harvest. It is widely assumed that this means that farmers are cheated because they will get a low value for their millet straight after harvest. In the WSDC survey the situation was very different. This was because the value put on the grain to be repaid was 'struck at the time of the loan.' The harvest that year was bad and the price at harvest was actually higher after harvest than when the loan was agreed. This illustrates the need to understand that the fairness or otherwise of this kind of credit cannot be judged *a priori* or even from a single year's survey data. In the uncertain environment of Darfur, both parties to the debt are taking a risk but both also have the chance to win.

The relationship between borrower and lender in Darfur is, in fact, very finely balanced. In some ways the borrower is the more powerful. He has no legal title to land which the lender could claim if he defaults. The lender has no legal right to interest, although it is paid without apparent resentment as an accepted fact in the area. Most important of all, the people of the region are highly mobile and it is a simple matter, and not at all uncommon, for a man to escape financial obligations merely by going away.

All this reflects the fact that, with land abundant and capital also relatively cheap, labour is the most sought-after commodity and entrepreneurs are forced to pay well for it, either directly or in the form of reasonable credit terms. One example was seen in 1985, in the first good season after a disastrous drought, when labour might have been expected to be cheap. On the contrary, those who had survived the drought were able to return to their own land and they were concerned only with their own crops so that commercial farmers could not find labour for hire in western or southern Darfur. In addition, a relatively minor cash crop, *kerkadeh*, which is exported to Europe as Roselle for use in herb teas, with a heavy harvest labour requirement, was enjoying a boom that year so that all spare labour was absorbed by that.

Linked to suspicion of capital is the idea that cultivators who enter the cash crop market will be made vulnerable to famine. In Darfur this is not the case. Very few farmers do not grow their own grain and all surveys show at least 70 per cent of the cropped area under grain. Almost all households store large quantities from good years as insurance against bad years and the proportion of household expenditure on grain is usually small (JMRDP Wet Season Survey, 1987). None of this is to deny that farmers remain highly vulnerable to drought and crop failure, especially in the poorer areas of north Darfur. Instead, it is to emphasize that their most effective defence is diversification into cash crops and other activities. Concentration on their subsistence crop only succeeds in concentrating the risk, besides reducing the potential rewards of a good year. That exploiting opportunities for reward is just as important as avoiding risks is a theme that will recur.

This is not to suggest that exploitative relationships do not exist in Darfur. They may even become more common, as land becomes more scarce and the better-off succeed in alienating the larger part of that land. Nor is it to say that farmers always achieve the best possible deal and are never cheated or misjudge the market. That would be to describe a market in paradise. What it does show, however, is that in Darfur in recent decades, the general run of market and credit relations are as fair and honest as it is reasonable to expect. There is one crucial exception: the widespread shortages created by government controls locally and at the national level. These have allowed the most widespread and rapacious exploitation.

Misallocation of capital is a common concern. In Darfur, the apparent separation between nomadic livestock owners, principally of Arab stock, and settled farmers, who are more commonly non-Arab, can give the impression that cattle and crops are divided by an investment barrier. In reality investment flows freely between the two sectors according to changing economic, environmental and personal circumstances. For some it is more profitable to invest surpluses from cropping in livestock. For others the reverse will apply. Among the Fur in the 1950s and 1960s there was a tendency to 'nomadize' as they found greater potential for investment in cattle than in their existing farm enterprise. In Radom, on the other hand, the Fellata cattle keepers were going against their traditional wisdom not to combine '*qurun* (horns) with *jurun* (granaries)' and taking up cropping because of high millet prices. Also in Radom, others were investing in livestock. Instead of 'nomadizing', however, the investors were putting their cattle out to hired herders (Haaland and Mustafa Abdel Rahman in Haaland, 1980). In short, the people of Darfur direct their investment and, indeed, their own labour efforts towards the most profitable activity at any one time. There is no over-investment in livestock relative to farming or anything else.

This leads to the last question, concerning a lack or otherwise of capital overall. At first sight, the evidence points in the opposite direction; that the true problem may lie, not in any shortage of capital to invest leading to 'unjust credit relations' nor in any sectoral imbalance between crops and livestock, but rather in a general lack of profitable investment enterprises. In years of better rainfall even the poorest may achieve a surplus in Darfur. It is in finding a profitable home for that surplus, to protect it from the bad years and allow it to grow, that the Darfuri faces his biggest problem. In essence he has only three options: livestock for breeding, extension of the cropped area by hiring labour or the purchase of trade goods to sell around the rural markets.

It is easy to look at the high level of activity and conclude that there is too much investment in all three sectors. The livestock herd is generally described as overstocked (although it will be argued later that the evidence for this is less solid than the received wisdom would indicate). There has certainly been a rapid expansion of crop cultivation. The numerous small and large markets of Darfur all have a surprising number of traders dealing in each particular class of goods. However, a high level of activity does not tell us anything about profitability. All those herders, farmers and traders may be competing furiously for fat profits and would wish to invest more. On the other hand, they may be struggling for ever smaller shares of low profits.

The correct conclusion, from the pattern of development in Darfur in the 20th century, would seem to be that availability of capital is not an issue. When the circumstances have been right, profits have been high, capital has been found without difficulty and substantial development has been achieved. In more recent years, however, there are signs of a serious slackening, but that has not been because of inadequate capital or in some imagined misallocation between the different sectors. Instead it has been the result of gross weaknesses in the macro-economy. And sure enough, the capital that once flowed into Darfur is now flowing out. Most of the larger traders who founded their wealth in the region have now fled to Khartoum, where the scope for investment may be no greater but where the access to political patronage is far greater.

Savings and Consumption

If there is one single indicator of the Darfur economy, it is what people spend their money on. To the outsider standards of living in Darfur still seem very low and it is easy to miss the extent of the changes that have occurred in the last 90 years. The local people are more aware of what development has brought them: 'God bless the [colonial] Government, it brought us matches, torches, soap, shibb and tea' (Shibb is alum from the Red Sea used to purify water) (Cunnison, 1966). Tea and sugar have had such an impact that they are now daily necessities and even more than that. Among the Baggara Arabs special tea-drinking associations with elaborate rituals called *baramka* have grown up.

It is not easy for the westerner to understand the impact of apparently minor imported goods; many of the things the Darfuri buys are so small, so much taken for granted in the west. In several cases they are no longer even used in the developed world. Washing blue, for example. It costs next to nothing. It went out of use in Europe 30 years ago, with the advent of washing machines and washing powders. It remains on every Darfuri's shopping list, if he can get it. Other examples include matches, small electric torches and the batteries for them and paraffin; all of them nearly forgotten in the west and yet crucial in a world without electricity. Tiny luxuries, sweets, dates, peanuts and so on, also have an importance that no westerner has felt since rationing during the Second World War. Such *tatatif* are also regularly on the shopping list.

Table 2.2 shows the level of weekly purchases of foodstuffs for the Darfur household in the 1980s in two areas of south Darfur. Both surveys covered quite a large sample of both the poorer and better-off households. The very poorest groups who are not easy to reach were probably not represented and neither were the drier and poorer areas of north Darfur. Nevertheless, the table gives a good picture of day-to-day consumption in the region. The first survey fell just before the famine of 1984, although harvests had already been poor for two years, while the second fell after the poorest season in the late 1980s which was otherwise a period of recovery. Both may be seen as typical of years with below average harvests but not outright famine.

The table shows a considerable reduction in consumption of what may be described as the staple luxuries of the Darfur household, those foodstuffs that are not absolutely essential to maintain life but which

Table 2.2: Weekly household purchases in South Darfur

	Unit	WSDC Area July–January 1983	JMRDP Area June–December 1988
Sugar	lb	4.16	1.96
Tea	oz	3.72	1.52
Oil	bottle	0.98	0.56
Salt	lb	0.39	0.41
Onion	lb	1.16	0.64
Chilli	lb	0.08	0.08
Salsa	lb	0.30	0.15
Waika	lb	0.07	0.15
Beef	kg	0.71	0.57
Goat	leg	0.20	0.20
Soap	bar	1.35	0.63

Sources: WSDC Consumption Survey, 1984, (Unpublished); JMRDP Wet Season Survey 1988

would not be considered a luxury in any except the poorest societies: sugar, tea, oil, onions, salsa, beef and even soap. The fact that onion and salsa consumption is lower in the JMRDP area, which is the major producer of these crops, is a particularly strong indicator of declining standards of living. Nevertheless, it is the drop in sugar and tea consumption that stands out: those goods for which the colonial government was most blessed and which continue to have immense political importance. They may be seen as the vanguard of the vent for surplus, a vanguard that is now in rapid retreat. Even in a largely subsistence economy, cash incomes are revealing. Figures for the JMRDP survey, which are typical at least for the main crop farming areas, were as follows:

Table 2.3: Rural household income in the Jebel Marra area

Source of Income	£S	Percentage
Crop sales	1,264	42
Livestock sales	473	16
Wages, remittances, etc.	432	14
Trade	712	24
Etc	96	3
Total cash income	2,977	100

Source: JMRDP Wet Season Survey 1988

Despite Darfur's long tradition of emigration, remittances contributed less than 3 per cent of income. One reason is that migrants usually bring their savings back with them as a lump sum or in the form of goods they have bought while away. This in itself reflects the extremely poor financial infrastructure. The banking system is not capable of handling remittances to small farmers. Another factor is the highly individualist nature of Darfur society. Husbands who emigrate are not necessarily considered to be responsible for the upkeep of their families. Nevertheless, the low level of remittances is also an important indicator of the acute constraints on the Darfur economy. What is the point of sending money back when there is nothing to invest it in and few imported consumer goods on which to spend it? The migrant is indeed well-advised to keep the money abroad so that he can buy goods to bring with him when he returns. He helps his family more that way.

There are two possible motives for saving: investment and insurance. Because of aid's obsession with capital and growth it pays far too much attention to the first and too little to the second. Every study discusses the capital constraint and every project includes a credit component. If the local people are to be encouraged to save, then it is to provide capital to stimulate the local economy. If savings are for investment this is logical. If they are for insurance it is madness. The last thing a Darfur farmer needs by way of insurance is further investment in the Darfur economy. His enterprise is already wholly exposed to the very high risks of that economy and such investment would provide no element of insurance against those risks. One of the greatest of all the myriad inconsistencies of aid is the way it lays such great stress on risk-aversion for poor people while wholly ignoring the simplest means of offering them security: external investment. If the World Bank were to open a branch in Nyala and offer Darfuri depositors the same deal it offers the major investors of the western world, namely good rates of interest with a high degree of security, it might well raise enough money to finance much of its investment in Darfur and reduce the aid requirement considerably.

The proof of this proposition lies in one fact above all, the very high stocks of grain held by Darfuri farmers. A series of three surveys in the JMRDP area illustrates this very well:

Table 2.4: Grain stocks held by Darfuri farmers

	Grain production kg per household	Grain in store kg per household
1987	822	200 (approx)
1988	1,399	45
1989	737	183

Sources: JMRDP Pre-Harvest Surveys, 1987, 1988 & 1989

The surveys were carried out at harvest time in each year and the grain in store at that time represented what was left in stock from the previous year. After a good season in 1986 there were high stocks left over at the time of the 1987 harvest. However, that was a poor one which meant that stocks were low by the time of the 1988 harvest and so on. Average household consumption is around 800 kg per annum. These figures suggest that, at the very least, households would like to hold 25 per cent more than they actually need in one year as insurance against a bad harvest the next. It seems probable that if they had two good years in a row they would build their stocks up even higher.

Another way in which the Darfur household adjusts to cope with drought is by shedding population. In 1988, after the poor harvest of 1987, the average household was smaller than it was in either 1987, after two good years, or in 1989, after one very good year. Other surveys show a similar pattern, with households shrinking during the bad times and expanding after. The destination of those who have to leave can only be guessed. The most likely possibility is that they go to seek work in the towns or in central Sudan.

In modern times, hessian sacks became popular for storage but these have become expensive and difficult to get in recent years. In 1983, 76 per cent of farmers stored in sacks, but after the good harvest in 1988 many were once again building the traditional mud storage bins, called *dabangas*, because they could not get sacks. Here is another example of the way a collapse of an economy's capacity to import drives smallholder farmers back from a new technique, itself very unsophisticated, to even older ones that are considerably more arduous (JMRDP Crop Protection Report, 1983).

The aid community has paid a vast amount of attention to food security in recent years. The most grandiose plans for national food strategies are drawn up and debated in the finest detail. Mission after mission tours the region searching for ways to improve storage and for the most suitable locations to place 'strategic reserves'. Elaborate schemes are devised to purchase grain from areas that are believed to be 'in-surplus'. The evidence is, however, that the majority of the Darfur population are quite capable of dealing with the storage problem for themselves, if the grain were available. If they could only buy sacks and possibly some simple storage insecticides they would become even more self-reliant. Without denying that the poorest groups may need special attention, the best strategic reserve is in the hands of the individual householder. Grain is by far the most dominant crop in the region. For a quarter or even more of that production to be tied up in store, as insurance, represents a massive reserve of capital which could be released if more effective forms of insurance were available. It seems reasonable to assume that a similar proportion of the livestock herd serves the same insurance purpose and to conclude that it is far more than just a quarter of the grain crop that is tied up as unused capital.

It will not be an easy matter to release that capital. It will not happen until some form of macro-economic stability is established in the Sudan as a whole. Three things will be critical: an end to inflation; a guarantee of open markets, so that if farmers sell their grain they can be sure of being able to buy some back when they need it; and a financial system that makes secure savings available to the majority of Darfuris. And these savings should not be invested in Darfur unless secure and high returns can be guaranteed. If there is a need for high risk capital in the region, which is debatable, then it should certainly not come from the people of the region.

Conclusion

The Darfur economy has demonstrated a potential for rapid growth of a rather straightforward kind. That growth has been led by trade but it has also resulted in greater integration of the region's economy and in very rapid urbanization. Simple and not so simple industries have expanded rapidly. Starting in the mid-1970s, however, the process has gone into reverse. The droughts of the 1980s have sharply exacerbated the problems and the pull of migration to the OPEC states has also contributed to the slowdown. Nevertheless, the prime cause for the collapse of the economy has been what can only be described as the slamming shut of the vent for surplus; by the inexorable decay of the railway system, by the increasing shortages of both inputs and consumer goods and by frequent changes of policy.

Many have drawn the conclusion that the famines of the 1980s reflect the impact of drought on an economy that has been made more vulnerable by monetization, cash-cropping and development in general. This is not the case. The droughts were made far more devastating than they need have been by the fact that they coincided with the reversal of development that has been described. Monetization and cash-cropping offer the only true way to greater security for Darfur, but they can only work when the Sudanese economy as a whole recovers from the much wider problems that have afflicted it since the 1970s. Even in the poorest parts of north Darfur, 'It was not their reliance on agriculture which pulled the Berti through the recent drought, but their dependence on international markets . . . Paradoxically, it is their very exposure to the outside world which makes possible their traditional existence as cultivators' (Holy in Johnson & Anderson, 1988).

3· SCRATCHING FOR KNOWLEDGE

> ... there come seven years of great plenty throughout all the land of Egypt: and there shall arise after them seven years of famine: and all the plenty shall be forgotten ... (Genesis 41:29–30)

We are told that the cropped acreage in Africa expanded by only 0.7 per cent per annum in the last 20 years. 'Assuming that the rate cannot be any higher in the future productivity must rise by more than 3 percent a year' (World Bank, 1989: Ch 4). It is suggested that this will be made possible by a 'more intensive use of chemical and organic inputs' and by the provision of an 'enabling environment' which would include better prices, security of land tenure and improved financial services.

Harnessing technology would form a key part in this process. A number of reasons are given for the fact that progress in this direction has been disappointing over the last 30 years: ' "off the-shelf" technology was frequently a failure', 'often farmers lacked the labour, capital or land necessary' and 'Farmers adapted slowly to using modern inputs and equipment. Chemicals for plant protection were not widely understood. High-yielding seed performed no better if not correctly grown.' It is concluded, therefore, that 'A new effort to harness agricultural technology to the needs of African farmers is now required.' Particular emphasis is laid on proper 'adaptation': for example, 'new varieties must be widely tested on-farm to make sure they perform' (World Bank, 1989: Ch 4).

What is striking about this analysis is how old-fashioned it is. The failures of 'off-the-shelf' technology transfer have been recognized for at least 20 years and agricultural research has been making strenuous efforts to 'adapt' new technologies to African circumstances for almost as long. The theoretical backing was laid out by Schultz as early as 1964, when he argued that poor Third World farmers are economically efficient but face especial difficulties in acquiring new, more profitable technologies. Agricultural technologies are not, he argued, 'amenable to transfer' and that is why off-the-shelf transfers did not work. Research and farmer training would, however, overcome the difficulty and so 'transform traditional agriculture'. In the years since then, vast sums have been spent on research in sub-Saharan Africa more than anywhere else in the developing world: ($360 million in 1980 as against $190 million in South Asia (World Bank, 1989: Ch 4). But the result has been little more productive than the earlier off-the-shelf transfers. Similarly, many, many attempts have been made to break perceived lacks of labour, capital or land, to little avail, and ever more complex systems of farmer training ('extension', as it is known in the jargon) have rarely managed to speed up the rate at which farmers have adapted to modern inputs and equipment.

Famine and food security are parallel themes, inevitably so given the repeated disasters of the 1980s. Once again, however, the conclusion is not new: that 'more attention must be given to developing the rainfed sector' (Bright in Maxwell, 1991). This prescription dates back at least to the early 1980s, when it went under the banner of help to the 'poorest of the poor'. The economists have found their justification for the same prescription in the fact that the rainfed sector uses very few imported inputs and is correspondingly valuable in cost-benefit analysis terms. All these arguments make the same mistake. They confuse the desired outcome – more food, help to the poor or greater net foreign exchange benefits according to taste – with potential.

A reasonable knowledge of Darfuri agriculture makes it easier to understand why it has proved so difficult to harness western technology; why potential has so often fallen short of desire. The first and most general reason is the relative abundance of land. This means that there is a gaping divide between the approach with which the research community is happiest and the wishes of the farmers themselves. Western researchers, and African researchers trained in western methods, are most concerned with land-saving techniques, that is to say, with technologies that will raise yields and maintain the value of the land. African farmers in areas like Darfur, where land is still available, are interested in only one thing: the return to their labour. Yields per hectare of land are secondary.

One reason for this difference of approach is simply that there is nowhere in the modern western world that is land rich. There remain no more reserves of land that can be brought into cultivation for no cost other than the effort of clearing it. The same is true for that part of the Third World where aid has had its greatest success, the green revolution in Asia. All the distortions of agricultural policy in the major western economies, whereby subsidies and quotas reward farmers for raising yield, greatly reinforce this tendency. A second reason springs from the power of the myth of the agricultural revolution in Europe. Every English schoolboy knows of Turnip Townshend, the man who was credited with the introduction of fertility-conserving rotations. Very few of them ever go on to learn that the turnip was, in fact, a regular field crop in Suffolk as early as the mid-17th century, a hundred years before Townshend, that 'the rise in grain output [in the 18th century] is believed to be due more to the increase in sown acreage than to improvement in yields' or that it was the 'generally rising level of prices between about 1760 and 1813 which encouraged and largely brought about the great increase in cultivated acreage and the more widespread adoption of better methods' (Chambers & Mingay, 1978: 39). The recent revolution in attitudes to environmental matters in the First World has added considerable new force to the concern for soil and moisture conservation and for a land-saving approach.

There is, however, a simpler and far more pressing reason for the failure of western technology in Darfur. It is not available. The problem is not that 'off-the-shelf' technology does not work but rather that the shelf itself is bare. The acute shortage of foreign exchange means that virtually no imports beyond the basic essentials are licensed. One reason, Schultz argues, that agricultural technology is not amenable to transfer is that merchants will not find it profitable enough to market it to peasant farmers. In modern Sudan, traders have neither the incentive to try nor the possibility of doing so. In earlier years, by contrast, Sudanese traders introduced many new technologies, most notably the Barberton groundnut variety on which the whole groundnut industry is now founded. There is, moreover, a widespread inheritance of the colonial 'nanny' tendency which places strict controls on the imports of new technologies. In earlier years this paternalistic attitude was justified on the grounds that African farmers were too simple to be allowed to try new technologies. They might get it wrong or they might be exploited by the traders supplying the technologies and buying the produce. The twin obsessions of the modern First World and hence of aid, health and the environment, have provided a new justification for this old attitude. The fear now is that farmers will mishandle equipment or chemicals, putting themselves or the environment at risk.

Added to that is the concern about exposing African farmers to excessive financial risks through involving them in untried and 'risky' technologies. It can, for example, be guaranteed that any proposal to introduce imported fertilizer to peasant farmers will meet objections on these grounds. Without questioning the need for strict controls on the truly dangerous chemicals, it should be recognized that current licensing systems in Africa place little or no control on the use of such chemicals, once they have been 'approved'. Instead they place considerable barriers in the way of approval for harmless items such as seed or fertilizer, merely because they have not been subjected to exhaustive tests by the appropriate authorities. Veterinary drugs in Sudan are an extreme example. They remain under the control of the Ministry of Animal Resources and are very difficult to obtain, whereas human drugs that would be on prescription in Europe are freely available.

The third and overriding reason for the failure of western technology lies in the choking off of markets for Darfur crops and of the supply of consumer goods. Darfur agriculture has shown spectacular growth using very few new technologies when the market was right; right in the sense that it offered consumer goods that farmers wanted at prices relative to local produce that made it worth putting extra effort in to raise their output of that produce. That growth has now been stifled and it is useless to expect farmers to take up new technologies when they cannot even fully exploit the ones they already have.

The opening premise of the aid prescription was that an extension of area faster than 0.7 per cent per annum is unlikely. This premise is not sound as far as Darfur is concerned, where a more rapid rate is still possible. It seems open to question even for Africa as a whole. The question then arises: Why has the rate of area expansion been so slow in recent years? In Darfur the reason is quite evident: that same stifling of growth by macro-economic problems.

Farming as a Gamble

Rainfall distribution is critical. A low annual rainfall spread over a whole year is of little use. At high temperatures the balance between precipitation and evaporation is always negative and no crop can survive. If, however, the same total is concentrated in a few months it becomes possible to farm. The difference between a good year and a bad one in Darfur often depends on how much of the rain falls in early or late months and how much in the main crop season.

A failure is still possible, even when the season is short and the total

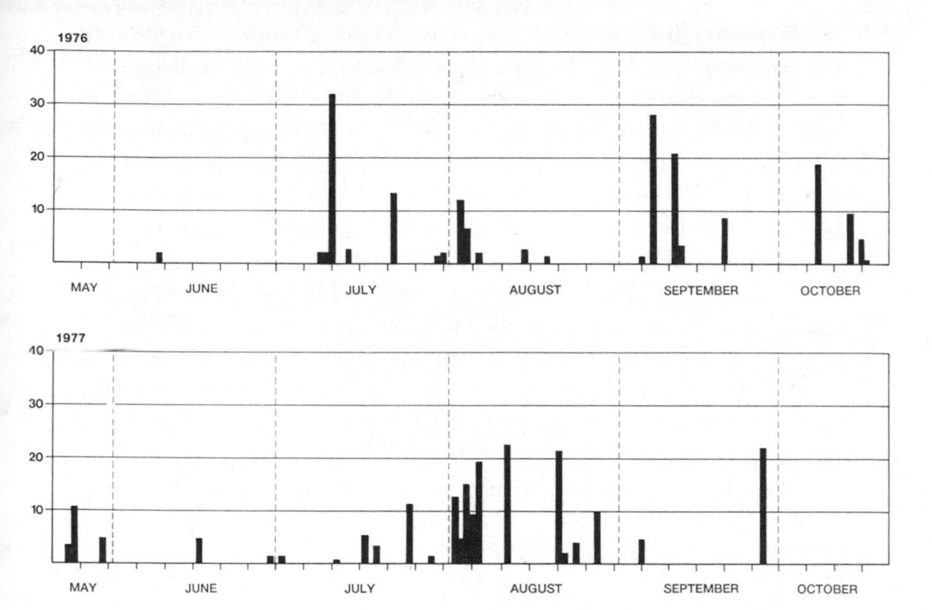

Figure 3.1 Daily Rainfall in El Fasher during the Season of Millet Cultivation

rainfall within the cropping period is adequate, because the rain may be spread out in numerous small showers, too small to provide usable moisture to crops, or because of long dry periods between each storm. Complex relationships between precipitation, evaporation, crop variety and soil type determine how much rain is useful, or effective. Rainfall in Darfur is relatively well concentrated seasonally and it usually takes the form of storms large enough to provide effective moisture. It is the second danger, that of long dry spells, or over-concentration in the wrong period that most often threatens crops in the region.

Figure 3.1 is a good illustration. Despite a long dry spell in September 1977, heavy, well-distributed rain in August, the key growing period, ensured a better crop than in 1976 when the annual rainfall was only 5 millimetres less but the few heavy and effective storms were widely separated and August was the worst of the three principal rainy season months.

Rainfall is variable spatially, as well as over time. An area that did better than its neighbours one year may do worse the next. This pattern has its benefits. It is only in extreme drought that all suffer a crop failure but, equally, it is only in very wet years that all are guaranteed success. And in wet years, the narrow areas of good alluvial soil along the wadis are vulnerable to floods. Strategies to cope with all these risks are central to the way farmers and stock keepers manage their activities.

The average cropped area is around three hectares per household. Over 99 per cent of holdings are managed by one farmer on his own. Most of the tiny remainder are worked in a partnership of one kind or another. In short, the vast majority hold their land without any form of rental. They either own it or have free customary use. In essence the farmers are almost all small but independent agents (Dept of Statistics, 1968). The table below shows the results from surveys in 1964 and 1976 and for two smaller surveys in south Darfur in the 1980s. After allowance for the different characteristics of the limited areas covered in the last two surveys, the table shows that little changed over the two decades. Millet is always more important than all the other crops put together and only sorghum and groundnuts are at all important among those others.

Table 3.1: Household cropped area by crop (rainfed)

	Darfur 1964 ha	S. Darfur 1976 ha	N. Darfur 1976 ha	WSDC 1982 ha	JMRDP 1987 ha
Sorghum	0.51	0.25	0.28	0.69	0.39
Millet	1.77	1.54	2.57	2.85	1.31
Mixed grain	na	na	na	–	0.17
Sesame	0.05	0.19	0.18	na	na
Groundnuts	0.45	0.63	0.18	0.83	0.26
Vegetables	0.03	0.08	–	na	0.20
Tobacco	0.04	–	0.05	na	na
Peas/beans		0.04	–	na	–
Maize		0.03	–	na	na
Pepper	0.10	0.04	–	na	0.05
Okra		0.13	0.14	na	0.08
Minor crops		0.05	0.05	0.23	0.22
Total	2.95	2.98	3.53	4.60	2.66

Note: 1. na for the WSDC/JMRDP surveys means that these crops are included in Minor crops. This is probably also true for the earlier surveys.
2. (Sources: Dept of Statistics, 1968; VRA/RMR, 1977.
WSDC Farmer Survey, 1983.
JMRDP Wet Season Surveys, 1982 to 1985 (average)

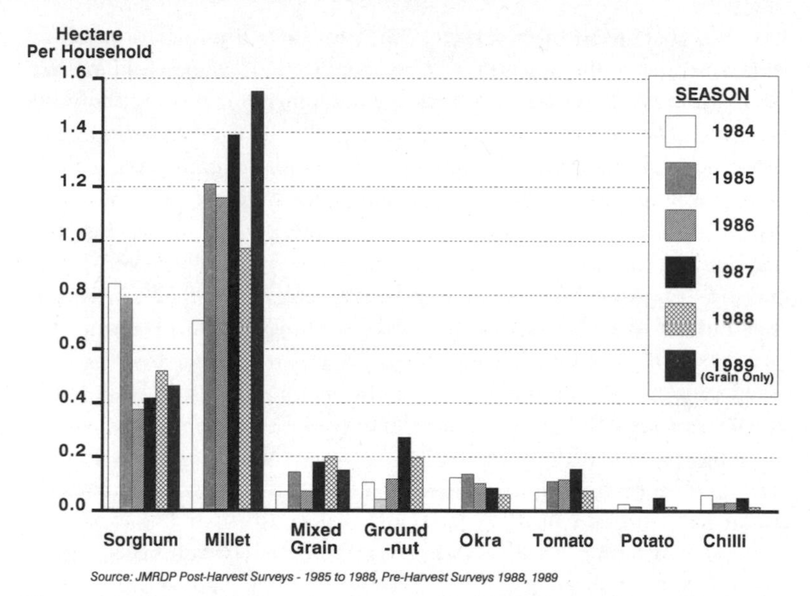

Figure 3.2 Changes in Cropping Patterns, JMRDP Area – 1984 to 1989

Mixed cropping is fashionable in the aid mythology; it embodies attractive ideas of non-chemical preservation of soil fertility and the value of Rural People's Knowledge. In Darfur mixed cropping is limited to specific areas and serves different purposes from the fashionable ones. Two mixes are fairly common: millet with sorghum on the basement wadis and millet with tomatoes on the Jebel Marra terraces. In neither case does the mix offer any potential fertility improvement. Instead the aim is to minimize risk. If the rains take one pattern then one of the two crops will do well. If they take another then the second crop's grain compensates for the first one's loss. Or one crop may be vulnerable to pests but will yield better if there are no pests. Another reason farmers quote for mixing their seed is to help with weedings their grain crop. Wild millets (ar *WeeWee*) and wild sorghums (ar *Adhar*) are common and it can be difficult to identify which is the crop and which is the weed. If there is a sesame plant next to the sorghum or a watermelon next to the millet, to quote the most common minor mixes, then the weeder can immediately tell his corn from the tares.

The fact that such a number of different crops are grown in Darfur should not be allowed to conceal the fact that very many farmers grow only one; apart from their *jibraka*, which is a small household patch of vegetables, they only grow grain. The prevalence of single cropping has very significant implications for the development of new agricultural techniques. In particular, it should be noted that it is cash-crops and cash-crops only that have allowed some relief to the grain monocultivation on the lowlands and more substantial relief on the Jebel Marra.

If aid believes that cash cropping is inherently bad or at least too risky for smallholder farmers in drought-prone areas, it believes just as strongly that drought-resistant subsistence crops are good. After the 1984 famine much emphasis was laid on the need for research into shorter season varieties of such crops. It was suggested that farmers would concentrate on millet before sorghum and grain crops before cash crops. Once again, things are rather more complicated. Figure 3.2 shows changing cropping patterns through six years in the JMRDP area starting from 1984. The first clear conclusion from the figure is that farmers grew more sorghum in 1984, not less. By contrast, millet expanded during the recovery phase. As far as cash crops are concerned, areas were down in the drought year but significant amounts were still grown.

A longer-term comparison can be made, between a 1976 survey of the same JMRDP area and the average for the six years between 1984 and 1989. Given the depression of exports since the mid-1970s and the steady, sometimes disastrous, decline in rainfall, a considerable change in cropping strategies might have been expected. Reduced cash crops and a concentration on subsistence grain seemed almost inevitable. It did not happen. As a proportion of the total cropped area groundnuts declined only fractionally between 1976 and 1985–9: from 6.6 per cent to 6.3 per cent. The proportion of the area under grain crops barely changed, indeed there was a slight decline from 78.6 per cent to 77.7 per cent. The proportion of the more thirsty crop, sorghum, actually increased considerably at the expense of millet. The proportion of minor cash crops, tomatoes, okra and so on, also increased (HTS, 1977; JMRDP Post-Harvest Surveys, 1985–90).

None of these changes was large enough to alter the overall pattern. Millet remained by far the dominant crop. Nevertheless, they are all in direct conflict with the intuitive beliefs about how farmers would react to drought – warning enough that policies based on self-evident intuition are bound to fail. Cropping patterns are determined by quite complex interactions of the technical and economic potential of each crop. If sorghum has increased in importance, for example, it is because the lower, wetter lands suited to the crop become easier to work in dry years while the light, sandy millet land is too dry to be worth planting at all. Besides, millet is the preferred food in Darfur. Although sorghum may yield more, that is only important when famine makes quantity more valuable than preferred quality. Similarly, more groundnuts may be grown in a dry year, because of price or because what rain there was fell at a particularly suitable time for the crop.

It is necessary to lose the mental baggage that most foreigners bring with them when they think about farming. To Europeans, and to many from the developing countries as well, land preparation is the most vital of farm activities. They think of a cultivation process that starts with one or more ploughings followed by harrowing, levelling and so on before any seed is planted. Almost universally, the plough is the symbol of farming. For the farmers of Darfur it should be the hoe; not merely because they do not have ploughs but, far more importantly, because they work their land in a different way and they cultivate for different purposes. The major grain crops are sown straight into the ground without any prior cultivation at all. Western experts have, in recent years, made much of the virtues of the supposedly new technique of 'minimal tillage'; that is to say the drilling of seed direct without ploughing. Darfuri farmers have been doing it for generations, indeed they have always done it.

A look at the language explains this. All land preparation/cultivation operations are grouped under one word: *hash*. This is linked to the word *hashshish*, grass or weeds, and *hash* is best translated as weeding, highlighting the farmer's major preoccupation. His problem is not the preparation of a seed bed for the crop nor is it the maintenance or release of soil fertility. It is not even the conservation of moisture. For the Darfuri farmer, these all pale into insignificance compared to dealing with weeds.

Again it is difficult for the outsider to believe that weeds can be a problem, in an environment that seems so barren for a large part of the year. In fact, it is precisely because the climate is so harsh that the local vegetation has adapted to be extremely aggressive, to germinate and grow very quickly, in order to take maximum advantage of the short rains. The problem for the farmer is not the inherent fertility of the soil, which he may not be able to change with ease, or the lack of rain, which he certainly cannot change. It is preventing the weeds from taking what little fertility and water he does have and completely choking his crop. The result is that weeding is universally the key constraint to an increase in production.

Crop establishment is critical. 'The commonest cause of failure is a rain sufficient to cause germination but insufficient to support early growth' (Tothill, 1948). Even in a good year like 1988, crops fail wholly or partially for a number of reasons. In poor ones, like 1987 and 1989, farmers may have to replant two or more times before the crop is established. Pests, especially grasshoppers, are just as likely to be the cause of failure as drought (JMRDP Pre-Harvest Surveys, 1989 and 1990).

Technical studies of agriculture in semi-arid conditions lay great emphasis on time-of-planting as a critical factor. Like so many aid recommendations, the reasons seem self-evident. If the crop is sown late it will have a shorter growing season and yield less. If it is sown early it may not get established or run into pest problems. Much research and extension effort has consequently been spent on determining the optimum planting time and on persuading farmers to plant at that time. The difficulties of crop establishment put a different angle on the question. Farmers know perfectly well what happens if they plant late or early but they also know that the pattern of rainfall is so variable that their only sensible strategy is to plant after every effective rain, early or late. An early planting may be lucky and produce a very good crop. If it fails, both the seed and the effort needed to replant it are relatively cheap, so not much is lost. At the other extreme, a late planting may rescue something from a disastrous year.

The whole strategy depends on flexibility. Which means that simplistic advice on things like time-of-planting is useless and that single track strategies such as telling farmers to shift to shorter season varieties are equally useless. It may help them to survive a dry year but only at the cost of losing the benefits of a good one. What they need is a choice of techniques and varieties so that they can choose their strategy season by season, indeed day by day during the planting period. This is the what they already do and it is only way they can keep the multifarious risks to a minimum.

Consider one field and what happens to it if almost everything goes wrong. Say that there are good rains in late May or early June. The farmer plants one *mukhammas* (approximately half a hectare) with a medium-to-long-season millet which mostly germinates well, but a severe attack by grasshoppers destroys half. He replants this half and once again it germinates well. However, there is a short dry spell and the plants on two sandier patches fail. Ants take the seed round an ant-heap in the replanted section. A month after the first planting, he thins out some of the well-established stands and uses the thinnings to fill in these gaps. After that the rains stop for the first three weeks of July and the whole field fails. Right at the end of July, the farmer plants a mix of short-to-medium-period millet and short-to-medium sorghum and that is the crop he finally harvests. This is an exaggerated example: a combination of all these disasters would be rare but far from impossible.

Just as with time-of-planting, the only way farmers can manage their weeding is to gamble. They do not sit down before the season and plan how much they can weed and fix the area they plant on that basis. Instead, they plant as much as they can. If it is a dry year they will be able to weed all of it. If it is wet they may have to abandon up to half of what they have planted because they cannot keep up with the weeds, but that does not matter. Planting is easy so little has been lost. 'The size of the harvest does not depend on the area sown but on how much land has been successfully weeded' (Holy in Johnson & Anderson, 1988). Here too, much aid-financed research and extension has been spent on trying to persuade farmers to weed better. The acres of unweeded and poorly weeded crops make the recommendation seem so obvious. It is just a pity it is actually pointless because they are already weeding as much as they can.

Groundnuts are the only significant crop apart from grain. It is grown using the same tools but the land is hoed before planting rather than after. It is significant that the same phrase, *hash murr* or 'bitter weeding', is used for this first hoeing despite the fact that the job is done before planting for groundnuts and after planting for grain. Second and subsequent weedings are called *hash jankab* for both crops. Because the *hash murr* is done first and because the sowing is harder work, the effort required at the early part of the groundnut season is higher and more concentrated than it is for the grain crops. More seed is used which is more expensive. For these reasons, groundnut is a riskier crop, in the sense that a greater investment has to be made early on. On the other hand, it takes only 90 or 100 days to maturity and this means that the crop can be planted when the rains are already well established. Groundnuts are also generally free from major pests. On balance, therefore, it is no more risky than grains.

Modern western agriculture uses sophisticated farm management techniques, linear programming and the like, to ensure that complex cropping patterns give maximum returns on limited land. Influenced by this approach, the idea that crops can be found that do not compete with one another for vital resources is another will-of-the-wisp that aid research has spent a lot of time chasing. Groundnuts seem to be a crop that matches this ideal. It should be possible to plant and first-weed the grain before hoeing for the shorter-period groundnuts and planting. At the other end of the season, the groundnut harvest could be completed before the major grain harvest began. Unfortunately it does not work that way and it is instructive to look at the reasons why.

As for most other things the answer is weeds. They have to be dealt with early, otherwise they create a vegetation so dense that it becomes more or less impossible to clear them by hand. 'It is not possible to influence the size of the harvest by extending the weeding period as any weeding carried out later than about two and a half months after sowing is useless. By that time the grass is so high and the millet so stunted that the millet could not ripen even if the grass were removed' (Holy in Johnson & Anderson, 1988). Because the weeding cannot be delayed there is little point in delaying the planting of the groundnuts.

As there is still abundant land, labour is the critical constraint preventing an increase in production. Rent is almost never paid for land and very few non-labour inputs are used, so labour costs are also the major determinant of profitability relative to yield. Labour requirements are next to impossible to estimate accurately. The variations from one area to another, from one season to the next and even from one field to the next are just too high. However, some broad estimates for the major millet crop illustrate the key differences: between the light, easily worked *goz*, the heavier wadi lands and the volcanic soils of the Jebel Marra itself. While similar surveys have not been done in north Darfur, the results will be similar with due allowance for the drier conditions.

Table 3.2: Labour requirements for a millet crop

	Goz	Basement wadis	Upper Jebel
		Man days per hectare	
Sowing	5	14	40
Hash murr	20	40	60
Hash jankab	15	30	40
Harvest	15	20	33
Threshing	6	15	15
Total	61	119	188

Sources: WSDC Farmer Survey, 1983; JMRDP Wet Season Surveys, 1987 and 1988; adjusted to a non-existent average year.

Accurate yield estimates are also difficult to obtain. The farmers' own estimates have proved as good as any and Figure 3.3 shows the results of a series of farmer surveys carried out between 1984 and 1987 in the JMRDP area. Figure 3.4 shows rainfall at Zalingei, the centre of that area. As might be expected, rainfall has a clear effect on yield. What might not be expected is that millet yields very little less than sorghum. The first figure also shows yields in the WSDC area, to the south and east of south Darfur. This is the major *goz* production area. What shows very clearly is that yields there are little different despite the much lower labour requirements. This is why *goz* cropping is so profitable.

Darfur pests are just as aggressive as the weeds. The biblical plagues of Egypt seem little more than myths to the European ear. Europe has not seen a plague since potato blight and vine phylloxera in the 19th century. In Darfur one plague or another is never far away. Good conditions at the breeding time for a particular pest can generate a plague very rapidly. The balance between pest and predators is also linked to the climate. Attacks in the years after the 1983–4 drought were particularly heavy as pest populations recovered more rapidly than those of the predators. There was a rat plague in 1985, for example. On the other hand, climate can also help to suppress pests; at least part of the reason that yields are heavier in wet years is because heavy and continuous rains suppress breeding insects.

The speed at which pest problems change is a special problem. The temptation to put extra resources into combating a plague that caused serious damage last year is strong. It is all too probable that this year another pest will have its turn. Aid, with its short-term perspectives and its desire for a 'successful campaign', is very vulnerable to this trap.

The millet head-worm, *nafaasha*, is a case in point. Its significance as an economic pest is new, not just in Darfur but in the Sahel and Sudan zones of Africa as a whole. It first appeared after the drought of 1972. *Nafaasha* is the caterpillar of a moth which pupates underground and then climbs the millet plant to feed when the grain is maturing. It bores a spiral pattern around the millet head, lifting the florets off just before they form grains. In wetter years *nafaasha* does not cause farmers much concern. Naturally a pest which does most of its damage during drought periods must be especially worrying but this should not obscure the fact that pests that are at their worst in wetter seasons may do just as much, if not more economic damage.

Vegetation harbours pests. At risk of caricature, while the westerner now sees a tree as an asset, a thing of beauty and a piece of the environment to be protected, the Darfuri farmer sees it as a source of birds and all the other pests that threaten his crop. Whatever the merits

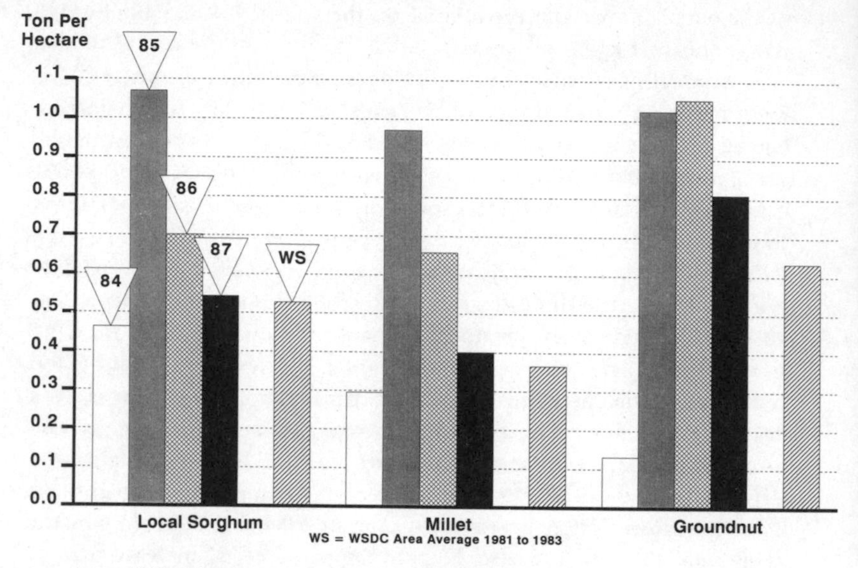

Figure 3.3 Changes in Crop Yields, JMRDP Area – 1984 to 1987

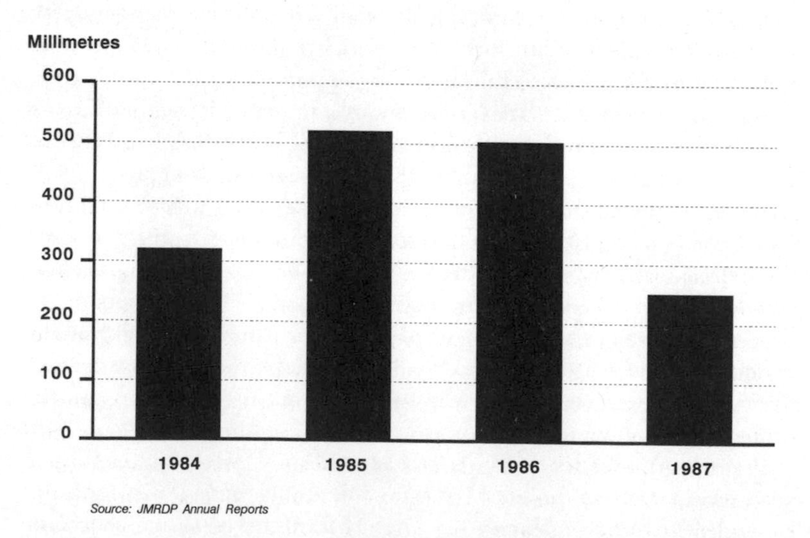

Figure 3.4 JMRDP Area Rainfall, Zalingei Town – 1984 to 1987

of the outsider's view in the long term, the farmer is undoubtedly right in the short term.

This attitude affects the way new cropland is developed. A lone farmer who tries to establish a small plot in an area of virgin bush risks having his efforts wiped out by pests. For successful settlement in new areas, it is essential for quite a large group to work together so that they can drive the bush back far enough to keep down the level of pests they all face. Proposed new cropping patterns which involve tree and crop combinations, either alley-cropping or tree/crop rotations, face serious problems for the same reasons, problems that have received little attention to date.

To sum up, Darfur farmers know what they are doing. They face a daunting problem in ensuring a subsistence crop from rainfed production but there is absolutely no reason to believe that anyone is going to better their existing strategies. They look scruffy and inefficient to those used to the well-groomed fields of Europe or rice-growing Less Developed Countries. Yes, they are scruffy but that does not mean inefficient.

Three Alternatives

There are three possible strategies for agricultural development. The first, summed up under the title 'Existing Resource Levels, Existing Resource Use Patterns', depends on the proposition that 'the application of a little science can provide solutions that have eluded thousands of farmers over many generations and that the major contributor to inefficiency in resource use is lack of knowledge' (Harvey, 1986). Whatever its faults the modern research community has, through its recognition of Rural People's Knowledge and the use of intensive techniques like Farming Systems Research, come a long way from this position. Nevertheless, it is still not unusual to find elements of it implicit in development programmes; those that urge farmers to pay more attention to time of planting, for example.

A good example of the second strategy, 'Existing Resource Levels, Modified Resource Use Patterns', would be the introduction of a fertility-conserving legume crop in rotation with the existing grain crops. Other examples, include closer integration of livestock and crops and alley-cropping of tree crops and field crops. There is some evidence that such practices would raise yields in Darfur, but one overwhelming piece of evidence that they could not raise yields by enough: the existing cropping pattern. Grain crops currently occupy around 80 per cent of the cropped land. If, in order to increase grain yields, it were necessary to rotate the crops, say one year grain to one year legume, then those yields would have to rise by two-thirds to maintain grain supplies. Quite simply, it is not plausible that the farmers of Darfur would have failed to notice and take advantage of yield gains of this order, if they were obtainable. This problem is particularly acute with agro-forestry, where the rotation is bound to be long and the ratio of grain to non-grain correspondingly low: at the lowest one to two and more likely as high as one to five, compared to one to one in the example.

Once again, the English agricultural revolution is a relevant example. Then, the driving force behind the introduction of rotations of grain and fodder crops was at least as much to meet growing urban demand for meat, dairy products and wool as it was to raise grain yields (Chambers & Mingay, 1978). In other words, rotations were a response to a market demand for the rotated crop, not to a need for greater supplies of the grain crop.

The last possibility is 'Improved Resource Levels, Existing Resource Use Patterns'. This depends on the use of imported agricultural equipment and inputs. However unreasonable, even illogical, that may seem for a poor region like Darfur in a poor country like Sudan, it is, effectively, the only way. All other approaches assume a degree of ignorance or even incompetence on the part of the Darfuri farmer and depend on western research discovering potential that the farmer has overlooked. The very small achievements of research in Sudan, and in Africa generally, make that seem extremely unlikely. One of its few solid achievements is, moreover, a wealth of evidence that the farmers of Africa have overlooked very little.

The result is a considerable dilemma. If an agricultural transformation depends on imported inputs, then the process will be totally blocked by a macro-economic collapse on the scale of that seen in Sudan in the last two decades. While that continues, research can only be largely academic. At best, it may develop new techniques which are not useful now but which will become applicable when the wider problems are solved. At worst, it will pursue concerns that reflect the current instability and not the true potential of the area at all.

Because it is working in this limbo between an existing, highly constrained situation, in which no real development is possible, and a situation of unknowable potential, when the wider problems are solved, it is extremely difficult to judge research itself. If it is the incentives and pressures of the market that provide the X-efficiency which generates knowledge and stimulates its implementation, then research will be particularly difficult when the market is stifled.

Research can be reactive, concentrating on solving problems that the existing situation has thrown up. Remember that Liebenstein found that two-thirds of commercial research done in the USA was for defensive purposes. That was reactive research. Alternatively, research can be anticipatory. It is then dependent on an ability to forecast what the future problems are likely to be. Although reactive research sounds less positive, it is likely to be much more fruitful and cost effective. The results can be put to immediate use, tested and amended to meet changing circumstances as they arise. Despite the modern emphasis on farmer participation and farming systems research, a great deal of agricultural research in Africa is anticipatory in the sense that it focuses on issues such as conservation, which may become important later but which are certainly not important in farmers' eyes at present; and in the sense that it depends on some future economic rehabilitation at the national level before it can be applied.

Rural People's Knowledge can also be particularly misleading when the processes of development are stifled. Because that knowledge embodies a vast amount of experience, it will include much that is not applicable at any one time. Western researchers who are, for example, concerned about environmental matters will certainly find local informants who can describe in detail the factors that cause environmental damage and who will agree wholeheartedly with the outsiders' concerns about erosion and so on. This does not mean that this knowledge is applicable at the time of speaking. There is a world of difference between knowledge and use of knowledge. And when the national economy is so constrained and markets are becoming less operative rather than more, there is just no way of telling whether that knowledge is ever likely to be applicable.

In Darfur, for example, farmers will generally acknowledge the value of trees like the *haraz*, *Acacia albida*, which provide fodder and shade and, possibly, maintain soil fertility. The fact is, however, that they do not conserve the *haraz*. They certainly do not plant the tree. When taking fodder from it they treat it extremely roughly and the number of trees which are 'accidentally' fired at their base, so as to kill them, is greater than coincidence can really explain. There is a strong modern tendency to attribute farmers' reluctance to pay more attention to conservation to population pressure, to drought and, especially, to the evil effects of modern, capitalist economic pressures. In answer to that it may be stressed that as early as 1958 there was a 'total lack of the younger class of [haraz] trees in those areas which are heavily farmed' (HTS, 1958).

Chambers quotes two anecdotes to illustrate the value of Rural People's Knowledge and the fact that 'professionals' ignore it. One concerns the mukau tree in Kenya, the seeds of which can only be germinated after they have passed through the stomach of a goat, and another about the winged bean in the Philippines (Chambers, 1983: 81–2). What he does not show is how this knowledge is of the slightest use in research or development terms, given that both the tree and the bean are wholly marginal crops. If there is one way that expatriate scientists are most successful at enraging their national counterparts it is by the elevation of these relatively trivial items of Rural People's Knowledge in a way that simultaneously devalues their colleagues' own status and tells them something of little or no importance. It is Rural People's Knowledge in action that matters: what they do and not what they say.

Research in South Darfur

The World Bank prescription on fertility focuses on shortages of chemical fertilizer and on the fact that farmers 'traditionally' use only limited amounts of organic nutrients. Fertilizer should, therefore, be made available, while the use of organic fertilizers should be 'encouraged'. Crop rotations and mixes and agro-forestry, which are both principally designed to maintain soil fertility, are also recommended (World Bank, 1989: Ch 4).

In Darfur, the largest single cropped area is on the least fertile soils, the *goz* sands of the south/east section of the region. The Western Savannah Development Corporation has been carrying out trials on these soils since 1976. It makes a fascinating case study: the 'Qoz land system is, of itself, a tough developmental assignment. The natural resources of the Qoz environment, at least in terms of soils, climate and crops, are not the stuff of which Green Revolutions are achieved' (Quin, 1989).

In Sudanese Arabic the word *goz* means no more than 'sand', but it is also used as a title for the extensive sand-sheets of Kordofan and Darfur. These are vast plains of wind-blown sands deposited at a much drier period. Nowadays, with better rainfall, the dunes have been fixed by broad-leaved bush or woodland savannahs. The *goz* is easy to clear and farm, which means that *goz* cropping is profitable even at low yields.

The following comparisons with standard levels of soil status illustrate just how infertile the *goz* is:

Table 3.3: Fertility status of *goz* soils in South Darfur

	Topsoil	Subsoil
Acidity	Weakly acid	Moderately acid
Cation Exchange capacity	Very low	Low
Exchange calcium	Very low	Low
Exchange magnesium	Low	Low
Exchange potassium	Low	Low
Exchange phosphorus	Deficient	Deficient
Exchange zinc	Deficient	Deficient
Exchange boron	Deficient	Deficient
Exchange manganese	Intermediate	Intermediate
Exchange copper	Adequate	Adequate

Sources: Data from HTS, 1974 and HTS, 1976

One might, naïvely, expect that all that would be required to raise yields substantially on such poor soils would be to add the missing nutrients, plus nitrogen which is always necessary. That might not be economically feasible, but technically it should surely work. Unfortunately it is not that simple. The relationships between soil, water and crops are extremely complex.

On a light, sandy soil rainwater drains away very quickly, but this does not necessarily mean that crops are particularly vulnerable to drought. Although the water drains quickly, it also penetrates the soil fast and to a considerable depth. On a heavier, less permeable soil much of the rain is lost as runoff or evaporation. Roots can also make their way more easily through a sandy soil, so the crop can reach further. Different soils have different 'suctions' which determine how much water they will release to the crop: 'sand has a smaller maximum water content but most of the water is held at relatively low suction' . . . 'The implication is that sand contains a smaller volume of water very readily available but quickly exhausted' (Winter, 1974). In a dry region water is often more important than fertility and *goz* crops can perform far better than the absolute fertility status might imply. Sometimes water is the limiting factor and sometimes it is fertility, but overall: 'The ease of cultivation of goz soil and the great depth which is available to water and roots make this intrinsically poor soil into a valuable agricultural asset. Though the nutrient status is low great volumes of soil can be explored by the roots' (Jewitt & Ferguson, 1948).

This combination of highly specific advantages in a harsh environment poses extremely difficult challenges to agricultural research. Three possible approaches have been fairly thoroughly investigated: chemical fertilizer, crop rotations and organic manure. The only positive conclusion had been that phosphate fertilizer, specifically Triple Super Phosphate (TSP), does raise yields; a result that has been matched in other sub-Sahelian countries. Relatively low applications, as little as 10 kilogrammes per hectare, raise millet yields in some areas by an average of 40 per cent. European farmers might use ten times as much.

Because the idea of sustainable rotations is so attractive, and so deeply rooted in western ideas about how agriculture should be, it is worth underlining how they are supposed to work. A rotation can only restore fertility if the vegetation produced by the rotation crop is returned to the soil. The nutrients are contained in that vegetation. This may be done directly, by ploughing it in, or indirectly, by grazing cattle over the crop so that it is converted to animal manure that stays on the land. If the crop is simply left standing, much of it withers and blows away in the hot winds of the Darfur summer. It does not rot into the soil as it would in Europe. The same happens even to manure, which dries hard and crumbles to dust.

Fodder crops are the classic example of a rotation that is both profitable and soil-restoring. The profit comes from the animals grazing over the crop while their dung returns nutrients to the soil and restores fertility. For this process to work enclosure is critical, to guarantee that the animals actually fertilize the field they graze over. (Enclosure was a central component of the English agricultural revolution.) In Darfur, the costs of enclosure are high and almost no fields are effectively fenced. Where a crop does have value as fodder, it is harvested and fed to the animals elsewhere. Otherwise the owner would see it quickly grazed off by his neighbours' animals or lose much of its value as it dried out in the field. Besides, the main need is to keep the animals alive through a long dry season. The fodder has to be cut and stacked somewhere safe so it can be rationed out to the stock. For all these reasons, 'It is unrealistic to consider that this crop [cowpea] could ever play any substantial role in restoring soil fertility because when biomass is removed from the land [as fodder], all the soil derived nutrients in that biomass go with it' (Quin, 1989).

The alternative is for the farmer to feed the fodder to his animals, away from the field, and bring their manure back later. Here too the trial results are not encouraging, showing 'little overall response'... 'While it is very attractive to consider the use of animal manure for crop production in a farming system that contains both crop and livestock components the trials of 1982 to 1985 do not demonstrate that the burden of work that is incurred with manuring actually is worthwhile' (Quin, 1989). Because farmers do not cultivate their land, so much as merely weed it, the additional work required to apply manure and plough it in is considerable: requiring much more than 'little overall response' to justify it.

Manuring is a good example of the problems with Rural People's Knowledge. In the central areas of south Darfur, farmers on the sandy *athmur* ridges used to ask herders to graze their animals over their fields after harvest and to enclose them on the field overnight. 'A herd of 30 cows produces enough manure to keep a mokhammas of goz fertile permanently if they are kept for 18 nights on the field, 3 days on the same campsite, 6 campsites on one mokhammas. This is done after the dukhn has been sown.' Payment to the herders was reported to be three *ratl* of sugar and tea per night (Haaland, 1980). This practice, called *diyarat*, is only really possible in the *athmur* area. The herds pass that way after the harvest anyway and water is available for the cattle. There are also plenty of thorn trees to make a kraal. None of this is true on the *goz* or in many other areas. Besides that, the cattle do not only graze the field they manure. It would not be enough to keep them for 18 days. There has to be other grazing available nearby. The work involved is considerable, especially in setting up a new kraal every three nights. The result is that *diyarat* is rare nowadays, illustrating the point that techniques included in Rural People's Knowledge are not of immediate relevance unless they are common practice.

What, then, happened to the positive finding, that phosphate fertilizer could improve millet yields by up to 40 per cent at low rates of application? The answer is, not much. TSP was unavailable in Darfur until the mid-1980s. Research in Sudan has been dominated by the large-scale irrigated sector, where it attracted great prestige and was able to give its recommendations something of the force of law. This was natural on large irrigation schemes, where all aspects of the cropping cycle are closely controlled and where the state had a major interest, but far less suitable for smallholder rainfed agriculture. One such recommendation was that phosphate was not a required input for the Sudan because the irrigated soils of the Gezira had shown little response to phosphate; that was taken to be sufficient evidence that it was not needed for any part of the country. As a result organizations in western Sudan had to direct their research first towards making an adequate case for the approval of TSP and their efforts towards winning that approval and arranging supplies. Even the FAO fertilizer programme in Khartoum had to fight to get licences to import phosphate and there is a story that in 1983 a donation of shiploads of the fertilizer from Japan was turned away from Port Sudan unloaded because the Ministry of Agriculture would not grant licences. By the time the potential of phosphate was recognized, Sudan's foreign exchange problems were so great that the only supplies ever to reach Darfur have been aid-financed.

The simplest, fastest and most cost-effective test of TSP would have been for adequate quantities to be made available over the whole of Darfur so that farmers could do their own tests and make their own adaptations, but it has still not escaped from the grip of the researchers. A wide range of arguments is given. There were the usual doubts about the whole concept of introducing 'risky and expensive' imported inputs. The fact that only small amounts are needed to gain a significant yield benefit was ignored. It also proved surprisingly difficult to persuade officials to recognize the fact that phosphate was different from a nitrogen fertilizer like urea; different in several ways that meant that the risks involved were much smaller. Urea has been available in Sudan for many years and is well understood, where TSP is not. Timing is critical with urea. Applied at the wrong time, it can 'burn' a crop or, because it is volatile, evaporate before the crop is ready to use it. Phosphate is far less sensitive. Even if grossly misapplied it is unlikely to damage a crop and it is not volatile.

There has been a tendency to chase after side issues in attempts to refine the recommendation rather than implement it as it stood. Despite the fact that good results were obtained with TSP, there were suggestions that rock phosphate, which is just a different form of the same nutrient, would be more suitable or that acidity and a resulting aluminium toxicity was a problem that could be cured by liming the *goz* soils.

The longest debate has concerned application techniques. There are two problems. First, the labour needed to apply the fertilizer costs the farms as much as the chemical itself, and that depends on how it is applied. Second, TSP can affect germination if it is in direct contact with the seed. As with manure, the fact that farmers do not cultivate their land before planting is critical because the easiest way to apply the fertilizer would be to broadcast it over the ground and then plough or hoe it in. If there is no cultivation, then it can only be applied in the same planting hole as the seed or in separate holes or drills.

There are other complications. By putting the fertilizer right by the seed, the dose per plant is kept high even though the rate per hectare is low. On the other hand, phosphate stimulates root growth and the roots may only go where they find the fertilizer, losing that major virtue of the *goz*: the way the roots can spread far and wide. One of the benefits of phosphate is that it persists in the soil and remains available for crops in subsequent seasons. However, if the TSP is put close by the seed in the first year, then the second year's crop will only benefit if the farmer manages to plant the crop in exactly the same place, which is near enough impossible. There is a trade-off between maximum economy in the first year and a greater residual benefit in the second.

The detailed arguments concerning TSP on the *goz* can be interesting, even fascinating, especially to researchers. Sadly, they are almost all irrelevant because none of them detract from the basic finding; that low applications of TSP can produce a significant yield response in the year of application. The research into the other issues appears to have blurred the clarity of that message, and it is still not wholly accepted that farmers should be encouraged to try TSP fertilizer. Instead, there is a wish for 'certainty', for an absolute and complete scientific understanding that will justify the research bureaucracy taking on the responsibility of encouraging farmers to try something new.

Such certainty is not necessary. In 1985, the EEC distributed TSP throughout Darfur in small quantities on the understanding that its value might not be fully proven but that anything that might assist a recovery from the 1984 drought was worth trying. One area where the fertilizer was taken up enthusiastically was on the terraces of Jebel Marra; not on the *goz* at all and in an area where the soils were assumed to be much more fertile. With hindsight, it is possible to see why. It is the one area where the fields are cultivated before sowing and where the seed is broadcast before being hoed into the soil. It takes almost no extra effort to broadcast fertilizer as well as seed and the application problem is therefore solved.

The very earliest trial that indicated a positive phosphate response was in 1948. The whole history of research in western Sudan seems summed up in that one trial: 'Owing to administrative difficulties the sowing was late and the test was further vitiated by attack of pests and birds' (Jewitt & Manton, 1951). A lengthy research process has, in the end, done no more than add refinements to that first finding. The message was quite clear early on and could, in fact, have been predicted as soon as the initial soil surveys were done. It may well be that the current understanding might have been reached more quickly, if the 'administrative difficulties' could have been overcome more often or if better rains and fewer pests had reduced the number of lost trials. However, such a speeding-up of the research process would not have added one iota to the impact of TSP. If it has not become established in the *goz* farming system it is because it has never been widely available and, possibly, because it is still not sufficiently profitable under current circumstances. These are facts that research cannot change. If, however, circumstances had been more propitious it is likely that farmers would, by their own processes of trial and error, have come up with adequate practical solutions to the problems that research has dealt with in such complexity. In other words, if TSP had been viable much of the research would have been unnecessary, despite the fact that our understanding of how TSP and the other nutrients in *goz* soil act remains very imperfect. We come to the central paradox: that it is a difficult and lengthy process to reach a full understanding, but that the achievement of that understanding will not provide any usable knowledge.

The above discussion has centred on the millet crop on the *goz*. No other topic has been researched in such detail and it is enough to say that there are no important additions or modifications to be made with regard to the influence of fertility on the other two major crops, sorghum and groundnuts, nor with respect to other areas of the region. One other result also illustrates the value of a 'rough and ready' approach. Trials on micronutrients, which are also very deficient in *goz* soils, showed that molybdenum in the form of sodium molybdate could improve groundnut yields. Only tiny amounts are needed: 100 grams per hectare, which is easily applied as a seed dressing. Rather than pursue further trials to prove beyond doubt how much yields are improved, a simple finding that on '3 occasions out of 4 (significantly so on only one occasion) molybdenum increased kernel yields in the absence of applied Phosphate' is enough to justify the use of the dressing. 'Admittedly the case was not absolutely proven. However, on balance (and not least because the innovation is cheap and has proved necessary in other groundnut producing areas in Africa) it was justifiable' (Quin 1989).

Varieties and New Crops

Variety improvement seems to offer an uncontroversial and low-risk means to increase agricultural production. Once a new breed is developed then farmers can grow it for themselves for ever after. There is no need to become dependent on expensive imported fertilizers and so on. For these reasons, variety research is immensely attractive to aid. The variety-led green revolution seems only to justify its popularity.

After a drought the recommendation is simple. What the farmers need is a better adapted variety: shorter season, more drought-resistant and so on. Naturally enough this leads to plans for accelerated research and breeding programmes. This strategy makes three mistakes. First, there are immense practical difficulties in any drought-prone area. There are so many causes of crop failure that research can be a slow and very frustrating business. It is doubtful whether such a thing as an accelerated programme is possible anyway. Second, the idea that there is one set of varietal characteristics that can solve the region's problems is false. Quite apart from the major divides between north/west and south/east, between wadi land and *goz* and so on, there is wide local variation over short distances. Even more important are the differences between the circumstances and wishes of one farmer and his neighbour and between what the same farmer may want one year and what he wants the next. It is not one variety that is needed but a range from which the farmers may choose according to their needs. Third, the green revolution may have been variety-led but it was based on a package involving higher inputs of both water and fertilizer, usually applied to relatively good soils. It is not at all clear that varietal research without these complementary inputs will lead to any great successes.

In the Jebel Marra area alone, some 280 local varieties of both millet and sorghum have been identified. These differ in a number of characteristics: period of growth, shape of head, colour of grain, disease resistance and so on. Figure 3.5 graphs the maturity distribution of sorghum varieties, showing the very wide range in just one characteristic. A similar figure could be drawn for millet. There is every reason to believe that this local population of millets and sorghums, adapted over generations to suit local circumstances, accurately reflects the optimum distribution. In other words, what is needed is not just a quick-maturing variety but a higher-yielding quick-maturing variety: a much more difficult task. If early maturity were all that is required it would be easy enough to find it from among the local stock. And that is in fact what happens. During the 1980s shorter millet varieties like *dimbi* drifted down from north to south Darfur. If the rains were to improve the drift would undoubtedly reverse. Varieties have also come into the area from further afield, especially West Africa.

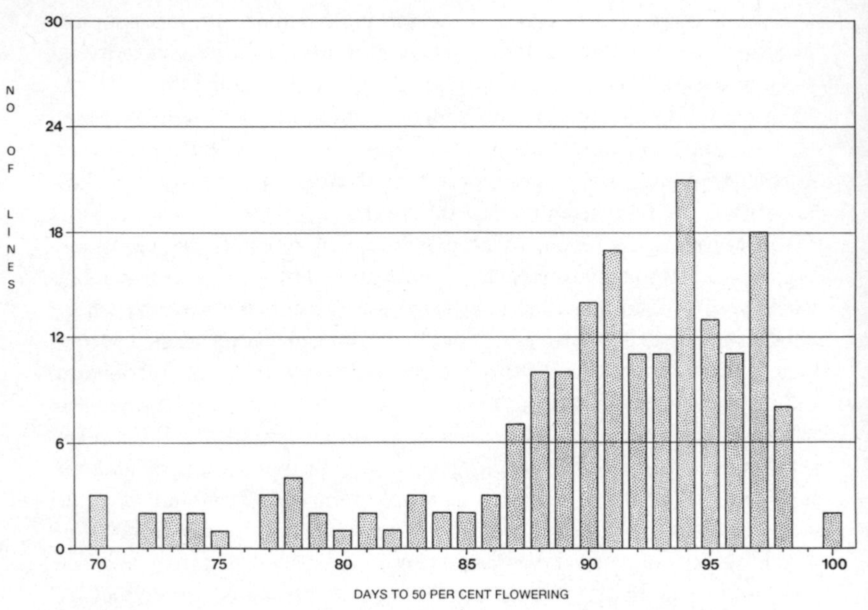

Figure 3.5 Maturity Distribution in Sorghum Local Collection

Taste is important. It is easy to forget, when the agenda is set by a perceived need for food security in a drought-stricken area, that even poor people have strong preferences over what is, after all, the very core of their diet. Anyone who has eaten millet or sorghum will quickly learn why. There are few things less palatable than dry bread made of red sorghum flour while white sorghum bread and white sorghum porridge can be very satisfying. As income rises in rural areas of developing countries, one of the major unobserved changes is a shift away from the least palatable sorghums and millets towards the more acceptable ones, even at the cost of some loss in yield. Threshing and milling characteristics are also important. Some sorghums have to be milled twice in the standard diesel hammer mill before an acceptable flour is produced.

Every farmer will put a different weight on the importance of all these and many other characteristics when deciding which of the range of available varieties suits him best. There is, however, one overriding reason why a wide range is important, which is that it allows the most flexible balance between two opposing risks: the risk of failure in a bad year and the risk of missing the rewards of a good one. For the same reasons, individual varieties have to be judged on their performance over a range of circumstances. It is no good seeking one variety that is 'best of class' in all respects. This is why the post-famine insistence on drought resistance is a such a serious mistake. It focuses exclusively on the risk side of the risk-reward balance. Research on sorghum, for example, has concentrated on short-straw, short-season varieties which are best suited to marginal lands and drier years. This is a perfectly valid research aim but it urgently needs to be balanced by the development of varieties for better soils and wetter years.

These ideas are difficult for outsiders and even for national researchers to accept. After all, the green revolution was largely built on one rice variety, IRRI Number 8, and the researcher has a natural desire for a clear-cut conclusion. Crucially, they also go against aid's inbuilt need for the big winner. They do not, however, go against practice in the First World, where it is common for seed merchants to offer ten or twenty varieties. Research into green revolution rice varieties also nowadays offers a variety for every circumstance.

Sorghum variety is probably the single most successful research intervention in Darfur. The first two varieties to succeed, principally in the JMRDP area, were called Dabar and Qadam El Hamam. Compared with local varieties, these are relatively short-strawed, medium-period sorghums which were developed by the national research authorities through selection from Sudanese varieties. They have been available in central Sudan for some time, where they were originally developed for mechanized farming.

Dabar grain is white and of good quality for *'asida*, the staple Sudanese porridge. Small quantities of these varieties were introduced as early as 1976, but the JMRDP only began wider distribution in 1982. Five years later Dabar was established as the second most important variety and it was grown on 19 per cent of all sorghum fields in the project area: firm evidence of farmers' willingness to take up new varieties that fit their requirements (JMRDP Post-Harvest Survey, 1988).

While Dabar filled a very useful niche in the farmers' armoury it was subject to limitations that illustrate very well the point that the requirement is not for one variety but for a range. It was always expected that it would be suitable for the drier, more marginal soils and it was a good choice for the drought years of the early 1980s. It did worse in wetter years like 1985 and 1986, when it proved vulnerable to fungal blight. Even though it was the second most common variety in 1987, it was

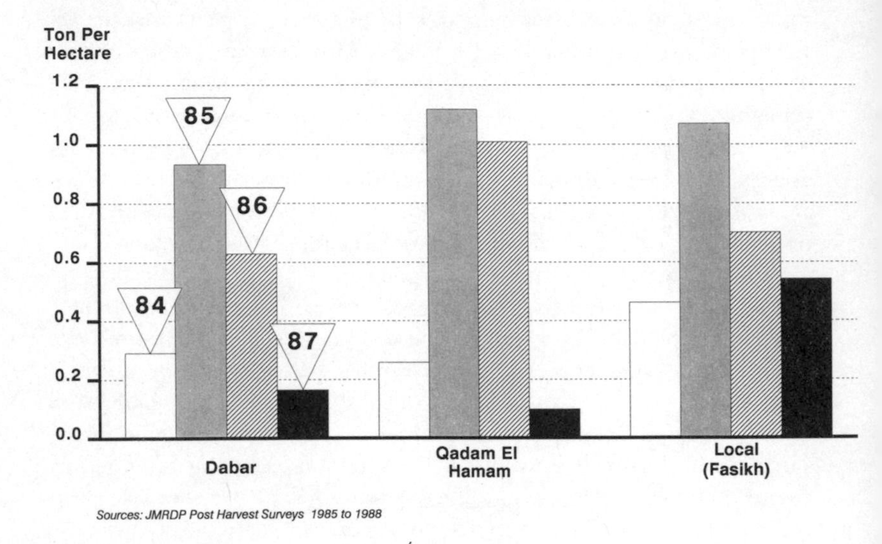

Figure 3.6 Sorghum Variety Yields, JMRDP Area – 1984 to 1987

sown on only half as many fields as the most common variety, a local one called Fasikh which is much taller and takes longer to maturity. Because it is sown on more marginal soils, Dabar yields are poor compared to Fasikh: only 160 kilograms per hectare compared with nearly 600 kilograms in 1987 (JMRDP Post-Harvest Survey, 1988). Figure 3.6 shows that neither of the two new varieties in fact outyields the local sorghum (predominantly Fasikh). They are, nevertheless, a success and they have been widely accepted by farmers. They may not outperform Fasikh on good land but they do allow sorghum to be grown on land that local varieties could not tolerate. As the figure shows, this means that the yields of these new varieties are worse affected by rainfall than the local ones, not less. In other words, the introduction of drought-resistant varieties did not reduce the farmers' risk. On the contrary, it allowed them to take on extra risk by planting sorghum on poorer land. Not at all the effect intended, but that is unimportant. The main thing is that farmers have found a use for the new varieties.

A number of even newer sorghum varieties have shown good performance in the JMRDP area. Trials varieties are known by unattractive numbers and P967083 was identified from trials supplied to the project by the national research authorities. It came originally from Purdue University in the USA, indicating the rather random way in which new varieties arrive for testing. It has been multiplied and proved popular with farmers. Survey results show, however, the great range of results achieved by just one variety, depending on location.

Table 3.4 Performance of a new sorghum variety

	Per cent satisfied	Yield
Mukjar	92.2	7.36
Garsila	96.3	4.48
Amballa	43.6	3.74
Tululu	36.7	3.46
Zalingei	53.3	3.75
Dankuch	25.6	2.11
Nyertete	19.0	1.83
Golo	26.1	0.54
Kabkabiya	9.7	1.29
Overall	48.8	3.54

Source: JMRDP P9 Survey, 1990

Groundnuts provide a good example of the pressure to conform with national research authorities. No new varieties have consistently outperformed Barberton, which was introduced into Darfur some years ago. The national authorities have, however, identified a variety called Sodari which has been approved for release to farmers throughout the Sudan. Unfortunately, Sodari has failed to perform in trials or on farmers' fields in Darfur. As it has been released there is little harm in its distribution to farmers, who will soon make their own minds up about it. As far as research is concerned, however, the time taken to assess Sodari has delayed attention being given to some other varieties which are not so well developed, in the bureaucratic sense that they have not been released, but which do show some promise. 'The varieties EC–5 and Spancross had yields greater than that of Barberton local on 6, out of a possible 10, occasions. On two of those occasions the differences reached [statistical] significance.' . . . 'By reason of some frequency of superiority, both EC–5 and Spancross may be alternatives to Barberton' (Quin, 1989).

To sum up, there are three key principles of adaptive variety research in hazardous environments like Darfur. First, the aim should not be absolute improvements in performance, which are unlikely, but 'some frequency of superiority'. Second, the goal should not be to replace existing varieties but rather to find alternatives that do better in certain niches. Third, early release to farmers ensures equally early indications of success or failure. The success of P9 sorghum on the JMRDP was quickly established by farmer response. A very helpful attitude from the sorghum breeders of the national Agricultural Research Corporation, who encouraged the project to distribute the variety to local farmers without insisting on formal release procedures, was especially important. A fourth principle, which has still not been widely accepted, is the need to be ruthless in throwing out varieties that have clearly not performed. Public relations efforts by research centres lead to over-estimates of the potential of new varieties and it then becomes difficult to admit their failure later.

Attempts to identify new rainfed field crops have not succeeded. Many crops which seem to offer attractive features have failed. 'It is very tempting to see pigeon pea as a valuable rotation crop on goz soils because of its potential for restoration of soil fertility and, as a hedge, acting as a windbreak. Nevertheless, [the research shows] that it does not do well on goz soils and cannot easily become a component of goz based cropping systems' (Quin, 1989). Among other crops tried have been guar bean, a source of an alternative to gum arabic, sunflower, fodder crops such as stylosanthes, cotton and rice. Some have been clear failures. Others have been technically successful but never followed up; rice, cotton and sunflower are examples.

As always, however, marketing is probably the major obstacle to any of these developments. The relatively slow progress of diversification at present should not obscure the fact that it may well be a major component of agricultural development if Darfur ever does break out of its overpowering constraints and starts to grow once again. Until that day comes, research is largely condemned to repeating itself without any result beyond deepening levels of sophistication and cost.

Pigeon pea continues to attract attention because it is a legume, theoretically capable of fixing nitrogen in the soil and so raising fertility. The aid bias towards 'hero crops' that can raise incomes as well as save the environment ensures that pigeon pea will continue to be tried again and again. This will be in the face of the 1940s finding that it 'was given a protracted trial for its rotational value as a deep rooter and a nitrogen restorer with negative results'. Even in 1948 researchers were wearying of trials work that led nowhere. 'This native of the far East [soya bean] has been tried continuously in the Sudan since the beginning of the century with seed and soil inoculants from various parts of the world. For many years it appeared that the fifty-seven values ascribed this plant by its advocates could best be attained by plants better suited to the climate but recent trials at Shendi have given encouraging yields' (Tothill, 1948). Despite those trials at Shendi, soya has still to show any potential in Sudan; and yet the attempts to prove that it has some continue.

Crop Protection

Crop protection is a major concern to farmers, second only to drought and weeds. Despite this it has received relatively little attention. Once again this reflects the western slant behind much agricultural research: a focus on fertility and conservation issues combined with a paternalistic suspicion of chemicals in the hands of peasant farmers, because of both the expense and the health hazards. 'There will be increasing demand for chemical pest and disease control material, much of which has undesirable environmental effects. Planned programmes will be necessary using limited quantities but increasingly relying on cultural and biological controls' (World Bank, 1989: Ch 4).

There is no doubt that where agro-chemicals are easily available in the Third World, mistakes are made and problems can develop. Nevertheless, this over-protective attitude, with its emphasis on 'planned programmes' and 'limited quantities', flies in the face of the realities of rainfed agriculture in difficult areas. Government services are desperately weak and incapable of managing planned programmes. But even if the national Plant Protection Department were much better equipped, Darfur agriculture does not lend itself to this style of organization. Different pests develop rapidly at different times and different places. They would test the speed of reaction of any organization. Besides, there is a basic contradiction between planned programmes and limited quantities. Planned pest control by government agencies inevitably involves major spraying campaigns over large areas. Some areas are bound to be sprayed which do not actually need it. On the other hand, small areas which need it very badly may not get sprayed, because the problem has not yet reached a level which justifies a major campaign. Either way the likelihood is that more chemical will be applied than if farmers were allowed to make their own decisions, however inefficiently they used it.

The 'planned and controlled' approach is particularly strong in Sudan, thanks to the influence of the major irrigation schemes which are naturally suited to large-scale campaigns and techniques like aerial spraying. The result is that certain major pests such as andat, or sorghum bug, African army worm, locusts and grasshoppers are classified as 'national pests': the specific responsibility of the Plant Protection Department. Given the natural tendency of bureaucracies to allocate turf, this is sometimes taken to mean that other agencies should not take steps to deal with these pests. It also tends to reinforce the idea that farmers should not be encouraged to act on their own initiative to spray their own fields. The lack of imported goods means that farmers cannot get crop protection equipment and materials, which reinforces the role of official agencies or, at least, prevents farmers from escaping their 'protection'.

Grasshopper bait is an example of the breakdown of the 'campaign' approach to crop protection. Grasshopper is the most widespread and persistent pest of all and there used to be an established system for the preparation of hopper-baits, made by coating groundnut shells with a pesticide. The collapse of state financed services has meant that baits have not been widely available for some years. During the drought years this did not have much effect, but grasshoppers caused major losses in the better years of the mid-1980s, another example of the dangers of ignoring non-drought problems even in marginal areas. As is now typical of most state supplied services, once this level of collapse has been reached, subsequent attempts to supply baits have been far from planned. Instead they have been almost wholly reactive, involving attempts by projects as well as the national Plant Protection Department to pool resources and win donor support to carry out a campaign. Since the essence of a successful bait campaign is having the materials available for rapid response to outbreaks, this reactive and *ad hoc* approach is almost bound to fail.

Crop protection provides some shining examples of the asymmetry between what the First World does and what it recommends for the Third World. Until 1990, Aldrex-T seed dressing was the single most popular modern technology among farmers struggling to protect their planted seed against termites and ants, until the crop was established (JMRDP Post-Harvest Survey, 1988). The quantity used is very small, as little as 60 grams per hectare, one-sixth of the rate European farmers used to use. The cost to farmers was equally small, some £S3 per hectare. Aldrex became established without any research work, spreading spontaneously throughout Darfur after being introduced for use in central Sudan. Unfortunately it contains aldrin, a chemical which has fallen foul of environmental concerns in the First World. Production stopped in 1988/9 and there was a race to buy the last stocks for western Sudan. Once those are finished, there will be no more Aldrex. An alternative which contains lindane rather than aldrin may prove to be effective, but it was certainly not as popular with farmers who tried both.

The western world used aldrin for decades, at much greater intensities than the Darfur farmer was ever likely to use, before it was suddenly abandoned. However genuine the aid community's concern about the environment, it is impossible not to see it as grossly inconsistent and asymmetric when it prevents the use of relatively harmless chemicals by poor farmers in areas that are unlikely to ever face a pollution hazard one-tenth as great as those that the west has still failed to adequately tackle, such as acid rain. This is particularly so when it has so far proved difficult to identify many other crop protection techniques that are immediately useful under the present situation.

The millet headworm, *nafaasha*, gives an idea, just as TSP did for fertilizer, of the practical complexities. During the dry years of the early 1980s, *nafaasha* was by far the commonest pest on millet, by far the most important crop. JMRDP trials did establish that spraying with a synthetic chemical called Ripcord could control *nafaasha* and raise yields by as much as 30 per cent. As always there was much concern about the wisdom of encouraging small farmers to use expensive chemicals, although the cost was not great. There were two more practical problems. One was how to identify when the crop should be sprayed to avoid spraying unnecessarily and yet not leave it too late. The other was labour. Millet grows up to two metres high and it can only be sprayed for *nafaasha* when it is fully grown. The sprayer has to carry a knapsack full of water through a dense crop and reach up to spray the ears of millet well above his head without getting the chemical in his eyes. Water for spraying is itself a problem. Even during the rains the majority of the millet fields are a long way from the wells, so spraying involves an extra trek to bring the water. For all these reasons it is an arduous job.

Various solutions have been tried. Ultra low volume (ULV) sprayers are much lighter and need only a little water, but the reluctance to propose more sophisticated techniques has meant that this option has not been fully explored. It is argued that it needs small batteries which might be expensive, although they are one of the few modern items to be found in every Darfur village where the hand-held torch is another of those simple tools that are almost obsolete in the west but which have changed life quite radically in a region without electricity. Another approach has been to advise farmers to plant their crops in neater rows, with rows of another low-growing crop like cowpeas at intervals so that it is easier for the sprayer to walk through the millet.

I have suggested that much of the research into optimum methods to apply TSP was not really necessary because it dealt with matters that farmers would probably have solved for themselves, if the fertilizer had been available in the market and if it had been economically viable. The same is true for nafaasha. When sprayers are widely available in Darfur, where millet prices are encouraging and when nafaasha is a problem, then farmers will work out for themselves how best to spray. Similarly, if both ULV and ordinary sprayers are made available they will quickly find out which suits them best. It is even likely that both technologies will find a market.

Cultivation Methods

Once again environmental concerns dominate. 'Full scale mechanization is not the answer', as it results in soil degradation (World Bank, 1989: Ch 4). Animal traction is the recommended alternative. The puzzle is, however, that animal traction has an impressive record of failure in many parts of Africa although it has been well established in many other parts of the continent since well before the aid era.

As populations grow, fallow periods are reduced and the land is cropped more frequently. Thus far most are agreed. The differences arise over the outcome. For the neo-Malthusians the result is ever-declining soil fertility and poverty. Only directed research can save the situation. The Boserup hypothesis argues, on the other hand, that reduction in fallows will stimulate the introduction of new technologies that offset the increased pressure on the land. In Europe this process started centuries ago although the very first stage, where two years cropping was followed by twenty years fallow, existed into the Middle Ages. Many parts of Africa, Darfur included, are still in the interim stages of a shorter bush fallow (Boserup, 1965).

The implications of Boserup are considerable. One is that African fallow systems are not the inevitable result of poor African soils, of an endowment which can only be used in this way. Instead, they merely reflect the balance between population and the resource at a particular time: the man:land ratio. '[Soil] fertility may be the result of the use of intensive methods of land utilization and not vice versa.' The other crucial implication is that technology is also a function of population density and that new techniques do not enable changes in cropping systems. Instead they follow them. 'The hoe is not introduced as a perfection of the digging stick. It is introduced when an additional operation [weeding] becomes necessary, i.e. when forest fallow is replaced by bush fallow.' Bush fallow is replaced in turn by shorter, grass fallows. Grasses are tougher to hoe and more cultivation is needed, so it is at this stage that the plough is introduced. At the same time the grass provides the fodder needed for draught animals. Fertilization techniques make a similar progression: from ash under forest fallows, through manuring in short grass systems, to chemical fertilizers. The key conclusion, very much at odds with aid perceptions, is that the absence of animal traction and fertility conserving techniques does not prove that land is in short supply but just the opposite (Boserup, 1965: Ch 2).

Without the plough, short fallows are avoided. Weeds are kept down instead, with long periods of continuous cropping giving the African eight-year-cropped, eight-year-fallow type of rotation. Pingali has found evidence Africa-wide to support Boserup, showing that the change from hoe cultivation to animal traction or to tractors depends on the level of intensity of the whole farming system, that the primary motivation is area expansion and labour saving and that 'all the farmer wants to do is substitute one power source for another *for a particular operation*' (Pingali, 1987, my italics). This description fits what is happening in Darfur exactly. Animal traction has not been widely successful, but it has found one or two single-operation niches where it has come into use. Such relatively marginal changes as this are not what aid is hoping for from research into animal traction, and most of them have happened without the assistance of research anyway.

Sudan has very large areas of mechanized farming, in the east of the country, and the negative side has received a lot of attention. A small group of people have become extremely rich growing sorghum on mechanized farms. They pay very low rents and it is widely believed that they are not farming the land but mining it, causing great environmental damage. Some even attribute a collapse of the subsistence economy to 'unplanned commercial development' which has left peasants and pastoralists dependent on wage labour in the mechanized sector and forced them to abandon 'sustainable agricultural techniques' on their own land. 'Having to compete with large scale commercial farming, very often with reduced family labour through migration, has meant that poor peasants have had to intensify their cultivation methods. This has resulted in the appearance of all manner of time saving techniques such as the decline in intercropping, crop rotation, strict sowing or weeding, extensive terracing and so on' (Duffield, 1990).

This sounds more like de-intensification, illustrating the shakiness of the underlying economics. The fact is that mechanized farming has, if its critics' own figures are to be believed, doubled the rainfed cropped area in Sudan without reducing the traditional sector. Both sectors now account for around 9 million *feddans* – some 4 million hectares (Duffield, 1990). To the critics, this means that the traditional sector has 'stagnated', a major reason for attacking the mechanized sector. Such a view, however, takes the massive increases in both production and employment provided by mechanized farming as more or less worthless. Only the ploughing and seeding is mechanized. All the other operations are done by hand and the employment generated is correspondingly large. The critical view also depends, by implication at least, on an assumption that the traditional, non-mechanized sector would have been able to produce a similar level of production. It is hoped that the discussion so far has helped to show how unrealistic that assumption is.

There is no doubt that mechanized farming can cause environmental damage. The extent is rarely clearly assessed, still more rarely analysed in rigorous economic terms. A critical distinction is usually ignored: between those effects of mechanization which are unavoidable and those effects which are entirely avoidable but which spring from bad management. There is every reason to believe that the environmental and even the social problems associated with mechanized farming in Sudan have everything to do with management, at every level, and little or nothing to do with the actual technology of mechanized ploughing. This point may be made more general by saying that the preponderance, in the development literature, of discussions of the choice of technology may be missing a far more significant area, namely the efficiency with which any one technology is put to use. In the words of the song, 'it ain't what you do, it's the way that you do it' that counts; the theme song of X-efficiency, perhaps.

Technically, there is little or no difference between mechanized farming and manual farming in Sudan. For both the main concern is weeds, and tractor ploughing is done after the first rains have encouraged the weeds to germinate so that they can be ploughed in. If the weeding operation or *hash* is the fundamental of traditional techniques, then tractor cultivation with the wide-level disc plough is nothing more than the ultimate *hash*. All it does is allow a larger area to be cultivated than could be achieved with manual methods. If there is any environmental damage, it is the result of the act of cultivation not of mechanization *per se*. Hand cultivation has exactly the same effect: it is merely a matter of scale.

The clamour about adverse side effects has obscured the fact that the economic case for the use of tractors in Sudan is strong. Land is relatively abundant and labour is short, especially since migration to the Gulf began. Intensification and the greater concern for the value of land that goes with it will not be attractive to the farmers of Sudan while this remains the case. The only way to achieve a rapid increase in standards of living is, therefore, to increase the area under crops. The fact that 60 per cent or more of agricultural effort using the hoe goes on weeding shows what could be achieved if only that crucial planting/weeding peak could be broken. Surveys have identified that critical labour constraint repeatedly since at least the mid-1970s. It is a measure of aid's resistance to, indeed fear of, mechanization and the whole idea of development by extension that little has been done to tackle it. Even the promotion of animal traction has been attacked on occasion, on the grounds that it helps only the better-off and threatens over-exploitation of a limited land resource, flying in the face of all the evidence (KTI, 1985).

If it is accepted that area extension is still a valid goal for for Darfuri agriculture, then the balance between mechanization and animal traction depends simply on their relative cost. Given the underlying bias against mechanization, the cost benefits of animal traction are frequently over-estimated. This is easy to do because the costs are not always obvious, especially to outsiders whose agriculture has been fully mechanized for many decades.

Using the acid test of Rural People's Knowledge In Action, the first question is: why is animal traction not in greater use already? The answer cannot really be that the people of Darfur do not understand the potential of animals. Camels and bulls have been used as pack animals for centuries. The introduction of the horse-drawn cart in the mid-20th century made a considerable difference to *goz* farming and both two- and four-wheelers provide much of the bulk transport around the larger towns like Nyala. Ploughing with camels is already well established around a town called Kas in south Darfur, a spontaneous development during the 1960s and 1970s.

The two large projects in south Darfur have both attempted to develop and extend the use of animal cultivation to a wider range of conditions and operations. Some progress has been made, but it remains a very long way short of a transformation. Just like Dabar sorghum and TSP, animal traction has found a niche in some areas but no more than that. And within that niche, developments owe almost everything to farmers' individual initiatives. Ploughing is still concentrated around Kas, where it first came into use, and even those who do plough do not use it on all their land. It is mainly used for groundnuts (WSDC Farmer Survey, 1984; JMRDP Post-Harvest Survey, 1988).

It is easy to assume that because Darfur is a major livestock producer animal traction should be cheap. After all there are millions of cattle, camels and donkeys in Darfur and hundreds of thousands of horses. However, there is a radical difference between herding animals for beef or even dairy production and keeping them for draught work. In the first case, the animal can be treated fairly casually, in the sense that it merely has to be directed towards good rangeland and water, according to the seasonal patterns, and protected against disease and other attacks. Otherwise, it looks after itself. For draught work, an animal has to be trained continuously, fed well and generally looked after. In countries where draught oxen are important, like Bangladesh, the calves are yoked into pairs almost as soon as they are born, so as to start their training. In Yemen, mature oxen are hand-fed. To maintain a really well-trained animal, this kind of attention has to be kept up throughout the year. On the other hand, the sowing period is short and unpredictable. It would take an enormous effort to keep a plough ox in good condition all year, to work for just a few weeks. This is one reason why camels are preferred for ploughing. They can be kept busy as pack animals outside the ploughing season, transporting crops to market and so on. As a result plough animals in Darfur are poorly trained. They are general purpose animals, and when they are not being worked they are often left to fend for themselves, grazing in the bush near the villages. It needs two men, or even three, to drive a single camel when ploughing. In a country which has a strong tradition of animal traction, one man can drive a pair of animals.

The fact that ploughing is only important in certain areas and that it is clearly linked with groundnut production partly reflects the influence of cost. Water and browse to feed a camel are relatively abundant in the basement areas around Kas. It is, however, technique that has really made camel-ploughing competitive with the traditional methods of the hand hoe. Ploughing has found its niche where it can be used to achieve the same object as the traditional 'minimum-tillage' hoe techniques for less effort, and that object is to suppress the weeds.

The technique is in fact exactly the same as that used on the big mechanized farms of eastern Sudan. The land is ploughed after the first rains have germinated the weeds, so as to bury them before the crop is sown. For grain crops, this is an important change because it means delaying the sowing until after cultivation and a consequent loss of a useful growing period. If, moreover, the rains fail and the crop has to be resown, then much of the benefits of the ploughing in suppressing weeds may be lost. For groundnuts, ploughing requires almost no change to the existing technique because, even when hand-hoed, groundnut fields are cultivated before they are sown. Ploughing is a straight substitute for that first cultivation. Because, moreover, groundnuts are sown close together, they can be drilled direct into the furrow behind the plough. The seed is then automatically covered over by the soil the plough throws over as it makes the next furrow. This saves a lot of labour. It takes nearly 40 man-days to weed and plant a hectare of groundnuts by hand (WSDC Farmer Survey, 1983). With three men and a camel plough it can take as little as six man-days. This 'plough and sow' technique is used by up to 70 per cent of those who plough (WSDC Farmer Survey, 1984).

Two other factors make ploughing particularly suitable for groundnuts. It is far easier to use animal traction on the light soils which suit groundnuts and the crop takes only three months to maturity, so the delay caused by waiting for rain and then for the weeds to germinate is not so important as it would be with grain.

The benefits of animal traction in terms of both yield and the suppression of weeds have been well established in trials, for grain as much as for groundnuts. Yield gains of up to 100 per cent have been measured and weed reductions, in terms of the weight at the time of first weeding, of between 40 and 80 per cent. Surveys have also shown that where farmers do use a plough, they manage to cultivate larger areas and those people who own a plough make extra earnings from ploughing for hire (Harvey, 1986). What is clear, however, is that those benefits are insufficient to cover the cost except where a particular set of circumstances provides a niche.

The ploughing technique came to southern Darfur before any research was done on rainfed agriculture in the area. The mouldboard plough used is based on a design which some farmers call 'Sini' or Chinese. Whether or not the original design came from China, it is simple enough and local blacksmiths in Nyala and Kas have been making it since the early 1970s. The first four were made in 1973 (HTS, 1974). What then has been the role of research, apart that is from building up a lot of evidence to explain why farmers were doing what they were already doing? One aim was to improve the efficiency of the existing method. Modern agricultural engineering, which reflects the influence of western mechanized farming, lays stress on correct adjustments to the plough to ensure that it enters the soil at the right angle and to the correct depth and so on. It was hoped that better design of the basic plough would allow farmers to make such adjustments. In addition, it was believed that more standard manufacture would make it easier for broken or worn parts to be replaced cheaply. Another approach has been to develop a seeder-weeder, in recognition of the fact that plough-sowing is the most important niche for animal traction.

A second goal has been to try to develop an animal-drawn weeding tool in the hope of overcoming the peak labour burden of all farmers. The idea of a multi-purpose toolbar, a frame of some kind that could carry both ploughs and weeding implements according to the farmer's need, has been pursued with virtually uniform failure throughout Africa. The attraction to outsiders, who perceive African farmers as desperately poor, is that it seems more 'economic': one tool to do several jobs. Any multi-purpose tool is, however, bound to be more heavy and cumbersome. For this reason farmers who have to carry and use such a machine and who have the tedious job of changing the plough for the weeding tines take a different view. (For much the same reason European farmers also tend to prefer single-purpose machines even if they cost more.) Besides, neither of the two techniques to be combined have been established independently in Darfur outside the limited camel-ploughing activity. A combined tool is only likely to prove valuable when both ploughing and weeding functions have established themselves separately.

After some years of work on multi-purpose toolbars, research came round to the need for a single-purpose, animal-drawn weeding tool. It remains to be seen whether it will find a market. A general problem for intercrop weeding is the fact that the crops are not planted to a tidy pattern. An animal-drawn weeder needs a clearly defined row to pass along. To the extent that farmers need to plant quickly, they may not find the effort needed to make neat rows worth their while.

Animal traction research has also been weighed down by the fact that it attempts to achieve two things simultaneously: to identify new designs suited to farming in the area and to stimulate local production of those designs. The attractions are obvious. After all, there is already an active blacksmith industry in Darfur and aid lays great emphasis on small-scale industry and the potential for linkages between industry and agriculture. However, the basic principles of mass production were not observed. In order to produce a standard design which will be more easily adjustable and which allows spare parts to be fitted off-the-shelf, then some form of mass production is essential. The ploughs must be built with standard jigs. If, moreover, the aim is to produce more ploughs and make them cheaper to farmers, then again a change in manufacturing technique is inevitable. The projects did attempt to encourage the Nyala blacksmith industry to raise its standards, by offering a standard design and contracts for reasonably large numbers. However, there is only one blacksmith in Nyala who is capable of undertaking such a contract and he can only do this by sub-contracting to all the other smiths. The inevitable result is variable quality and high cost. This is a case of the dilemma discussed in Chapter 1; whether to concentrate on the short term and on providing the best possible assistance to the farmers, which might be better done by contracting plough manufacture to the bigger engineering companies in Khartoum or even overseas, or to provide them with a rather poorer service in the hope of establishing a local plough manufacturing industry for the longer term.

Some of the most successful industries in Third World countries have in fact found their place in the production of the simpler agricultural equipment and supplies, which may not represent the most up-to-date western technology but which cannot, at the same time be described as 'intermediate'. The Indian diesel engine and irrigation pump industry, for example, may be simple but it still uses all the basic mass production techniques and equipment: power lathes, drills and grinders. The fact that animal-drawn ploughs are an intermediate technology for the farm does not, in any way, constitute a sound argument for them to be produced using basic smithing techniques which barely qualify as intermediate. In Europe it was the introduction of mass-produced animal-drawn equipment that marked the first step towards integrated development of agriculture and industry, not the introduction of new designs for manufacture by craft blacksmiths.

Tractors have also been tried in Darfur, mainly on the *naga'a* soils of the southern alluvium. These are more fertile than the *goz*, but they are too hard for hoe agriculture. Even with a tractor they can be difficult. Partly because they are so hard, they tend to become completely bare. If the grass cover is lost, as a result of sheet erosion compounded by grazing, the *naga'a* becomes so hard that the vegetation cannot re-establish itself naturally. Once this happens it is utterly useless, although it makes a nice smooth service to drive a car over or even land an aeroplane.

As early as 1973 it was demonstrated that these soils can be ploughed with a standard, 90 horsepower tractor using heavy chisel ploughs (HTS, 1976). Provided the ploughing is done to an adequate depth and providing there are no prolonged droughts, heavy crops of sorghum can be grown. As always with mechanization, these findings have been treated with great suspicion. Tractor ploughing is seen as 'costly and difficult to sustain' . . . 'Although the methods are effective they do restrict the potential utilization of naga'a to wealthier farmers. In the absence of any alternative practices this means that the majority of the farming population absolutely cannot utilize the naga'a lands' (Quin, 1989). Once again the potential consumer and employment benefits of increased sorghum production are arbitrarily ignored. More prosaically, the belief that tractor ploughing is outstandingly expensive is not really justified. WSDC analyses in 1984–5 indicated that a reasonable and affordable rate, comparable with hire rates for hand cultivation on the *goz*, could be charged, provided that the hire service was managed efficiently. On that basis the corporation expanded the limited hire ploughing service it had been operating in the *naga'a* areas.

Given current circumstances in Sudan, that proviso about efficient management is a major consideration. As throughout, this is not an issue that can be decided with any certainty while almost all the imported goods needed to run a tractor are in such short supply in Sudan. It is impossible to make a realistic assessment of the true cost or to judge how profitable it might be. However, it is worth emphasizing that surveys in no way support the idea that *naga'a* ploughing is a wealthy man's prerogative. In 1984, the average *naga'a* plot size was only 1.77 *feddans.* Some plots were as little as half a *feddan* and less than 20 per cent used any hired labour at all. This is hardly comparable with the 1,000-*feddan* blocks farmed by the sorghum millionaires of eastern Sudan (WSDC Naga'a Survey, 1984).

Irrigation

Irrigation illustrates the way in which preconceptions about development strategies can obscure significant possibilities. The first studies were sponsored by the Ministry of Mines and Irrigation, looking for large-scale gravity-fed irrigation using dams. This was found to be uneconomic

omic. During the 1960s and early 1970s, under the aegis of the Horticulture Department of the Ministry of Agriculture, a number of large tube wells were drilled. These were to be used to irrigate three Pilot Development Areas, each one of some hundreds of hectares. This approach was dropped in its turn, because there was not enough irrigable land per tube well and because there were difficulties with the concept of farmer organization that was proposed. In the meantime, private companies promoted irrigated Virginia tobacco, rather more successfully. Many of the wells dug by tobacco farmers at that time are still in use, mainly for growing onions. (The tobacco business has more or less disappeared. It suffered from government intervention, but southern Sudan also proved more attractive in the period when there was peace in the south.)

In the public sector, the lack of progress on the larger irrigation schemes led to a complete change of strategy with the establishment of the Jebel Marra Rural Development Project. In keeping with the concerns of the 1970s, for help to the poorest of the poor, attention turned to the rainfed sector. Emphasis was laid on subsistence grain production and irrigation was dropped altogether. JMRDP has, subsequently, become involved in support to small-scale irrigation, but this was against advice from both expatriate technical assistance staff and the preferences of the major donor, the European Development Fund. It is only on the insistence of the Sudanese management that the project now sells pumps to private farmers. To sum up, it has taken thirty years for public sector research on irrigation to escape from a series of preconceptions, first on how it should be done and then on whether or not it should be done at all, before retreating to a sensible role: that of giving farmers what they want.

No major sources of groundwater have been found at accessible depths, and irrigation depends on the relatively narrow and shallow aquifers that run beside and under the larger wadis. Existing well construction technologies are simple and in many cases the wells do not even exploit those aquifers to the full (JMRDP Hydrogeology Report, 1988). There are three ways to raise production in these circumstances: improve the wells, cut water losses, or raise the yield of the crops for a given amount of water applied. The techniques to do any of these things are well established worldwide and many have been proven in Darfur. Even with limited aquifers more water can be made available by improving well design and construction. Water losses can be cut by lining irrigation channels and so on and, especially, by irrigating only when the crop needs it. Yields can be raised with fertilizers, pesticides and in many other ways.

Irrigated farming in Darfur is very inefficient by international standards. For expensive diesel pumps, the area irrigated is, at 0.62 hectare per pump, far below the capacity of the pump. In one survey, each pump was only operated for 19.7 hours per week; about 40 per cent of what might be considered full capacity on an eight-hour, six-day week. There are many countries where even that would be considered a low level of operation. Pumps are run at slow speeds, which reduces their performance still further below the optimum. And farmers do not seem to be making very efficient use of the water they do get. They do not vary the rate at which they apply the water to the crop, as they should do for the greatest efficiency, and the field channels and ridges are not constructed with any great care. Fertilizer and pesticides are rarely used to raise yields and farmers do not normally apply manure. Only 15 per cent of onion plots had any fertilizer applied in 1987 and only 22 per cent had pesticides (JMRDP Irrigation Survey, 1988).

Irrigation is a relatively new business in Darfur and this may be one reason for the poor performance. On the other hand, some farmers have been growing irrigated crops for twenty years or more and there is a wealth of irrigation experience to be gained from central Sudan. The true explanation for the failure to progress beyond the simplest techniques is the economic choking-off progress. The lack of consumer goods and the high price of those that do reach the market mean that labour costs are high, a strong disincentive to more intensive methods. Add to that unreliable supplies, especially of fuel, which has been extremely difficult to get for many years. To get diesel almost always involves dealings either on the black market or with the bureaucracy. Fertilizer and chemical supplies are even more erratic. On the output side the onion market has been affected by repeated changes in the rules over export to Chad and Central Africa and by the fluctuation in competing supplies from central Sudan. That competition is almost completely unpredictable, because it depends on the state of transport between Darfur and the east which changes wildly from day to day depending on whether Sudan Railways is functioning and whether there is any diesel for the trucks.

Farmer surveys show how these market uncertainties deprive research of a market for its work. In early 1987 farmers reported that a lack of water was the biggest obstacle to increasing their irrigated area. In early 1988, despite the fact that the 1987 rainy season had been drier than 1986 and the aquifers were if anything less full, water had dropped to fifth place in importance. Fuel and cash, to buy that expensive fuel and to hire labour, were the main 1988 constraints. Farmer interest in techniques to save water or to get more water out of their wells or to raise yields was swamped by the need to keep their pumps operating at all (JMRDP Irrigation Survey, 1988).

Constant change is part of the problem. If one constraint, be it water or labour or fuel, was dominant every year then it would be possible to adjust strategies to suit and research could focus on methods to enable such an adjustment. The inability to know which problem is going to be at the top of the list in any year means that farmers have to concentrate on simple techniques that avoid excess exposure to any one problem. The result is that irrigation, which should be a more secure form of agriculture in Darfur, albeit more expensive, is actually just as risky as rainfed or even more so.

Extension

If the lack of a market for new technologies under the present economic situation has prevented progress for research, the same is true *a fortiori* for the Extension Service, which is supposed to 'sell' farmers the new technologies developed by research and, in reverse, to inform researchers about what farmers want. Extension services which are in difficulty are characterized by two features: a lack of popular 'extension messages', i.e. technologies, to offer to farmers and inadequate contact with the farmers themselves; features that may be seen throughout Africa.

The standard diagnosis emphasizes extension methods and organization: 'management and supervision are typically lax, links with research are weak and feedback from farmers is almost non-existent.' The most famous solution offered for these problems is the Training and Visit (T & V) system whereby 'supervisors check that fieldworkers are visiting farmers while regular training sessions and links with research allow extension workers to be continually upgraded and to feed results and farmers' questions back to researchers' (World Bank, 1989). If, however, there is no effective demand for new technologies, and there are no technologies available anyway, this diagnosis is addressed more to symptoms than to causes and T & V offers no solution. The lack of strong links with research and the poor feedback from farmers do not reflect any inadequacies in the Extension Service itself, but are simply the result of a lack of demand for what it is offering.

The Sudanese Extension Department of the Ministry of Agriculture suffers from the acute shortages of all government services and lacks the capacity for any large-scale activity. In Darfur, it is only the JMRDP which has had a full extension service to offer its farmers for any length of time. In an area with approximately 90,000 farm households, the project has around 60 Extension Agents or one for every 1,500 households. This may be compared with the national Extension Department which only has around 200 agents for the whole of the rest of north Sudan.

This immediately poses the first problem with extension: the cost. Even at the density of coverage at the JMRDP's disposal, backed with an equally intense level of supervision – one supervisor for about ten agents – the project cannot, in a large area with very scattered population, reach every household even occasionally, let alone provide intensive support. In 1987, some 70 per cent of households knew of their Extension Agent and 45 per cent had been in touch with him in the last 12 months (JMRDP Post-Harvest Survey, 1988). Given that each agent has to deal with as many as eight different villages, up to 12 kilometres away from his home, and given that he had only a donkey or a bicycle to visit his farmers with, this should be considered a good performance. Yet it is clearly not enough to allow him to give detailed help to more than a few farmers during the short peak of the farming season. Even so, the cost of a service at this level of intensity is almost certainly beyond the capacity of the government of Sudan to sustain without aid finance. It has to be doubtful, moreover, whether it will ever generate sufficient extra production, and hence income, to pay for itself and so enable government to afford it once aid finance ceases. Long-term sustainability is a serious problem for extension.

A simple calculation reveals the problem. In 1988 the total value of field crop production in the JMRDP area was some £S 250 million, of which £S 220 million was in millet. That year the total project budget was around £S 20 million, which heavily undervalued the foreign exchange components. Even so, the project cost 8 per cent of the total gross value of production in the area. This is a bit unfair, as it makes no allowance for the contribution in other areas (transport and fruit production, for example), but it helps to make the scale of the problem clear. Much of the methodology of extension has been developed in large, intensive production schemes. On a major irrigation scheme growing an export crop, for example, extension may be both necessary and profitable. Under smallholder circumstances in poorer areas it is far more difficult to find a way between the twin perils of unsustainable cost, on the one hand, and an extension service that is spread so thin that it really serves no purpose, on the other.

An Extension Agent can do three things: farmer training and advice, supply of inputs, or provision of credit. It is often argued that there are difficulties in combining these roles. It is felt that an honest teacher and advisor might be compromised if he is also an input salesman. Above all, there is the fear that if the Extension Agent is made responsible for credit provision, farmers will so resent his assessing who is credit-worthy and, above all, his pursuing them for loan repayment that they will not trust his advice. More simply, an Extension Agent who is running a large store of inputs and the paperwork for numerous small-farmer loans will not have much time for farmer training. The only way to avoid these problems would be to have separate networks for Extension and for Input Supply/Credit, implying a doubling of the cost.

Various ways of getting over these problems have been suggested and tried out. The appointment of local farmers as 'Leading Farmers', or subsidiary Extension Agents, is one way in which costs might be reduced. This would leave the officials of the extension service more time to manage supplies and credit. Training the leading farmers then becomes the major difficulty. Another alternative is to keep credit separate, under a credit bank such as the Agricultural Bank of Sudan, or to subdivide the credit business between Extension Agents and the Bank. The former deal with the more positive aspects, such as assisting farmers to make loan applications, while collection remains the problem of the Bank. Credit banks find it very difficult to undertake such a role among small farmers with no formal security. The pressure to insist on extension playing a more formal role in collection is strong. In the JMRDP's case the Agricultural Bank insisted on a formal guarantee from the project before it would become involved in pump loans.

Gender is another problem that has received much attention in recent years. It is widely believed that male extension workers either have difficulties contacting female farmers or are not interested in so doing, especially in Muslim societies. Once again, a solution would imply the establishment of a parallel Female Extension Service at greatly increased cost. Social pressures among the educated classes pose a further problem because those women who might qualify to be Extension Agents are, by convention, less free to move around than either the female farmers they are to serve or their male colleagues. It would not, for example, be 'good form' for an educated Sudanese lady to travel by donkey between eight scattered villages, still less by bicycle. It might not even be wise for her to do so.

Certainly women farmers have less direct contact with the Extension Service. In a 1988 survey, only 4 per cent of female-led households received an extension visit compared with 16 per cent for the male-led. The majority of women farmers are members of male-led households and may be presumed to have access to extension through the men, but 17 per cent of all households are female-led so there is room for concern (JMRDP Post-Harvest Survey, 1988). Attempts to overcome this problem have included the establishment of more concentrated women's training programmes working in a different style from the Extension Service. Special, women-only farmers' meetings at which a suitably chaperoned male Extension Agent can make contact are another suggestion. Despite the statistics, there is clear evidence that the barrier to contact with female farmers is far from rigid. Some male agents appear to manage to make good contact with women farmers, even to the extent of appointing them as 'lead farmers'. Monitoring and Evaluation staff, who interview female-led households and women farmers on exactly the same basis as men, have never reported any difficulty on this matter. There is also a danger that Extension Agents themselves feel it appropriate and modern to report difficulty in reaching women, a factor that is especially prevalent in Muslim societies.

However, all of these problems diminish in importance if the underlying situation is remembered: a lack of demand for what extension has to offer. Farmers are quite willing to put up with Extension Agents' involvement in credit if the equipment offered on credit is of interest to them. JMRDP has an admirable record on credit recovery for irrigation pumps, in contrast with a history of failure with credit for animal traction implements. Similarly, women farmers find no obstacle in obtaining an input like Aldrex-T seed dressing from the Extension Agent if they want it. As far as the perceived clash between farmer training and advice and input supply is concerned, it is clear from surveys that inputs are the principal motor behind farmers' contact with the Extension Service. Attendance by farmers at extension meetings is not high and the agent's ability to reach the farmers individually, in the fields or at home, is limited by the sheer numbers and the distances involved. The biggest single way in which the agents meet their farmers is when they come to the agent's store to buy inputs (JMRDP Post-Harvest Survey, 1988).

And this leads back to the central conclusion. If a wide range of effective technologies was available, and if farmers were likely to be able to use them profitably, then a healthy and effective Extension Service would be easy to establish. Farmer demand would keep the Extension Agents busy without the need for the apparatus of Training and Visit. Clearly some supervision would be necessary to prevent abuses and it might be that the gender problem, for example, would turn out to be serious. At the moment, however, the Extension Service is tied to the promotion of some technologies for which it never has enough inputs, most notably crop protection, and others for which the demand is, at best, patchy like animal traction. Under these circumstances, it is impossible to judge which of the many suggested difficulties with extension are real and which are merely expressions of an underlying lack of effective demand for the service.

Farming Systems Research

The Farming Systems Research methodology represents the apogee of the development knowledge business. This multi-disciplinary approach requires agronomists, economists, sociologists and other researchers to work together to understand the 'Farming Systems' of the local people. In order to ensure that the new technologies they develop are appropriate for the farmers, the area or region being studied is divided up into 'recommendation domains' of homogenous groups of farmers, in the expectation that a different package of new techniques will be required for each domain. Divisions between recommendation domains may be based on technical factors, such as soils, rainfall or topography, or on social or economic factors such as sex or wealth.

Farming Systems Research, universally abbreviated as FSR, developed as a reaction to the failures of earlier attempts at finding new agricultural technologies for Africa. Those are categorized by the description 'on-station', implying that the researchers tended to confine themselves to carefully controlled trials on official research stations. As a result, it is alleged, the techniques they developed were not adequately 'adapted' to farmers' actual circumstances and duly failed. In order to avoid this, FSR lays great stress on farmers' participation, on 'on-farm trials', as opposed to 'on-station trials' and on the gathering of Rural People's Knowledge.

FSR is an all-embracing approach which aims at a comprehensive understanding of the way rural farming works and of the society in which it is set, in the belief that science will be able to use that understanding to develop the technologies or recommendations that farmers need. The considerable volume of research work done in south Darfur, starting as long ago as the 1950s, means that there is plenty of material for Farming Systems analysis. Soils, vegetation and even land use maps are available. Several comprehensive farmer surveys have been carried out using a variety of approaches. Researchers from a number of disciplines have worked together for years at a time. And yet the results, in terms of new technologies developed, seem small and far from specific as regards 'recommendation domains'.

FSR appears to have found Darfur both too simple and too complex. It is too simple because farming across the whole of the region is so homogenous that it might almost all be considered one Farming System: almost everyone grows millet with a little sorghum or groundnuts as well, and everybody uses hand hoes to do so. It is too complex because of the immense range of subtle variations in the way that millet is grown from one place to the next, and especially from one year to the next, depending on the rains, the pests and a thousand other factors. 'The definition of recommendation domains in the area is exceedingly complex . . . in any one village several land types are represented from marginal upland soils through to various types of alluvial soil. A single farmer may have fields on several or even all of the land types, but the recommendations and by implication the research requirements for each differ considerably. Thus the domain either becomes a catch-all losing the focus for which it was intended, or many more domains must be created in which individual farmers of households are multiply represented' (Harvey, 1986).

Table 3.5 summarizes some of the indicators that have proved most effective in showing a distinction between one 'domain' or another.

One weakness of FSR is a tendency to discover the obvious, at considerable expense. Some of the distinctions between these different domains are perilously close to trivial; the differences are so manifest, and the reasons so clear, that they would probably have been obvious to the chance traveller, if he kept his eyes open. Between the *goz*, the basement wadis and the high Jebel, clear and simple differences in technique and in cropping pattern tell almost the whole story. Obvious differences in the environment explain that story. And if the traveller would not have spotted those differences, any researcher who works in the area would be able to spot them without need for any complex surveys or the paraphernalia of FSR.

Attempts, however, to deepen the analysis and to identify more subtle distinctions run very rapidly into a morass of minor distinctions and

Table 3.5: Farming systems indicators

	WSDC Area 1983		JMRDP Area 1988		
	Qoz Maaliya	Central Area	Basement Wadis	Upper Jebel	Female H'holds
Household Size	6.02	6.26	5.79	6.65	4.06
Female Household Head %	2	12	21	4	100
TECHNIQUES					
Precultivate millet	NO	NO	NO	YES	na
Prerain planting millet	23%	NO	NO	MOST	na
Hoe type	Hashasha	Hashasha	Tawria	Julmai	na
Ploughing %	0	16	30	22	na
Hired Labour Used %	74	19	7	13	na
CROPPING PATTERN – Ha	8.5	3.7	2.7	3.2	1.7
% Millet	70	56	50	67	51
% Sorghum	8	20	20	3	14
% Groundnuts	22	15	13	2	10
% Other	0	9	17	28	25
LIVESTOCK OWNERSHIP					
Cattle % Owning	71	61	32	17	18
Av Number Owned	29	30	6	4	4
Goats % Owning	50	60	73	51	64
Av Number Owned	9	11	8	3	5

Sources: WSDC Farmer Surveys, 1983 & 1984; JMRDP Wet Season Surveys, 1987 & 1988

subtle variations in degree that do not clarify anything. Prolonged surveys of labour inputs in the Jebel Marra area, for example, show no clear pattern and no improvement on the straightforward understanding gained in the first surveys. The degree of overlap, even between domains which the prime indicators show are clearly different, is considerable. 'Within the large land system strata there is great variation especially between areas in the middle of each system and those on the margin with a neighbouring system. Each village is by contrast relatively homogeneous. The villagers all face roughly the same environmental constraints and opportunities' (WSDC Farmer Survey, 1983).

Nevertheless, Farming Systems analysis clearly works, in the sense that significant differences in technical and socio-economic patterns can be identified and 'domains' defined on that basis. Where, then, are the 'recommendations'? The answer is that they are few and far between and that they are rarely domain-specific. One explanation that is frequently put forward is that the full recommendations of FSR are not being followed. This is usually said to be because the different technical disciplines do not co-operate properly: the agronomists do not listen to the social scientists, who do the initial identification of the domains, for example.

Experience provides a different answer, which is that FSR may succeed in identifying different domains but it has yet to show how that knowledge is of any use in the development of new technologies. The reason is that the differences between the domains do not imply any significant difference in the farmers' technical requirements. There may be variations in degree, but the binding constraints in all domains are the same, peak weeding labour above all, and the technical potentials of all domains are very similar. The only exceptions to this are where the distinctions between major domains are overpoweringly obvious; that is to say where soils and topography are clearly different and where farming techniques are different as a result.

Conclusion

The foregoing account does not do full justice to the research work done in south Darfur nor to Farming Systems Research, a concept that has developed a large literature. It is enough, however, to explain the case for a different approach, for a substantial change of emphasis.

The Introduction mentions the Boserup hypothesis, which states that new agricultural technologies are brought into use naturally enough when the time is ripe and that it is the balance between population and the land available that decides when that time will arrive. It was suggested that much of the case for aid depends on the belief that the Boserup mechanism cannot work fast enough, so action is needed to speed it. Darfur amply demonstrates that the hypothesis is correct. Aid research and extension efforts are failing because they are aimed at a situation that has still not arrived. This exactly matches Boserup's observation of the failures of research and extension in the late colonial and early independence eras; failures that were not due to any cultural inertia, because many new crops have been very successful. It was merely that many of the innovations being promoted were just not profitable (Boserup, 1965).

A useful distinction may be drawn between 'recommendation domains' and 'niches'. A domain is expected to be broadly homogeneous, so that there are major differences between the farming system on one domain and that on another. As a result, research is expected to form a package of different recommendations for each domain. By contrast, a niche exists where two broadly similar farming systems differ in only one respect. The use of camel ploughs only in some parts, and only on some crops, of the basement wadi farming system, is a good example of a technology occupying a niche. Some very different approaches to research depend on whether the aim is to develop technologies for whole domains or to concentrate on looking to fill niches.

The hazards of rainfed agriculture in western Sudan make the concept of 'frequency of superiority' important. Because it is unlikely that research will identify technologies that are unambiguously superior in all circumstances, it is necessary instead to seek out those that perform reasonably well, reasonably often. For the same reason, breadth of range is also critical. Where there is no one technology that is unambiguously better under all circumstances, it is vitally important that there should be as wide as possible a choice of 'frequently superior' but different technologies. That is the only way to have a good chance of there being at least one which does well, at any given time and in any given place. This is one of the central reasons why the weaknesses of aid's short-term bias are so obvious in Africa. For the outsider to make a useful contribution in a situation where the range of circumstances to be tackled is so wide, there is no substitute for reasonably long experience of the changes between years and over a large area.

There is a particular danger in excessive detail. For triple superphosphate it has meant that a technology of some potential has become bogged down in a series of refinements. There is equal danger in attempts to identify high priorities. The short-term significance of the *nafaasha* caterpillar, which was most damaging during the drought years, diverted attention from other equally damaging pests that appear in better years. Above all, it is essential to balance reward against risk. In a hazardous environment, exploiting the good years does more to cut down the overall risk than avoiding damage in the bad. In all cases, the pressing need is not for one technology but for a range that allows maximum rewards as well as minimum risks.

If the aim of research is to promote the most effective technique, then it should not be constrained by attempts to develop local capabilities at the same time. If this means purchasing animal traction equipment from overseas rather than from local blacksmiths, then so be it. If it means using imported TSP, instead of attempting to demonstrate the virtues of rock phosphate because there might be a source of it in Kordofan, then so be it. It is not irrelevant that the importation of the Chinese plough was probably the biggest single boost the Darfuri smithing industry ever received. It gave the smiths something to copy and created a market for them; but it had to be imported first. Similarly, if TSP ever developed a demand for phosphate, then it would have prepared the market for Kordofani rock phosphate.

In other words, researchers and workers on agricultural projects should be ruthless in support of their primary clients: the farmers. The goal is the best and cheapest technology for them. If government wishes to support local industries, then that should be a separate exercise. The most likely way for an intermediate farming technique to succeed will be if it is developed and produced using the most up-to-date manufacturing methods. It is a harsh truth that the least likely way is for it to be designed by volunteers learning their trade and manufactured by blacksmiths using traditional techniques on scrap material.

Equally to be avoided are attempts to guide research from social, economic or environmental first principles; especially where that means avoiding areas that are believed to be 'dangerous'. There is not such an abundance of development possibilities in Darfur that any of them can be ignored. It may well be, for example, that mechanized farming has social and environmental costs as well as production benefits, but it is impossible to calculate the balance between them in advance. Not to research into mechanized farming will not stop the introduction of tractors. If the market favours them they will be irresistible. It will, however, ensure that a chance to find out how to use them efficiently will be lost, which will only make it less likely that the benefits will outweigh the costs. Similarly, statements that 'an economic threat to the groundnut and sesame producers on goz soils such as the promotion of sunflower for [mechanized production on] naga'a [soils]' should be avoided, represent no more than the wilful abandonment of a promising opportunity for wholly speculative reasons (Quin, 1989).

The cliché analogy with evolution is unavoidable, not in the sense that evolution is a gradual process but rather with respect to the way it works. Evolution depends on a proliferation of possibilities – call them variants – and on the forces of natural selection to weed out the less well adapted variants and allow the best adapted ones to grow. This process looks wasteful, because it depends on natural selection destroying so many variants in order to select one good one. In fact it is 'cost-effective', because it is cheaper to develop a thousand variants and identify the best than it is to try and 'design' that best one from first principles. The research described in this chapter may be summed up as just such an attempt to design technologies for Darfur from first principles, with all the apparatus of surveys and FSR intended to develop the data on which such a design might be built. It has not worked.

The history of the few successful developments in the area seems much more akin to an evolutionary model, in which a new variant technique appears, more or less independently of any preliminary research, and is found, by selection, to fit into a particular niche within the overall farming system. The TSP story is, perhaps, the clearest example, in that the fertilizer was distributed throughout the region in 1985–6 and found its niche on the Jebel Marra, but the pattern has been similar for camel ploughing, for potatoes and oranges grown on Jebel Marra, and for several other techniques.

But proliferation is just as important as selection in the evolutionary process and this has been more or less completely choked off. Selection needs as many variants to choose from as possible if it is to have the best chance of finding a good one. In the Sudan, the supply of new variants is very, very small indeed: mainly because of the acute economic constraints and but also of the aid-financed research bureaucracy's insistence on thorough testing before now techniques are approved for release to farmers.

If these barriers could be broken, the aim should be to provide a flood of possibilities for farmers to try out for themselves. This would not involve complex 'on-farm' trials and participatory relationships between researchers and farmers. Instead, as many farmers as possible should be given the opportunity to get on with it by themselves. They might not all get it right, but enough would, if the technique were any good, to ensure that it would establish itself on the local scene. Sheer volume of numbers would make up for scientific rigour in the testing process.

In effect the choice lies between the many small losses and small inefficiencies that would happen in this evolutionary process and the cost of the research needed to avoid those losses and, most importantly of all, the time that would have to be lost while that research is carried out. If the experience of research in Darfur and, indeed, in Africa generally has anything to show it is that both the costs and the time losses involved in the search for certainty are very high indeed. The scale of the risks on the other side are not so easily measurable, but there is no obvious reason why they should be especially large, given that none of the technologies that are likely to be applicable in smallholder agriculture are especially expensive or capital intensive.

Capital is important. If, as the aid orthodoxy has it, farmers are very short of capital, then the cost of asking them to make even a small investment in trying out new technologies might well be high. If, on the other hand, capital is abundant and the farmers' principal problem is a lack of useful ways to use their savings, then the cost of any investment in what is, in effect, their own research will be low. Clearly, there are some poor people in Darfur who cannot afford any kind of additional risk; additional because risk is such an overwhelming factor that no one, rich or poor, can avoid it. Equally clearly, there are plenty of people who make small investments and some who make large ones. The risks they face are, by First World standards, enormous, but if the Darfuri investor may be considered to have a portfolio, part of the reason it is risky is because it is very narrow. The range of options is very limited. For this reason, the chance to diversify into any new technology, however unproven, may actually reduce the risk of the overall portfolio. There is little reason to hesitate in allowing farmers to try out new technologies for themselves, provided of course that they do so of their own free will.

Research still has a role: in identifying and developing new technologies, in making sure that they fall within the range of likely requirements for the area and in providing farmers with an outline of their characteristics. Indeed of attempting to develop a 'super-technology' which meets all possible requirements, the emphasis should be on proliferation, on the development of as many reasonably promising technologies as possible.

Where the evolutionary approach does suggest a major cut-back in research is in precisely those areas that have developed most recently: adaptive research, on-farm trials and the whole apparatus of FSR. All of these represent attempts to enhance the researcher's certainty in order to reduce the farmers' risk. In so doing, they substitute the slow and expensive processes of scientific technique for the rough and ready strengths of the farmers' own 'will to search'. At various points through this chapter, mention has been made of the 'nanny tendency', that paternalistic wish to protect the farmer against all possible risk. This tendency is very strong because it provides a major part of the justification for the whole of the aid-financed knowledge business.

The fact remains, however, that effective research, whether it is set in an evolutionary framework or takes a more 'scientific' approach, cannot be carried out in a vacuum. It needs a market for its findings, a demand for its wares. This is not merely because without a use for its results research is reduced to an academic exercise, but also because research itself desperately needs the feedback. It is only by testing them in that market that new technologies can be finally proven and adapted in the light of wide experience. The evolutionary approach will only work if the selective force of farmers buying one technology and refusing to buy another is allowed to function. Unfortunately, this market demand for research in Darfur and many other African countries has been stifled by the wider economic crisis. Inputs are not available, markets for product are unreliable, supplies of consumer goods to make the effort worth while are both expensive and unreliable.

The result has been that instead of being reactive, that is to say subject to market demands and stimulated by them, research has become increasingly anticipatory, in the sense that it is forced to focus on issues that may be useful in the future but which are not applicable now. Because it is operating in this kind of limbo, the pressure to divert research into areas that are of concern to the First World organisations that finance it but not of immediate interest to the farmers is difficult, if not impossible, to resist. The very shift into the safety-first, all-embracing style of research which has been, somewhat unfairly, summed up here as FSR, reflects the fact that research is operating in this kind of limbo. To put it another way, the fact that agricultural research in Africa has developed into what is the most sophisticated, sensitive and knowledgeable system ever, while being the most expensive and least productive one at the same time, is the result of the constraints that lie outside its own capacity to deal with. It may be noted that FSR had little part to play in the green revolution, for example. It is not beyond the bounds of possibility that FSR before the green revolution would have predicted the negative effects, especially the social ones, and recommended that it should not happen. However great those negative effects, that would not really have been the right answer.

One can continue to hope that a 'super-technology', such as new varieties of millet, sorghum and groundnuts which spectacularly outperform the local varieties under all circumstances, will emerge from the longer-term processes of selection and breeding. The likelihood is, however, that the 'super-technologies' will be a long time coming. Until they do, the only way forward is to exploit the thousands of more minor opportunities to raise production, the niches. And the only way to achieve that is to allow the farmers themselves to find the best technology to go into every niche by offering them the widest possible range from which to choose.

Aid likes slogans. Let us call for a shotgun approach to research, where the aim is to offer as many different technologies as possible, in the hope that each one will bring about some improvement in production, somewhere or at some time among the hundreds of different combinations of circumstances that the hazards of rainfed agriculture in Darfur can throw up. Just as the shotgun does not aim to kill with great accuracy but rather by a combination of width of scatter and weight of numbers, so should research concentrate on achieving as wide as possible a scatter of opportunities, taking only sufficient care over aiming to ensure that the general direction is correct.

4· DROUGHT AND DESERTIFICATION

'You know, James, I sometimes think we are trying to plough the ocean with a caterpillar tractor – probably the Pacific.' Sudanese director-general of a large conservation-oriented project.

Outsiders can often be overawed by the impact of recent events which seem less devastating in a longer perspective. Even in perspective, however, the pace and extent of environmental change in Darfur over the last few decades is extraordinary, even shocking. Big game, which was so abundant that lions were designated a pest right up to the Second World War, is no longer seen. Vast areas of climax savannah woodland have been cleared. During the last two decades rainfall has rarely come close to the average for the period up to 1960. In 1948, Darfur villagers were described as extremely well off compared to many people in Europe: 'for the poorest people there is peace and security and sunshine: there is an ample food supply and a good variety of foods; milk and good water and fuel for cooking are available to all' (Tothill, 1948). While allowance must be made for some colonial self-congratulation and for the impact of the Second World War on Europe, it was not an unfair description. The contrast is stark for an area that saw famine in 1984–5 and, according to some reports, is about to do so again. But famine was always on the horizon in Darfur. The starker contrast lies between Darfur as it was in 1948 and a modern Europe which has raced ahead to a position where famine is more or less unthinkable.

All of which makes the modern concern with the environment seem entirely correct: 'The more people there are, the more they destroy the long-term potential of fragile environments and the poorer this makes them and their descendants.' Chambers's neat summary of this point of view makes clear the kinship between environmental concerns and Malthusian economics. In fairness, some key difficulties are well recognized: the fact that 'conservation will fail unless it appeals to the farmers' self-interest' (World Bank, 1989: Ch 4) and the poor quality of the 'long-term potential' itself. It may even be that the only option is to 'mine' what small potential there is for the maximum short-term production. To do so is no different from pumping oil from an oil field which must one day run out. 'The environment exists for man, not man for the environment' (Chambers 1983: 148).

In the end, therefore, the problem is technical: how great is the potential, how long can it last, what techniques can sustain it and so on? The first step towards an answer to these questions is to measure the pace of environmental change. Which is difficult. The next step is to explain it. Which can be close to impossible. Aid is rarely willing to recognize these difficulties. Instead it takes refuge in appeals to high technology or to attractive generalities. Some call for a 'minimum framework that links a set of satellite [environmental] accounts to the conventional System of National Accounts', something that is not done in any First World country (World Bank, 1989: Annex). Others present tortuous analogies such as Chambers's 'epigenetic landscape' that gives 'attention to timing and irreversibility'. The implicit assumption, that effective technical answers can be found if only enough technology is applied and enough really 'appropriate' consideration is given to the problem, has little to support it. The Darfur experience has shown that what is happening can be convincingly described, with some difficulty. The problems of analysing why and how it happens remain near enough insuperable, let alone those of making a prediction of future potential and deciding on timing and irreversibility.

In Darfur both cropland and rangeland for grazing are near enough open access resources. There is some concept of community or tribal ownership, but it is weak. Livestock, on the other hand, are individually owned and farmers work as individuals. The classical theory of the 'Tragedy of the Commons' argues that this combination of an open resource and individual management is a primary cause of environmental degradation because it leads to overuse (Hardin, 1968). If grazing land is open to all, 'the communal grazing system gives no incentive to the individual pastoralist to reduce his herd in the hope that he will be able to feed them better, for there is no assurance that his action will improve grazing as long as others continue to increase their herds' (HTS,1974). On cropland, farmers will not be able to maintain a rotation with fallow because other farmers can take over and crop the fallow land. At the extreme, it is even argued that farmers are forced to grow uneconomic crops merely to maintain their right to land. The logical solution is to give the cropland to individual farmers or groups and to allow individual herders or groups to enclose grazing land. In other words, to replace open access either with much tighter communal ownership or with private ownership.

Many attempts have been made to do so but they have created more problems than they solve, especially where vulnerable groups lose customary rights in the process. This has been recognized for some time. 'The transition to land titling should be attempted only in response to demand by rural people' (World Bank, 1989: Ch 4). Nevertheless, the belief that social institutions are the root cause of the over-exploitation of the environment remains strong and the 'Tragedy of the Commons' thesis continues to dominate. One reason for the resilience of this belief is that it offers a way out of the difficulties of technical measurement and analysis. If the root cause of the problem lies in the social arena, then it is far easier to justify and even plan developmental action on *a priori* grounds, without the need for any firm technical evidence.

To accept that institutions like land tenure are the cause of the problem implies that they are permanent and immutable, or at least slow to change. Part of the Boserup hypothesis described earlier is that this is not the case; tenure forms adjust to changing resource endowments. The central questions considered here, therefore, are whether or not resource endowments have changed enough to justify a change in tenure and, if they have, whether or not the autonomous Boserup adjustment is taking place without undue difficulty. This enquiry is made against a background in which it has been generally assumed that the answer to the first question is definitely positive and the answer to the second almost as definitely negative.

Drought

The first and overriding difficulty in interpreting environmental change is to distinguish any effect of human activity from the immensely powerful effects of climate. Figure 4.1 shows rainfall for western Sudan as a variation against the mean. Like the rest of the Sahel and much of Africa, there has been an unprecedented period of poor rainfall, starting in the mid-1960s, which shows no signs of coming to an end. No more does the debate about the causes of this drought, which is more noteworthy for its lack of conclusions than for anything else:

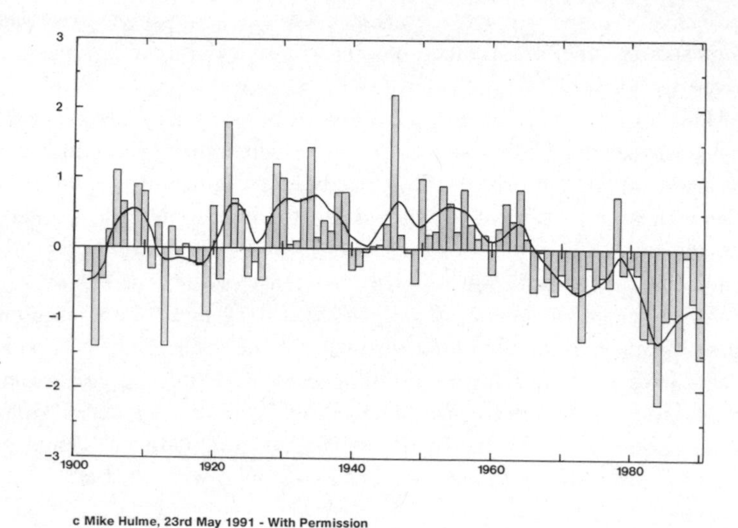

Figure 4.1 Mean Normalized Rainfall Anomaly, Western Sudan – 1902 to 1990

The most obvious gaps in our knowledge are:

We do not know why the present drought exists;
We do not know why droughts have occurred in the past;
We do not know how long the present drought will last (Farmer & Wigley, 1985)

This list of our ignorance is pretty comprehensive. Of the various possible causes – global warming, deforestation, ocean temperatures and the greenhouse effect – recent research has only lightened this gloom in one respect. It now seems reasonably well established that there is a link between the African monsoon and changes in the temperature balance between the world's great oceans. The El Nino system of the Pacific is part of this wider pattern.. It is most probable, therefore, that the driving force behind the drought is external to Sudan. 'In a semi-arid environment like Sudan most moisture originates from outside the region and hence land cover change can have only a marginal effect on moisture recycling' (Dr M. Hulme, personal communication). Attempts to impose anti-desertification strategies on the people of Darfur at this stage should, therefore, be treated with deep suspicion. It will only add to their problems if they are asked to take part in a losing battle with a desert that is being driven forward by global forces.

> The upper portion of this part in the west, where the rest of the land of the Tajuwiin is, is all pure desert. There used to be much water in it and pools. There are now no inhabitants in it because there are moving sands which are shifted by the wind from place to place and no one has a permanent habitation in it, because the sands pass over it and the winds blow strongly in it.

This description sounds as though it comes from a television programme describing the 1984 drought. In fact, the Tajuwiin are believed to be the Daju, the earliest recorded inhabitants of Darfur, and the quote comes from Al Idrisi, an early Arab geographer who died in AD 1153 (quoted in Arkell, 1952).

The Tragedy of the Commons

The Tragedy of the Commons works through congestion. When too many people use a given resource, they get in each other's way. The classic example is a narrow road which becomes congested when too many drivers use it. For grazing land, congestion occurs when the number of livestock becomes so great that each animal has less food than it needs and grows more slowly or produces less milk as a result. For cropland, congestion leads to pressure to reduce fallow rotations and hence yields. The problem with such common access resources, a road on which anyone can drive without charge, rangeland open to all herders and cropland without tenure, is that the individual is not charged for the cost his presence imposes on others, for the congestion he creates.

In Darfur the offtake rate for cattle is around 8 per cent (WSDC, 1985). A simple model would be for an area that is fully stocked when it carries 1,000 head of cattle and produces 80 for sale. Then a herder, usually known in the jargon as a 'free rider', who already has 100 head decides to buy ten more. Because there is no spare fodder this means that all the cattle have less to eat and the offtake rate drops, say to 7.5 per cent. The situation thus changes from the 'before' case to the 'after' case, as shown in Table 4.1. (The third, 'Coase', situation is discussed later.)

Table 4.1: A model of rangeland production

	Before	After	'Coase'
Communal herd	900	900	900
Communal offtake	72.00	67.50	71.75
Free rider's herd	100	110	100
Free rider's offtake	8.00	8.25	8.25

The tragedy is that the other herders' only defence is to do the same, to buy more cattle and try to recapture some of what they have lost to the 'free rider'. In this way, the whole herd becomes far too large, production is actually reduced and, at the extreme, long-term damage is done to the rangeland. (The model will be developed below.)

The logic of this is powerful and it has fitted outsiders' perceptions of what is happening on the African ranges so well that it has dominated the debate since long before the aid era. Only in the last decade or so has there been any serious attempt to break away from it, an attempt springing from the evident failure of programmes designed to tackle the 'Tragedy of the Commons'.

To the economist, this is a problem of externalities; the free rider is imposing an external cost on the other herders. Modern analysis of externalities has revolved around the Coase theorem. This states that it should always be possible for the loser from an externality to make a deal with the gainer. And that is the third situation in the example. All the other herders could pay the free rider not to buy his extra ten cows. He would get just as much but they would lose less. Importantly, the total offtake or the production of the community as a whole would stay at the maximum 80 (Coase, 1960).

Lipton has set Coase in opposition to the games theory model of the Prisoners' Dilemma. In this parable, two prisoners are accused of a crime. The prosecutor tells them that if they both confess they will go to jail for ten years; if neither confess they will both get two years; if only one confesses then he will get just one year while his fellow prisoner will get 20. If the two of them could only contact each other and agree their strategy, they would both deny the crime and get two years each. Because they cannot negotiate, they may well both confess, to betray the other and avoid being betrayed themselves. They end up with ten years each. Lipton argues that 'a major task of governments is to convert PDs [Prisoners Dilemmas] into COs (Coase Outcomes)' and that there is a drift in the Third World towards 'PD non-cooperative outcomes' (Lipton in Matthews, 1985). He suggests four causes for this adverse trend:

- Population growth 'increases the number of transactors', so raising the cost of negotiating a Coase deal, the so-called transactions cost.
- Developmental change reduces the number of times that similar decisions have to be made and this makes it less likely that repeated plays of a PD game will reveal the costs of not co-operating.
- Risk aversion will lead actors to prefer the least bad, safe result over a better one that depends on others sticking to their word.
- Lastly, what he calls a 'transition of trust' is under way as the 'old chiefly authorities and clan-like decisions are challenged by centralized governments and codified laws'. Individuals are losing respect for traditional restraints but they are still unimpressed by the new authorities, so mutually beneficial deals are less easy to strike.

The first of Lipton's points is central not merely to this particular discussion but to the whole of this book. It is, in effect, the anti-Boserup hypothesis set in the social arena. Hayami and Kikuchi have drawn exactly the opposite conclusion and described a social Boserup hypothesis, linking institutional change to the balance between population and the available resources. 'The distribution of income [between] landlords, tenant operators and landless labourers responds to changing resource endowments through adjustments in the institutions governing the use of land and labour.' Water rights, financial and market institutions also change in response to 'changes in resource endowments, technology and government policies'. Such institutional changes involve costs and those costs, depend on the 'tightness' of institutional structures, which is itself a function of population density. The social Boserup hypothesis thus runs: 'We hypothesize that the basic force underlying the tightness in community structure is relative resource scarcity – the scarcity of non-labor resources to labor. So far as a resource is abundant, there is no need to coordinate its use among community members. The need arises only when the resource becomes scarce' (Hayami & Kikuchi, 1981: Ch 2). In other words, it is when population density rises that effective social institutions appear to manage resources as they become more scarce.

In the example it is clearly unfair that the free rider should be able to blackmail the rest of the community in the way he does. Coase-type rules on compensation for externalities take no account of fairness and may not work for this reason. 'Unless there is an all powerful autocrat, rules perceived as very inequitable will be widely broken' (Lipton in Matthews, 1985). The free market approach to externalities offered by Coase still depends, therefore, on a social institution, call it government, to negotiate a consensus on the rules and to enforce them. The most likely way to do this would be by arranging an allocation of specific rights. In the example, if the free rider had a right to graze 100 cattle then he would have to buy the right to graze more from the others. If, on the other hand, he had a right to graze 110, then the other herders would do best by buying the right to the extra ten off him. Total production would be the same either way; the difference would lie in the distribution of the output between the community and the free rider.

But negotiation is not the only way to reach the Coase optimum. The alternative is enclosure, which means abandoning co-operation in favour of a minimal level of agreement to respect one another's fences. Enclosure was in fact the route taken in most developed countries and it is implicit in the many development programmes based on giving farmers and herders individual or group tenure. As many of those programmes have found, the more powerful are always likely to win the race to enclose, whatever the safeguards. For this reason, Lipton dismisses enclosure, on the grounds that its equity implications are unacceptable. But he is looking for policy prescriptions. Here the aim is to analyse whether or not the community is trapped in a Tragedy of the Commons and, if it is, why it has not found a way to escape from it. Of the two routes to escape, negotiation and enclosure, the latter is the more likely. Take the situation where, in Lipton's words, 'extra-economic power can lead one party to disregard, without penalty, promises to abide by a socially optimal solution.' Such power might well stand in the way of a co-operative agreement to control stocking on the rangeland. On the other hand, 'extra-economic power' would be just what is needed to enable the powerful to enclose and so capture all the benefits of destocking for themselves. The socially optimum level of production would be achieved despite the fact that the distribution of that production would be very far from optimum.

Either route involves costs. For the negotiated solution there are all the 'transactions costs' of doing a deal and policing it to make sure that it is obeyed. For the enclosure solution there will be the cost of fencing. In the Coase column of the example the community saved 4.25 head by bribing the free rider not to increase his herd. If, however, the effort to negotiate that bribe cost 4.25 head or more, then there would be little point in making the deal. It is, therefore, the balance between the transactions cost and the size of the externality that is critical. If an increase of ten head of cattle on the rangeland results in a large reduction in offtake, then the incentive to negotiate will be strong. Everyone will be willing to pay a high transactions cost. The socially optimum solution depends, therefore, on the strength of the 'temptation of goodness'; the incentive for each Prisoner of the Dilemma to choose the optimum (Lipton in Matthews, 1985). It could just as easily be the strength of the 'temptation of badness'; the incentive for each herder to enclose an area of range unilaterally, in breach of customary law, and so capture the benefits of destocking for himself.

There are four phases to the Tragedy of the Commons. In the first phase there is so much rangeland that the expansion of an individual herd does not affect the others at all. In the second phase, the gains to the individual who expands are greater than the communal losses he imposes on others. In the third phase, the communal losses are greater than the individual gains but the difference is not enough to cover the costs of a solution. At last, in the fourth phase, 'losses exceed gains enough that the light-grazing solution, if enforced on all, produces so much more total herd output than the heavy grazing solution that the difference suffices to pay the cost of social institutions to ensure the light-grazing solution' (Lipton in Matthews, 1985). Although Lipton clearly prefers a 'good', social-management route to the light-grazing Coase outcome, it is equally possible that in the fourth phase the difference becomes large enough to pay what may be called the 'fencing cost' of the 'bad' enclosure route. In what follows, an attempt is made to identify into which phase the crop and livestock sectors of Darfur fall.

Aid is now based on the premise that the African environment is under immediate threat from overuse and that open access or communal tenure, exacerbated by population growth, by rapid development and by political weakness, prevents a change to more productive and less damaging patterns of use, in other words to sustainable development. Lipton's model stands as the theoretical manifesto of this diagnosis. Superficially, Darfur seems a classic example. The decay of law and order seems all too evident. There has been extraordinarily swift environmental change. Populations have grown rapidly. Both cropland and grazing land are largely common access resources.

It is, nevertheless, nothing of the sort. First, the evidence that the Darfur rangelands are overstocked is, in common with most of Africa, extremely weak while it will be shown below that the pressure on the cropland has actually decreased. Second, despite all the customary laws that say it is not allowed, farmers and herders in Darfur are finding little difficulty in converting common land into more or less private tenure – the standard solution for the Tragedy – where it is worthwhile.

And the truth is that it is not generally worthwhile. The problem is not one of population pressure, developmental change or transition of trust. It is the lack of any strong incentive or 'temptation' either way, partly because of the technical factors controlling returns to farmers and to livestock owners but more importantly because of the overall stifling of the Darfur economy.

Range and Livestock

There are two questions. Is pastoralism and, by association, free access to rangeland economically inefficient? And does it cause degradation? Initially, evidence was deemed almost unnecessary. 'So many documents, officials and even scientists repeat the assertion of pastoral responsibility for environmental degradation that the accusation has achieved the status of a fundamental truth, so self-evident a case that marshalling evidence on its behalf is superfluous if not in fact absurd, like trying to satisfy a skeptic that the earth is round' (Horowitz, quoted in Anderson & Grove, 1987). Well into the 1980s this remained largely true and there are still many who will argue in support of the basic premise that African herders keep too many cattle for maximum economic returns, and so many that the range is damaged. Traditional range science held that it was possible to estimate a safe, sustainable carrying capacity. More recent studies have concluded that 'the Carrying Capacity concept is of questionable validity in livestock production systems in Africa, that it is virtually impossible to accurately estimate CC, and that the concept cannot be meaningfully applied in pastoral systems' (Bartels *et al.*, 1990).

The processes of degradation are easy enough to describe in theory. Some plants are more attractive to grazing animals than others. On overgrazed ranges these good species are eliminated. The next stage comes when the vegetation as a whole is reduced. The soil is bared to wind and water erosion, which means that plants cannot re-establish themselves. A threshold of irreversibility has been passed. It has proved far more difficult to analyse the process in practice. 'Direct examination of rangeland vegetation does not, on the whole, provide an unequivocal answer. Rates of soil loss and other deleterious changes in the soil may prove to be more reliable than vegetation change as an indicator of irreversible rangeland degradation.' But even when soil loss can be shown, as in Botswana studies, it is slow, giving a 'residual soil life of 400 years' and the lost production from cutting cattle numbers to try to stop it would be considerable. 'Put simply, the immediate costs to producers of destocking would be heavy. The long-term gains in terms of reduced range degradation would be slight. In eastern Botswana, destocking is not worth it' (Behnke & Scoones, 1991). This does not mean that economically significant degradation never occurs, but Botswana is one country that has seen decades of attempts to halt perceived degradation.

Ambiguous evidence has not hindered the debate on the causes of overstocking. Once the axiom that African herders keep too many animals is accepted, the scope for discussion becomes infinite. A supposed difference between western and African pastoralist 'management goals' has been a frequent feature. In its early form, the idea was that there was an 'East African cattle complex', whereby African herders put social values on cattle ownership over and above the financial return. Latterly, there has been a shift towards more 'rational' explanations – for example, that western ranchers prefer low stocking rates that give maximum growth rates for young animals because they want rapid production of high quality meat. 'The [African] subsistence pastoralist is more likely to see as optimal a stocking rate which supports a larger number of animals [with] a higher output in terms of the much wider range of desired products – milk, calves, subsistence and security for a large number of people' (Homewood & Rogers in Anderson & Grove, 1987). Although superficially logical, these ideas are irrelevant to the problems of congestion and degradation. Inadequate fodder will have just as great an impact on a milk cow's production as on a heifer's weight gain and would almost certainly raise the risk of losses. There is no *a priori* reason why degradation should not affect both western beef herders' and pastoralists' future returns from the same resource equally.

There is a more straightforward and more convincing explanation. 'African pastoral systems, with high labour but low capital and fossil fuel inputs, have a higher output per unit area of land than extensive Western ranching enterprises' (Grandin, 1987). In other words, differences between African and western systems reflect straightforward economic factors, principally massive differences in the returns to labour. One implication of this should be underlined: that a shift from African to western systems will result in a reduction in output and hence in incomes. Even if the African way is not sustainable, such a change cannot really be advocated.

Another 'rational' explanation of African overstocking is risk. It is suggested that subsistence pastoralists have to keep large herds to ensure their minimum needs in a risky environment. It is even suggested that cattle become a 'store of value' and monetarist analyses of cattle stocks have been attempted. It is more revealing to look at the balance between risk and reward: 'a conservative stocking rate always carries a cost – the forage which cannot be consumed and the livestock production which is thereby foregone in good years because livestock numbers are insufficient to consume all available feed. As Sandford has shown, this cost increases as the variability of rainfall increases' (Behnke & Scoones, 1991). Less conservative stocking is more efficient because it captures the benefits of good years, but it does lead to inevitable die-offs in bad years. It is these die-offs that give observers trained in western livestock management the impression that African herds are constantly on the point of disaster and that the African range is grossly overstocked.

To argue that there is no 'cattle complex' does not invalidate the basic mechanism of the Tragedy of the Commons, which explicitly assumes rational economic behaviour. What it does do is remove some of the extraneous explanations for the failure to reach a Coasean solution. Similarly, the growing recognition that the perception of universal overgrazing may be false does not explain why institutions to control stocking, be they social controls or enclosure, have not developed naturally, nor why they have been such abject failures when introduced. Even where common access does not lead to a catastrophic decline in the quality of the resource, it may still act as a barrier to investment and prevent the introduction of more intensive and profitable techniques. It can also lead to misallocation of resources. Because no rent is paid for the range, too much labour and capital may be employed in livestock management (Gould, 1972).

To sum up, there have been three approaches to the question of overstocking. One is to attempt to measure directly the balance between the number of animals and the capacity of the range to support them. The second has been to try to demonstrate that African herders will have too many cattle simply because of the assumed special conditions they live in. Those conditions may be social, such as that they suffer from a 'cattle complex', or socio-economic, where they are risk-averse, subsistence pastoralists. The third is the 'Tragedy of the Commons', another *a priori* argument but a more general one. The evidence from Darfur does not support any of them.

Livestock Management in Darfur

Western Sudan is one of the most important livestock-producing areas in the whole of Africa and Darfur is the most important in Sudan. In the 1977 census, the region held 23 per cent of all cattle in the nation, 16 per cent of sheep, 21 per cent of goats and 15 per cent of camels. The Darfur cattle herd was nearly twice the size of that of any other province (VRA/RMR, 1977). Well over 40 per cent of Darfur households own cattle and as many as 60 per cent own goats. Some 20 per cent own camels and 10 per cent sheep (WSDC, 1985).

Because of the climate, mobility is critical. In the south/east section of south Darfur, the most important cattle-producing area, over 50 per cent of farmers who own cattle trek their herds a significant distance away from their cultivation for at least part of the year (WSDC Farmer Survey, 1983). The herders' strategy is to take maximum benefit of the wet season and to survive the dry season. In south Darfur this means taking the herds on to the higher basement areas during the rains. The majority of calves are born in the late dry and early wet season: 77 per cent between March and June in 1973 (HTS, 1974). The herds' peak production period follows. Milk is plentiful and the animals gain weight as they make the most of the good rainy season grazing on the basement. Much of this becomes inaccessible later on, after the pools of standing water dry up. Even if it were accessible, the quality of grazing falls off fairly rapidly once the rains stop. The sheer volume of fodder remains the same but the grasses lose protein value rapidly as they dry (HTS, 1974). Western experts bent on conservation suggest that herders should reduce the pressure on the wet season range and save some of it for the dry season, when it will be in short supply. Even at this seasonal level, however, Sandford's point stands; that it is better to 'track environmental variation', grazing as much as possible during the rains and aiming to do no more than survive the dry, rather than struggle to find some optimum, steady level of production through the year.

During the wet season, the low-lying alluvial areas are avoided. As they flood, movement becomes difficult and flies become a major pest. The farmland is also closed to all livestock during the rains, once the crops are established. It is opened again after the harvest is over, a moment called the *talaqa*. During the dry season, it is essential to get to an area with enough grazing in reach of reliable water before it is too late. Once the herds reach one dry season area it may become impossible for them to move again because there is no grazing or water on the way to another.

'Rainy season migration is a lot more flexible than was previously thought. Migrations can no more be described in terms of lines of movement but more in terms of a diffuse kaleidoscopic pattern' (HTS, 1974). The movement can be divided into three levels. Some herds do not move far, grazing just outside the cultivated area during the rains and moving back into it after the *talaqa*. Then there are herds which move greater distances during the rains but which also return to a base in the area of settled farming during the summer. Lastly, there are the herds which travel away from the cultivated area in the dry season as well as the wet. Many of these go considerable distances to find good reserves of dry season grazing and water. The movement of the Rizeiqat herds south of the Bahr al Arab and of the Fellata and Taaisha south and west into the Central African Republic are the best known. As might be expected, it is the larger herds that are most frequently trekked, often with hired herders.

The sandy *goz* lands of the south/east, which are so important for cropping, are poor grazing. In the dry season there is no water to be had, except expensively at boreholes. During the wet, the basement offers better grazing. In the western world, agricultural development has sprung from the integration of livestock and crop farming, allowing manuring, fodder rotations and all the other yield-enhancing improvements of the agricultural revolution. The special nature of the *goz* – profitable cropland but poor and waterless grazing – is only one of many factors that make it unlikely that the western experience can be repeated in Darfur.

Many of the boreholes drilled in the eastern half of the region were intended for livestock use, with the aim of easing pressure on the rangeland, long believed to be overstocked. Nevertheless, herders avoid the boreholes because of the cost. For the greater part of the year they depend almost entirely on standing water in pools. In the hot summer months when the pools dry up the majority use hand-dug wells. In 1984, 70 per cent of nomadic herders used wells during the dry season and 60 per cent of stock-owning farmers. Although they are cheaper than water bought at a wateryard, it still costs money to get the wells dug and it is very hard work to raise enough water for a large herd from an average depth of five metres. At the height of the dry season some wells may be in use 24 hours a day (WSDC Nomad Survey, 1984).

As in much of Africa, discussions of livestock in Darfur have focused on nomadism and on groups perceived to be nomads. An ethnic dimension is added by virtue of the fact that the majority of the Arab tribes of Darfur call themselves 'Baggara', cow people, or 'Jammala', camel people. The reality is, however, that most of the herd is in the hands of farmers, that is to say those whose interest in cropping is significant and in most cases greater than their interest in livestock. In 1970 and 1971 the largest number of cattle sold in Nyala, by far the greatest market in south Darfur and one of the largest in Sudan, came from the Fur tribe, who are neither Arab nor Baggara (HTS, 1974). Even among the Rizeiqat, the most famous Baggara tribe of all, only half were identifiably nomadic in 1976, in the sense that they were living in 'nomadic dwellings', the famous Bayt al Arab tent of woven mats (Adams, 1982). The truth is that it is impossible to draw a clear dividing line between nomad and settled management of livestock. There is a continuous spectrum between the wholly sedentary herder whose cattle do not move at all during the seasons and the wholly nomadic one who never stops moving. Individuals shift position along that spectrum according to their own circumstances, more or less regardless of tribe.

One reason the distinction between 'nomadic' and 'sedentary' was believed to be important was the fact that comparisons appeared to show that nomads are better managers of livestock. Nomadic herds had higher calving rates, 65 per cent against 40, and lower mortality. As a result, production was nearly twice as high: 0.057 kg of meat per breeding female compared to 0.023 (Adams, 1982). The evidence that nomadic herds do better is not beyond question. The figures quoted were taken in 1973, a dry year when sedentary herds might have been expected to suffer. They ignore milk production, when milk for the household is proportionately more important for the smaller sedentary herd. Surveys from a later period showed exactly the opposite results: higher calving rates among sedentary herds than among transhumant ones (WSDC, 1985).

Nevertheless, it seems probable that on average herds that move further will produce more. They will be able to reach better grazing during the rains and will be less likely to come under stress during the dry season. To conclude, however, that nomads are better managers of livestock is to misunderstand the meaning of efficiency; which is not properly measured by the calving rate or by mortality. The true measure is the total return a household gets from the effort it puts into managing not merely its livestock but all its enterprises. A farming family is sensible to concentrate on its crops at the expense of its livestock. And the argument is reversible. It would be equally wrong to accuse the nomads of being bad farmers because their yields are lower. They too would merely be making the decision to concentrate their effort on their animals without abandoning crops altogether.

The nomad–sedentary divide was given further emphasis by the belief that disputes between herders and farmers indicated serious tensions. 'Cultivated areas often represent an obstruction out of proportion to their size and yield, both because of their location across migration routes and because graziers are obliged to give them a wide berth.' The result was that at one stage it was intended to rationalize land use by resettling cultivators out of the nomad herds' way and so 'polarize the rural economy into a predominantly transhumant livestock sector and a crop sector with supplementary livestock enterprises' (HTS, 1976). It will be argued below that the level of farmer-herder disputes was not in fact anything out of the ordinary and that the resurgence of tribal fighting had other causes.

The 1970s surveys in south Darfur did show very clearly, beyond any possible doubt, that the 'East African Cattle Complex' was dead and buried. Livestock herders are as aggressive profit maximizers as any Wyoming rancher. This is true throughout the region, in the far north-west just as much as in the central cattle-keeping areas of south Darfur. 'The predominant interest that the Zaghawa have in their livestock is as economic assets; there are no indications of the kind of relationship associated with the East African "cattle complex" ' (Tubiana & Tubiana, 1977).

Earlier studies in Sudan emphasized social aspects of stock-keeping, especially among the most famous cattle people, the Baggara Arabs. 'In kinship, in marriage, and in politics, cattle serve a common purpose in that by investing in them a man is investing in social relationships; he is attaching followers to him. In short, cattle are power' (Cunnison, 1966: Ch 3). A better understanding came from the realization that even groups with a supposedly strong 'baggara ideology' frequently made investments in agriculture even to the extent of putting their major efforts in that direction and that, conversely, cultivators were major stockholders and sometimes even took up a strongly nomadic pattern of life as a result. Ideology is secondary to economic motives (Adams, 1982).

This recognition went considerably further than a mere acknowledgement that pastoralists had a rational approach to maintaining their subsistence, Herders were found to be deeply involved in the market. It is usually argued that the pastoral family has a minimum subsistence requirement of milk and meat which only a certain size of herd can meet. As a result, 'it is rational for a herder to accumulate a large herd to produce milk for his family as well as to provide an insurance fund and portable bank' (Dahl & Hjort, quoted in Eicher & Baker, 1982: 166). The Darfuri cattle owner is not of this class at all. Not even the most nomadic herders subsist merely on meat and milk. They buy grain by selling their cattle. Cattle are rarely slaughtered for domestic consumption, outside ceremonial occasions, and the strongly seasonal pattern of calving and the lack of grazing in the dry season mean that a year-round milk diet is impossible. Many herders will admit that a milk-only diet is boring, anyway. In 1983, even among households operating larger herds over the rather longer transhumant cycles of south-eastern Darfur, that is to say households towards the 'nomad' end of the spectrum, grain consumption was as high as among settled farmers. On average they purchased 12.8 sacks of grain per household and they grew 5.9 sacks themselves, giving a per capita consumption of over 200 kilograms, when the average for Darfur is usually estimated at around 150 kg (WSDC Nomad Survey, 1984).

Once market exchange is involved it becomes impossible to calculate a 'subsistence' herd size because it will depend on the relative price of grain and cattle, which is highly variable (Eicher & Baker, 1982). Darfuris are well aware of this, and some can recount in detail how they built up their herds by growing grain when it was expensive and could be exchanged for large numbers of stock and then sold the cattle off again when stock prices rose. The extraordinary increases in offtake during both world wars are extreme examples of that process.

Herd management is clearly intended to achieve the maximum sales earnings. 'Herd structures are generally well adapted to the physical environment and to the marketing constraints' (Adams, 1982). Those who believe that the range is overstocked almost always suggest that herders keep their animals too long. If they were to sell them younger, then the same or even a higher production might be achieved with fewer animals on the degraded range. Many livestock development projects in East Africa have tried to bring about greater stratification of livestock management, whereby herders are persuaded to sell their animals to specialist fatteners at a younger age, thereby reducing the size of the herd on the range (Bennett, 1984). In Sudan the Livestock and Meat Marketing Corporation was established partly with this objective, with

World Bank money. The price structure of the Darfur market gives no incentive for stratification. The market for young stock is restricted because it is only when a bull reaches maturity and is in good condition that it can make the long trek to Omdurman, to be slaughtered for the Khartoum market or even to be exported. These were prices cattle owners actually received for the various classes of cattle in 1984:

Table 4.2: Sale prices of cattle in Darfur, 1984

		Average £S Per Head
Madmun	(12–18 mths)	83
Jad'	(18–24 mths)	103
Tani	(2–3 years)	215
Raba'	(3–4 years)	232
Adult	(> 4 years)	212

Source: WSDC-unpublished data

Selling an animal under two years meant passing up £S100. Keeping it for yet another year earned an extra £S15. Drought and rinderpest in 1983/4 meant that herders were keen to sell and the price gradient is probably steeper in better times.

While the return from keeping an animal until it is older is high, the extra cost of doing so is negligible. Grazing is free and cattle taxation is low, when it is collected. Other running costs include watering, herding and animal health but these did not exceed £S4 a head in 1983/4 (WSDC Nomad Survey, 1984). As would be predicted from these figures, less than 30 per cent of cattle sales are of animals less than two years old. Over 50 per cent are over three (WSDC, 1985). Also entirely in keeping with hard commercial sense, males are sold first. The proportion of adult males in the herd is small, around 7 per cent, and adult females for breeding form the core of the herd, over 40 per cent. There is, however, one important potential cost to keeping animals for longer: the risk of losses. If that risk is high, it might well be sensible, for example, to sell a three-year-old, Tani bull. To hang on for an extra year would mean risking the loss of over £S200 worth of bull instead of gaining an extra £S15.

It is often argued that risk is a major reason for keeping large livestock herds, as an 'insurance fund and portable bank'. Here too, the argument only holds for the subsistence case, when the pastoralist is presumed to be out of the market. If, for example, a household has to guarantee itself ten cows in milk to survive and if mortality is high and calving percentages are low, then it will have to keep a large breeding herd to ensure that its needs are met. By contrast, where the household is producing cattle or milk for sale, a larger herd merely becomes a bigger gamble on a risky proposition than a small one. If the owner could find a safer home for his money, then he would do better to sell a portion of the herd and so lessen his exposure to the risks of drought, disease and poor markets.

Darfuri cattle owners are very much in the exchange economy. If, therefore, their cattle are an 'insurance fund', then the risks being insured against are outside the livestock sector. That is to say that they may be balancing the risk of a poor crop harvest against the separate risk of poor livestock performance, in the hope that the two do not coincide. Livestock have one advantage in this respect and that is that they can be moved. Even if the rains fail on the farm and the crop is lost there is some chance of reaching grazing elsewhere before all the herds are lost.

The conclusion is that Darfuri livestock owners are entirely rational and that they keep the numbers of animals they do for the good reason that it is profitable. If they do treat them as a store of wealth it is because there is no alternative investment which provides any better combination of security and return. If the Darfur range is overstocked the reason does not lie in any 'cattle complex' or in the special strategies of subsistence or risk-avoidance.

Livestock Population and Carrying Capacity

The difficulties with the concept of carrying capacity have been described and Darfur is no exception. To demonstrate overstocking it is necessary to know what the livestock population is and to compare it with what the rangeland can safely and sustainably carry. It has proved extremely difficult to measure either the population or the carrying capacity.

The only comprehensive estimates of total livestock numbers in Darfur date from the 1970s and earlier. Clearly, there may have been considerable changes since then, above all as a result of the 1984 drought, when there must have been some reduction in the numbers, especially in north Darfur. It is impossible to assess how great the reduction was or how rapid the recovery had been. It has to be emphasized, moreover, that all estimates of livestock numbers are hugely imprecise. Several attempts were made to count livestock in south Darfur. Two used similar aerial census techniques and others the completely different approach of sampling numbers at waterpoints. The results were all hopelessly inconsistent, summed up in the despairing comment that 'no useful purpose is likely to be served by any further direct counts of livestock in the project area in the foreseeable future' (HTS, 1981). The most comprehensive survey was the aerial census of 1977. Table 4.3 at least gives some indication of the scale of what is being discussed:

Table 4.3: Livestock numbers in Darfur, 1976

Cattle	3,600,000
Goats	2,300,000
Sheep	2,600,000
Camels	370,000

Source: VRA/RMR, 1977

A central plank of the overgrazing argument has been that the livestock population has seen explosive growth in the 20th century. It is argued that the Africa-wide rinderpest epidemic of the late 19th century, combined with smallpox and the wars and movements of people during the period of the Mahdia, reduced both population and livestock numbers to very low levels at the start of the Condominium era, in 1899. The extent to which this represents colonial propaganda against the Mahdist regime is impossible to assess. Under the Condominium, the situation was very different. 'By the end of the 1930s, the increased use of motor transport by veterinarians and the discovery of certain vaccines, together with political stability, enabled the livestock population to expand. About 1945, livestock numbers were probably on a par with carrying capacity; in 1955 Harrison reported that the Baggara territory was 20 per cent overstocked. Between 1953 and 1976, the cattle population more than trebled' (Adams, 1982). The pan-African JP55 Rinderpest vaccination campaign of the early 1970s may be seen as the last step in the expansion of livestock populations assisted by security and veterinary advances.

Similar statements may be found about many other parts of Africa. 'From 1930 on Baringo [in Kenya] is repeatedly identified as having a major land-use problem, with erosion surveys rating it among the worst in the Colony' (Homewood & Rogers in Anderson & Grove, 1987). However, few of them show quite so clearly as the Sudan reports the inconsistency between a report of 20 per cent overstocking and a subsequent continued massive growth in numbers. What, after all, can 'overstocking' possibly mean if numbers can still be trebled without reaching a catastrophe?

On the figures given to back up this argument, the period between 1953 and 1976 saw cattle populations increase at 5.8 per cent per annum. Over roughly the same period human population was growing at only 2.7 per cent. Although it is possible that the rate of human population growth is underestimated, it is unlikely that it was much over 3.0 per cent, which still leaves a considerable gap. Such a wide divergence is difficult to believe. Pastoral herding is relatively labour intensive and an individual household can only manage a certain number of animals. The 20th century has also seen a rapid expansion in crop farming inside Darfur and vastly improved opportunities for labour elsewhere in Sudan or abroad. The proportion of labour devoted to herding must have decreased as a result. The only reasonable conclusion is that the rate of increase in livestock populations is unlikely to have exceeded the rate of population growth. It is more likely that the average herd owned by each family is smaller than it used to be, that is to say that livestock has expanded less rapidly than the human population.

This does not mean that the pressure on the range was not considerably increased. If, for example, livestock populations grew at 2.5 per cent between 1953 and 1976, then the Darfur herd would have been 76 per cent larger at the end of the period. It is difficult to reconcile such a large increase with the reported 20 per cent overstocking in 1955 or with the fact that overstocking had already become an issue 20 years before that, in 1935 (Gillespie, 1966). Vaccination, which was supposedly meant to be the major factor behind the growth in stock populations, was actually restricted, for fear of overstocking, as early as 1944 (Fisher, quoted in Adams, 1982).

In the 1970s intensive attempts were made to estimate carrying capacities in terms of standard livestock units (lsu) equivalent to 300 kilograms of herbivore biomass. In 1976/7, the National Livestock Census showed stocking densities of 11.8 1su per km^2 in south Darfur and 3.3. for north Darfur (VRA/RMR, 1977). As averages these conceal the fact that the better areas are more heavily stocked while others are of little use for grazing. Nevertheless, range surveys at the same time estimated that a stocking rate of 10 1su per km^2 in the better areas of south Darfur would prevent further range degradation. That is to say that the 'safe rate' on the better areas was less than the average rate for all areas, good and bad. It was estimated that on the two most important zones for livestock, the basement and the baggara alluvium, the stocking rate was about twice the safe level (HTS, 1974 and 1976). This is not quite as 'embarrassing' as a report from Somalia of 'rangelands chronically overstocked at rates 8 times in excess of their capacity' but it is still quite implausible (Behnke & Scoones, 1991).

The conclusion was, nevertheless, that the region was massively overstocked and that the hardier and more prolific classes of stock, above all goats, were expanding at the expense of cattle. Survey results appeared to show such a shift, with the implication that livestock production was in long-term decline. Expansion in the first part of the century had put excessive pressure on the range. Increasing population was diverting rangeland to cropping. The drought of the late 1960s and early 1970s was only accelerating an existing downward trend. Furthermore, the ever-decreasing performance of cattle herds would force more owners to turn to cropping, so the process was actually self-reinforcing. Disputes over cattle movements, crop encroachment on stock routes and so on were all seen as evidence of this same trend.

The premise that the Darfur ranges are overstocked is still widely accepted, as it was in most of Africa until very recently. All development plans since the 1970s have been based on that belief. Given the difficulties of measurement it is unlikely that the case will ever be decided on direct evidence. Indirectly, however, overstocking is looking increasingly implausible. The Darfuris themselves are indifferent to the issue and stock numbers just keep on growing, despite the fact that the range was supposed to be overstocked more than 50 years ago.

The 'Temptation'

To assert that Darfuris are aggressive, market-oriented keepers of livestock does not conflict with the Tragedy of the Commons, which predicts that overstocking will occur even when economic agents behave entirely rationally in the search of maximum profit. Nor do doubts about the extent of environmental degradation disprove the contention that communal rangeland leads to significant economic losses from congestion or a combination of congestion and degradation. One way in which this might be measured is to return to Lipton's twin parables of the Prisoners' Dilemma and the Coase Outcome, to see if the value of the temptation to shift to the 'light grazing solution' can be estimated.

In Table 4.1 above, there was a community of herders using a common range, one of whose members was a free rider who would always increase his herd at the expense of his neighbours if given the chance. By reversing the before and after situations the example can represent what was believed to be the situation in Darfur. The free rider has increased his herd, negotiations have failed, the range is overstocked and the offtake rate has been reduced from 8 per cent to 7.5 per cent. The community wants to destock and to restore the productivity of their herds and they are willing to share the reduction proportionately between themselves and the free rider. The table then reads as follows:

Table 4.4: The rangeland model revisited

	Before	After
Communal herd	900	891
Communal offtake	67.50	71.28
Free rider's herd	110	109
Free rider's offtake	8.25	8.72

The shift from 'before' to 'after' here represents the outcome of a successful attempt to raise range productivity by destocking. Once again, the example shows that it should be possible to do a deal. Both parties are better off if they all destock. A failure to do so presumes that neither of the two possible routes to escape from the Prisoners' Dilemma of non co-operative misery can be taken:

1. for either or both sides to unilaterally fence off their share of the common area and so break out of their dilemma by going their separate ways. This might happen amicably or by force. One of the two parties might, for example, be able to make an investment in 'aggressive overstocking', so as to drive the other off the range. Once he had done that he could capture all the gains of destocking for himself. Perhaps more likely would be for one side to use simple *force majeure* to achieve the same thing.

2. for all parties to negotiate a rational arrangement for stocking control.

There are two possible explanations for the failure to take one or other route in Darfur. One is that the traditional consensus in favour of open access to rangeland is simply too strong to allow enclosure. The other is that political and economic changes might have destroyed earlier arrangements under which the larger tribal groupings controlled movements between their respective areas of rangeland by agreement. Post-colonial biases against the nomads and the relatively intensive efforts made by the Condominium authorities to manage tribal relations counted against those arrangements. 'Any policy which tolerated nomadism was dismissed as colonial' (Adams, 1982). This is a reversal of an argument put forward to explain similar problems in East Africa, especially Kenya, where it is argued that it was colonial penetration that first destroyed the 'adaptive' tribal institutions that prevented abuse of the rangeland (Bennett, 1984). There remains, however, a more fundamental problem. The cattle owners of Darfur do not appear to regard the range as being overstocked, at least not so much as to wish to tackle the problem. They certainly appear to take a more relaxed attitude to range quality than most outsiders. Under the WSDC programme single villages were encouraged to enclose relatively large grazing reserves and given considerable support in so doing, including all the necessary administrative measures to ensure their legal rights to enclose. It did not lead to any obvious measure of destocking. More importantly, the people of the community allowed outsiders to bring their cattle inside the enclosure, more or less destroying the point of the exercise. This parallels experience elsewhere. 'The Samburu [of Kenya] voted out all grazing schemes when given the opportunity to do so in the late 1960s' (Bennett, 1984).

The customary position on rangeland is summed up in the saying that three things are free: 'Al Hawa wa Al Ma′ wa Al Kala' – air, water and pasture. 'It is customary for any member of a tribe to have the right to graze his animals at will over the tribal land of his tribe providing that they cause no damage to cultivation or to gum gardens. The responsibility of keeping animals out of cultivation and gardens is on the herdsman. Grazing boundaries exist between tribes where ill-feeling has made them necessary. Similar boundaries may exist between subsections of a tribe or adjoining villages but they are an exception to the common practice. Strangers are required to gain permission to graze their herd' (Tothill, 1948).

Contrary to later views on Sudanese developments and, more generally, to Lipton's argument that change has undermined 'old chiefly authorities and clan-like decisions', the situation at the end of the colonial era was very loose. This was at a time when the tribal leaders' authority, which had been supported by the Condominium, was at its height. Despite this the only restrictions on the movement of livestock were those required to avoid damage to crops, except where there were special reasons for tribal tension. The situation has not changed. Livestock herders are still required to avoid cropped areas during the season and farmers should not crop on acknowledged livestock routes. The principal routes (*ar murhal*) are defined by custom and latterly enshrined in local government orders. They are supposed to be 40 ropes, or 120 metres, wide. Each main route has many subsidiaries branching off it and even running parallel. Stock usually travel quickly along the major routes running between cultivated areas in order to reach the more open range where the herds can spread out and settle to graze. Farmer – herder clashes are mostly the result of a herder losing control of his stock in transit, not because of direct competition over grazing land. (That is not to say that the 'loss of control' is always innocent.) For the same reason, herders resent cultivation because it blocks access to grazing or, especially, to water, not because of the loss of pasture. In normal times, there are acknowledged procedures for negotiating compensation for damage done to crops by livestock. A few hours' inadvertence by a herder can result in his having to sell two or three head of cattle to pay compensation.

To sum up, the customary procedures mediating between herder and farmer were designed to facilitate movement, not to control stocking. It is not irrelevant that one of Coase's examples of how the market can handle externalities is precisely that of cattle trampling crops, and Darfuri customary arrangements that are still in place prove his point; that given clear rules compensation arrangements can and do work (Coase, 1960).

On the other hand, the well-defined customary position, that rangeland is free, is being breached quite widely. Both communities and individuals are establishing enclosures of which the purpose is clearly rather more than just the protection of crops. These enclosures are known in the local phrase as *Zara'ib al hawa*, or 'enclosures of air', a sarcastic reference to the traditional wisdom that three things are free: air, water and pasture. In the mid-1970s at the village of Diri, west of Nyala, 'about 30 people worked for 10 days constructing a communal enclosure for the village herd.' There were also individual attempts to 'enclose pasture by Zeribas' (Haaland, 1980).

Behnke, working in the same area in 1984, went further, showing that the degree to which rangeland was being enclosed and cropland acquiring more individual tenure depended on the distance from the major urban centre of Nyala, an important market for fodder (Behnke, 1985). In the JMRDP area, a relatively recent trend is the gradual extension of a plot cleared from virgin bush, year by year, until it includes an area of fallow. The cropped area is then rotated within the fenced area and the fallow produces a crop of natural grass which may be cut and stored (JMRDP/HTS, 1985). In yet another part of the WSDC area, the alluvium of the southern district, transhumant herders reported that they had bought the right to graze over enclosed land, in most cases pure grassland not just cropland left to lie fallow (WSDC Nomad Survey, 1984). All the above instances indicate a move towards the enclosure of rangeland by groups or individuals to conserve fodder, in many cases for sale rather than for the household's own livestock.

To sum up, neither traditional structures nor Lipton's four factors of population growth, development change, risk aversion and 'transition of trust', adequately explain why the Darfur herders have failed to escape the Tragedy of the Commons. Where it is worthwhile, Darfuris are perfectly capable of finding both escape routes from the Prisoners' Dilemma: negotiation and enclosure. Negotiation forms probably the biggest single part of Darfuri social action and there is no solid reason to believe that the proportion of failed negotiations is any greater in Darfur than it is in the developed world. Where there is a need for rules to organize negotiations over externalities to control transit damage by livestock, they exist and usually work. Similarly, where enclosure is likely to be worthwhile, Darfuris are happy to do it, regardless of the overt consensus against it. It should be stressed, moreover, that there is no evidence of attempts to resist these enclosures. Given the ample evidence that Darfuris are willing to fight and kill in defence of their interests, and given the lack of customary or legal support for enclosure, this is a strong indicator of the weakness of that consensus.

There is really only one conclusion left, that the incentives to tackle

Table 4.5: A games theory model of destocking

		The Community	
		No change	Destock
No change	Herd	900:100	810:190
	Output	72.0 8.0	64.8 15.2
	Total output	80	80
The free rider			
Destock	Herd	–	810: 90
	Output		81.0 9.0
	Total output		90

Note: for simplicity, output is assumed to be an adequate indicator of returns net of costs.

overgrazing are too weak: that the benefit to be gained from controlling stocking is too small to justify the effort of enclosure or of negotiation.

A return to the Prisoner's Dilemma helps to illustrate the possibilities: The columns show the choice taken by the community, to keep stocks high or destock. The rows show the free rider's choice. (It is assumed that the free rider will certainly not destock if the community does not, so the bottom left box is empty.) In each box, the situation that results from the combined choice of both parties is shown, the community's herd size and output on the left and the free rider's on the right. The current offtake rate if neither party destocks is 8 per cent. If the total herd could be cut by a tenth, that would rise to 10 per cent. If the free rider decides not to co-operate, he will increase his herd to take up the slack created by the community's destocking and total output will not change. Instead the free rider's share of the total, overstocked, output increases.

What would happen if the community offered the free rider a trade? To do this they might have to offer him as good a deal as he would get from increasing his herd to 190 and capturing all the gains of their destocking. Can they do it and would it be worth it? The answer is yes:

Table 4.6: Trading the gains from destocking

Community's cooperative gain:	81.0 – 72.0	= 9.0
Free Rider's non-cooperative gain:	15.2 – 8.0	= 7.2
Free Rider's cooperative gain:	9.0 – 8.0	= 1.0
Community bribe to Free Rider:	7.2 – 1.0	= 6.2
Community gain minus bribe:	9.0 – 6.2	= 2.8

How implausible is this? In some ways, very. The community's net gain is small, only 4 per cent of their original offtake. In the real world, moreover, the transactions costs between a community of thousands and potentially hundreds of free riders would be very high. However, the real point of the model is to emphasize the very narrow range within which the Tragedy of the Commons can be operative; the narrow range in which the externality is relevant. A relatively small change in the assumed improvement in the offtake rate can shift the numbers either downward, to where it is not worth anybody's while destocking, or upward to a position where even the free rider unambiguously gains from co-operation.

In the example it is assumed that a 10 per cent reduction in the size of the herd will generate a 25 per cent improvement in the herd's performance: from 8 per cent to 10 per cent offtake. If herd performance improves only 11 per cent it is not enough to compensate for the reduction in numbers and offtake does not increase at all. On the other hand, if the performance is doubled by destocking, then the free rider gains just as much from co-operating as he does from stealing the community's reduction in numbers:

Table 4.7: Destocking gains relative to offtake rates

Offtake	Community's	Free rider's gain		
rate – %	cooperative gain	Coop.	Non-Coop.	'Bribe'
8.9	0.0	0.0	7.2	–
10.0	9.0	1.0	7.2	6.2
11.0	17.1	1.9	7.2	5.3
15.0	49.5	5.5	7.2	1.7
20.0	90.0	10.0	7.2	0.0

Well before the position is reached at which the free rider is unambiguously better off, the amount needed to bribe him to co-operate becomes diminishingly small compared to the community's gains. To sum up, the Tragedy of the Commons position is essentially unstable; changes in costs, returns and technical productivity are all likely to push it down, to a position where there are no relevant gains to be made from the establishment of institutions to control over-exploitation of the free access resource, or up to a position where the gains are so great that the incentive for all parties is towards resolving the problem.

One of the classic solutions to the problems of free access resources is taxation. Theoretically, it would be difficult to calculate the correct level of tax and the tax would have to be applied to the correct factor of production. Taxes on output do not have the right effect. Despite these difficulties, 'quite crude approximations may be rewarded by significant efficiency gains' (Gould, 1972). It is worth noting that the colonial system of taxing livestock numbers was the best theoretical option. The decay of that system in more recent years is correspondingly regrettable. Because it is easier, government now focuses its livestock taxation on sales, that is to say on output.

The conclusion is that there is nothing to support the belief that development in the livestock sector can be brought about by better management within the existing resources. Despite the logical power of the Tragedy of the Commons thesis, the evidence is that the livestock owners of Darfur do not perceive adequate benefit from attempts to control stocking and that they are almost certainly right. One last piece of indirect evidence that they see little value in extra rangeland is the fact that attempts to extend it by providing extra water supplies from *hafirs* (tanks) or from boreholes have almost always failed because the herders are not interested in maintaining these facilities. This contrasts with farmers who make strenuous efforts to keep their water supplies going (Adams, 1982). Herders also make every effort to avoid paying for water for their herds, regardless of the fact that to do so might gain them access to better grazing.

The conclusions of a report from Mali in the early 1980s seem entirely supported in Darfur: 'The suggestion that a smaller herd will produce more in an absolute sense is not true for rangelands such as the Sahel that are dominated by annual plant species whose production is mainly determined by the availability of nitrogen. Nitrogen losses from the vegetation are already high without grazing. When more cattle are kept less nitrogen is lost by volatilisation and fire so that animal production is almost proportional to herd size. Experience with perennial pastures on soils with reasonable fertility may also have led to the idea that better pastures are those with higher biomass. Applied to the Sahel where nutrients limit the production of annual grasses this is a mistaken idea that leads to overestimation of the value of wells, boreholes, fire control, fodder conservation, rangeland regeneration and other important management ideas' (Breman & De Wit, 1983).

Just as was the case with agricultural research, no gains can be made from 'the improvement of range and herd management alone *without external inputs*' (Breman & De Wit, 1983, my italics). Whether or not there is overstocking and whether or not the range is in danger of serious degradation, the way out of the problem depends on the development of new techniques using imported inputs and almost certainly linked to new market opportunities. There is every reason to believe that if those do become available, the herders and farmers of Darfur are capable of making all the necessary adjustments to both their techniques and to their social arrangements. (Justice and administration are important exceptions here, as discussed later.) Sadly, it must be concluded that most of the work done in this area represents no more than an attempt to tackle the wrong problem in the wrong way, possibly a wholly non-existent problem.

This has happened because the evidence has been consistently misinterpreted.

> They make scarce any manure for their corn fields . . . but when one piece of ground has been exhausted by continual cropping, they clear and cultivate another piece of fresh land; and when that is exhausted, proceed to a third. Their cattle are allowed to wander through the woods and other uncultivated grounds, where they are half-starved; having long ago extirpated almost all the annual grasses by cropping them too early in the spring, before they had time to form their flowers, or to shed their seeds . . . A piece of ground which could not maintain one cow, would in former times have maintained four, each of which would have given four times the quantity of milk.

These comments could have been made at any time in the last 50 years by any one of hundreds of experts bewailing the disastrous environmental impact of rising population on African common lands. It comes in fact from a European visitor to the English colonies of north America in the mid-18th century; a visitor who could 'with difficulty discover there the character of the English nation, so well skilled in all the different branches of agriculture' (Smith, 1776). Yet Adam Smith's conclusion was not that the American colonies were on the brink of environmental catastrophe, or that some mystery of the new Americans' psyche made them spectacularly poor farmers, or even that they were facing a Tragedy of the Commons. It was merely that land was abundant and that more intensive agriculture was not yet profitable: 'It is late in the progress of improvement before cattle can bring such a price as to render it profitable to cultivate land for the sake of feeding them; yet . . . they are perhaps the first which bring this price; because till they bring it, it seems impossible that improvement can be brought near even to that degree of perfection to which it has arrived in many parts of Europe.'

Smith would have found many other parallels between modern Darfur and his own Scotland. Just like Darfur, Scotland was a poor region newly attached to a more prosperous land and, just like Darfur, Scotland was feeling the impact of rapidly expanding markets for its hardy highland cattle. Since the 18th century, the Scottish banking business has been far more important than such a small country would warrant. The earliest days of that business were built on the cattle trade. The Tragedy of the Commons depends on the absence of a 'temptation to goodness' to negotiate range controls or a 'temptation to badness' to enclose the rangeland. That temptation is measured by the rent a piece of land can command. 'The union opened the market of England to the highland cattle. Their ordinary price is at present about three times greater than at the beginning of the century, and rents of many highland estates have been tripled and quadrupled in the same time' (Smith, 1776).

In Darfur the first signs of shifting range and livestock management patterns can be seen in the development of fodder and dairy enclosures near to the big towns, especially Nyala. Smith describes precisely the same pattern: 'in the neighbourhood of a great town the demand for milk and for forage to horses frequently contribute, together with the high price of butcher's meat, to raise the value of grass above what may be called its natural proportion to that corn.' The outstanding question is why a simple interpretation of livestock development in Africa along the lines described by Smith has never been adopted and why more complex interpretations have survived in the face of much of the evidence.

Saving the Savannahs

With some exceptions, cropland is a free access resource in Darfur just as much as rangeland. In areas that are not already occupied anyone can settle and clear a farm without any formalities at all. Even where a pioneer group has already established a claim, by virtue of prior occupancy, newcomers are usually allowed to take over land that has been abandoned or to clear new land with a minimum of negotiation. The mechanism of the Tragedy of the Commons should, therefore, be just as destructive on cropland as on the range; more so, in fact, because the act of cropping changes the vegetation and the soil far more radically than even the heaviest grazing. Concerns about erosion, degradation and exhaustion of the croplands have a history almost as long as that of overstocking on the range.

The strongest concern has been about the *goz* savannahs of the eastern parts of Darfur. This has been partly because the *goz* is the poorest soil and vulnerable to wind erosion, partly because the effects of drought are most obvious on the *goz* farming areas of north Darfur and partly because the impact of new borehole water supplies has been mainly confined to the *goz*. That impact has been rapid and highly visible.

The pessimistic belief is that before population pressure built up, the *goz* savannahs supported shifting cultivation in which relatively short periods of cropping were followed by long fallow periods during which the vegetation recovered to its original climax condition of relatively dense savannah woodland. This long fallow restored fertility. Then, as population pressure built up, farmers were forced to shorten the fallow period. An individual farmer could not prevent this because the right of free access meant that some other farmer could take over and crop his fallow. This is why land tenure, or rather the lack of it, is so important to this argument. 'When fertility is exhausted and the land abandoned to bush fallow, the cultivator has no easy way of ensuring that others will not reclear the land before the planned period of bush fallow expires. As population pressure increases, especially within easy access of watering points, this problem becomes acute and soil erosion and exhaustion sets in' (HTS, 1974).

In a closed system, where population has no escape, through migration for example, this becomes a vicious Malthusian circle. 'Population increase led to excessive cultivation, which in turn led to enhanced soil erosion and soil impoverishment. To make amends for this the population which is increasing at an annual rate of 2.5 per cent had to increase the area cultivated with millet. This meant a fresh wave of desertification' (Ibrahim, 1984). That description came from north Darfur and the flow of people driven out of the north increased the pressure on the wetter south, which might not see desertification but soil exhaustion would have the same effect. Vegetation was seen as a critical indicator. Farmers stated and observation confirmed, to some degree, that apparently exhausted areas of *goz* carried a high proportion of the species *Guiera senegalensis* (*ar ghubeish*) (HTS, 1976).

On the other hand, it seemed that farmers could use the gum arabic tree, *Acacia senegalensis* (*ar hashab*), to counter the whole process of decline. In the colonial era it was reported from Kordofan that 'The [hashab] trees are cut down, when they become too old to produce gum, to make way for grain cultivation. Five years later the land becomes too exhausted to produce grain and is left fallow. After an interval the acacias begin to reappear, without human effort, and in five years or so are big enough to be tapped for gum' (Davies, 1957). It came to be accepted that 'ideally the land is cultivated on a rough 4 year cultivation – 12 year bush fallow [gum] rotation.' As early as 1950, however, it was reported from Kordofan that 'population increase and the tendency of well fields to dry up has resulted in concentrations of population round permanent water supplies, where, consequently, the fallow period has largely disappeared' (Jewitt & Manton, 1951).

The earliest experiment to test these ideas was in 1948 when the presence of a gum forest that had been protected since 1920 next to land that had been cropped for 30 years allowed a comparison. 'The comparison is an extreme one, between land cultivated for 30 years and land under Acacia forest for a similar period.' As always with trials in western Sudan, the most important aspect was lost to the everyday hazards of agriculture in the area, the 'two grain crops being destroyed by pests and birds'. Nevertheless, the experiment did show clear differences in yield for sesame and groundnuts and responses to fertilizer on the exhausted land, although the 'experiment was not replicated and it is unsafe to draw firm conclusions from the yields' (Jewitt & Manton, 1951).

Those words of caution were to be forgotten in the eagerness to find a sustainable cultivation system. Besides, hashab appeared to have all the fashionable virtues. It formed part of a traditional rotation sanctioned by Rural People's Knowledge and technically it has all the characteristics of an ideal rotation crop. It produces a commodity of value and it is by nature a legume. Leguminous crops have the capacity to fix nitrogen in the soil, although not all of them do so, and hashab should, therefore, have a beneficial effect on fertility. (As with measurements of livestock carrying capacity, the debate on how, when, where and how much leguminous trees contribute to fertility is enormously complex and hedged with scientific qualifications.) (Vetaas, 1992.)

No experimental work in the subsequent four decades has made it possible to make any firmer statement about the effect of a hashab fallow on yields. And therein lies the fundamental problem. It may be possible to recognize 'exhaustion' from the vegetation and from the tendency of the soil to wind erosion, but it has proved impossible to put any significant economic value on it. If, after all, it is possible to crop these soils profitably for 30 years, then the rate of yield decline must be very small indeed. Why then was there any traditional rotation between hashab and grain? A possible answer is that during boom times in the gum markets it was hashab that was the principal crop and grain that was the rotation crop. It was not soil exhaustion that encouraged rotation at all, merely the fact that the hashab trees periodically became too old to produce gum.

Whatever its contribution to fertility, hashab did play an important role in land tenure. Because gum arabic had such high value, the ownership of the trees was important: British district officers in Kordofan spent a considerable amount of their time adjudicating on disputes over hashab gardens and many of them were formally registered (Davies, 1957). To this day, there are many areas where hashab is the only registered form of tenure.

The 1970s saw a massive acceleration in the rate of bush clearance in south Darfur as new borehole wateryards made new areas accessible. The impact of the wateryards was extremely visible. On aerial photographs and later on satellite images the radiating rings of clearance, cropped land and abandoned land were more eyecatching than even the largest of the natural topographical features. Driving overland, the traveller crossed from the enclosed world of mature savannah woodland, where the view is confined to the patterns of shade and light cast by the tall broadleaved trees on the scanty grasses underneath, over a frontier into another country, the bare plains of the cleared land. There the view over the mix of crops and dense grasses and low shrubs on the fallow had no limit except the dark line of the next block of uncleared land on the horizon.

In 1975, a study of some 150 wateryards in the eastern half of south Darfur revealed that so much land had been cleared, since they were opened in the late 1960s and early 1970s, that in some areas, 'at the present rates of exploitation it is likely that this small amount [of reserve land] will be exhausted by 1981 and by 1986 the vast majority of cultivation will have been abandoned' (HTS, 1976). In the western half of the province, on the Goz Dango, the frontier of the cleared land advanced at the rate of one kilometre a year up until 1984. By 1987 it was estimated that 61 square kilometres of natural climax vegetation were being cleared every year (WSDC/HTS, 1989). Even in 1987 there were still large reserves of uncleared land on Goz Dango, over 9,000 square kilometres. There are also uncleared reserves on the southern half of Goz Maaliya/Rizeiqat in the east. Despite this it was easy to see the situation as being similar, in its smaller way, to the wholesale destruction of the tropical rainforests of the Amazon basin, for example.

In one sense, the 1976 prediction that the reserves on the sandy *athmur* dunes of the Baggara Alluvium and in the northern half of Goz Maaliya would be 'exhausted' by the 1980s was more or less borne out by the 1987 study. By then, less than 12 per cent of uncleared climax woodland remained on the area of *goz* studied and just over 15 per cent on the Baggara *athmur*. At many individual wateryard sites there was no climax woodland left.

To sum up, there seemed to be compelling evidence of a Tragedy of the Commons in process, and development strategies of the late 1970s were founded on that belief. These included a programme of 'controlled settlement' on uncleared *goz* savannah areas of south Darfur carried out by the Western Savannah Development Corporation. Although the first phase of the work was considered to be a pilot programme, it involved

$20 million expenditure over three years and represented a very major attempt to tackle the perceived problems of development on the *goz*. Four settlements were established, each based around a newly opened borehole water supply. Farmers were allocated 30 hectares of land each. This was rented to them on condition that they did not crop more than six hectares at any time. It was expected that a rotation with hashab would develop and that research would identify an increasing number of more intensive techniques to enable incomes to increase without encroaching on sustainable cropping intensities. The key feature was that the secure leasehold tenure would ensure that there was no obstacle to farmers taking up those more intensive techniques and making the necessary investments to support them. As already discussed, research to identify more intensive techniques was not a success but the settlement model proposed was not wholly dependent on new techniques. The benefits of land tenure on its own were expected to be substantial.

The strength of the belief that population pressure on a free access resource was leading to soil exhaustion through declining rotations diverted attention from some important technical facts about cultivation on savannah soils:

- [shifting cultivation] 'The attitude of the shifting cultivator to the soil is quite different from that of a farmer in a less spacious environment. The system is not designed to preserve the land for posterity – that is an attitude which evolves when there is no more room to expand. Nor do farmers attempt to achieve maximum yields on a given patch regardless of effort.'
- There is no doubt that the increasing effort of keeping land free of weeds is often the primary reason for a patch of land being abandoned. If land is abundant, clearing can be easier than weeding. Especially as it can be done in the off season, which weeding cannot.
- In the savanna there are many examples of three years cropping being followed by only three years fallow for many years, though fertility declines to a very low level at this intensity.
- For any form of intensified production in the savanna, whether by shifting cultivation or by permanent cropping, fertilisers, especially nitrogen and phosphate, are essential. Without them the vicious cycle of poor fallows leading to poor crops cannot be broken.
- In high-grass savanna soils very low in nitrate, nitrogen content is low for leguminous species generally, and recent work in Australia indicates that the growth of Rhizobia [bacteria which fix nitrogen

in the roots of leguminous plants] may be severely restricted by periods of water shortage.
- It seems likely that one of the main functions of the fallow on phosphorous deficient soils is to mix the phosphorous availability chiefly through the ash added when the fallow is cleared (Nye & Greenland, 1960).

All this implies three things: that fallows on savannah soils are of small value, that they are not necessary to sustainable agriculture, since farming can continue profitably at very low yield levels, and that the driving force behind shifting cultivation is not soil exhaustion so much as weed infestation. The prolonged and painful research experience described in Chapter 3 confirms this description in almost all respects, notably in the fact that the only clearly established research result was a yield response to phosphate. The whole concept of 'soil exhaustion' was probably a misinterpretation. Dense stands of bushes like *Guiera* on abandoned land do not mean that the land is 'exhausted'. Instead, it is the density of the infestation itself that forces farmers to move on; the bushes become so thick that it is pointless to continue planting a crop.

The very act of farming creates weeds. 'Many weeds are plants that under natural conditions would not be able to survive competition with the natural flora. Under cultivation, however, where the natural flora is kept in check and competition is reduced to a minimum, they are able to thrive' (Tothill, 1948). Small shrubs like *Guiera* are too tough to pull up by hand, so the farmers have to work around them. Even the animals do not graze *Guiera* and an infestation is encouraged to build up almost unopposed.

If it were not that the concept of increased pressure on shifting cultivation systems was so central to the aid analysis of environmental problems, this discussion would almost be irrelevant. Shifting cultivation may not be any indication of soil exhaustion, but true shifting cultivation, with a short crop period followed by a move of residence, is uncommon in Darfur anyway. In 1983, 'At least 25% of the population have never moved their residence. Almost all the movement can be attributed to the pressure of population growth and cropped area expansion. Even in the goz areas significant numbers have never moved.' Even for those who did move the periods of residence were long and 'It seems unlikely that many have moved more than once in their life.' The conclusion was that 'In the absence of population growth stable cultivations systems would be the rule [on the *goz*] too' (WSDC Farmer Survey,

1983). In other words, as communities expand they inevitably outgrow their immediate environment and some proportion has to move regardless of whether the cultivation itself is shifting or not and regardless of whether the soil is 'exhausted' and yields declining. A 1976/7 survey showed that 99.4 per cent of south Darfur households had always lived at their present site and 89.7 per cent of north Darfur households (VRA/RMR, 1977).

In most of the areas opened up for farmers by the provision of borehole water supplies the pattern of development was similar. Initially population built up very rapidly and the land closest to the water source, the focal point, was cleared to absorb it. At this stage most of the cleared land was cropped, meaning that the ratio of fallow to cropped was low. The cultivation intensity was high. New areas were constantly being cleared. There was usually a belt of land under clearance, where the trees had been cut but the farmers were waiting for the wood to dry out. Then they could burn it and start cropping the new land. As the first cropped land was abandoned the farms moved on to the ring of newly cleared areas surrounding it. The belt of clearance itself moved still further out. Cultivation intensities started to decline as more and more land was abandoned to fallow.

While this process was going on the site could continue to absorb more population; as the radius increased so did the area available. However, once the circle reached its limits, dictated by the distance water could reasonably be carried, no more population could be absorbed. If there was exhaustion and if yields did start to decline because farmers were forced to start reusing fallow before it had fully recovered, the village might even have begun to need to shed population. Nevertheless, at some level of population, an equilibrium would be reached at which fallows were long enough to ensure yields adequate to support the community. It appeared that the cycle from zero cultivation through to a stage at which population levelled off or even started to decline took about 25 years in the Goz Maaliya in the circumstances of the 1980s (Scott-Villiers, 1984).

In effect, the pessimistic analysis of what is happening on the *goz* depends on the belief that no stable equilibrium between population, fallow and yields can be reached. Because the community cannot shed population it will be forced to crop more than is sustainable and to reduce fallows below the necessary level. Without denying that this might happen in the long-term, the evidence is that it has not happened so far. A detailed study in 1987 compared land use in 1971, 1975 and

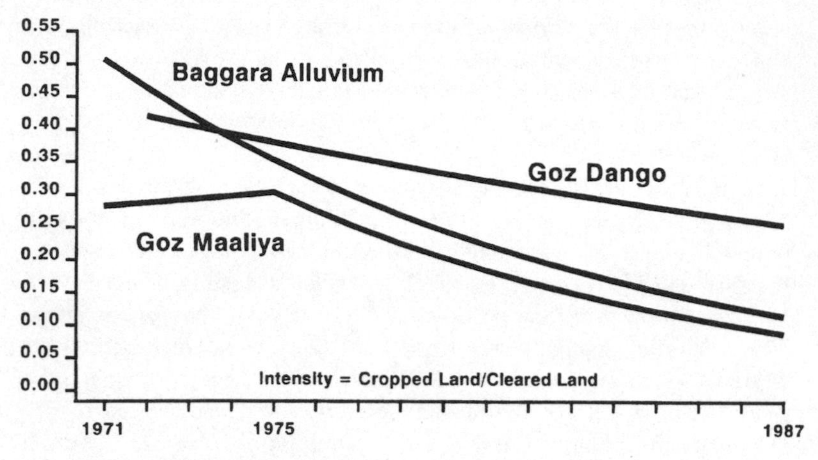

Figure 4.2 Changes in Cultivation Intensity, Three Areas of South Darfur – 1971 to 1987

1987, using aerial photography from 1971, ground survey in 1975 and satellite images for 1987. Figure 4.2 graphs the cultivation intensity in three separate areas of south Darfur using the data for the three measured years and interpolating for the intervening periods. Although the interpolation makes it appear smoother than it really was, the trend was the same in all three areas: an unambiguous decline in cultivation intensity. In other words, the quantity of fallow land relative to the cultivated area increased very substantially. The vast areas of woodland that were cleared during the 1970s were not cropped ever more intensively until exhaustion set in. Instead, they have been cropped extremely extensively. On average, the land that was newly cleared does not seem to have been cropped for more than two or three years.

What this means is that right at the end of a period of spectacular expansion in cultivated areas and of serious drought and famine, which drove population down from north Darfur into these relatively better-off parts of south Darfur, the ratio of fallow to cropped land was substantially higher in areas of uncontrolled clearance than it had been in the past. It was also higher than the various strategies aimed at preventing a Tragedy of the Commons were recommending. The WSDC controlled settlements required tenants to maintain a cultivation intensity of 20 per cent: six hectares cropped out of 30 hectares. The traditional 'ideal' grain to gum arabic fallow rotation of 4:12 implies a cultivation intensity of 25 per cent. In two of the 1987 study areas of uncontrolled settlement, the Goz Maaliya and the Baggara Alluvium, the cultivation intensity was only 11 per cent and 13 per cent respectively. Even on the Goz Dango, which was the most newly developed area and still under active clearance, the density was only 27 per cent. It should not be forgotten, moreover, that these areas had absorbed population from the north, thus lowering cultivation intensities there. In 1987 there remained reserves of uncleared land, so there was no particular reason to believe that the decline in intensities would be reversed in the near future.

Here, in more extreme form than anywhere else, we once again have a situation in which the development strategy proposed was addressed to a problem that might or might not occur in the future but which was not in any way a matter for concern at the time the strategy was being put into effect. To repeat, that strategy was based on the idea that in a situation of free access to cropland population pressure would mean that farmers could not fallow their land for long enough and would not be able to invest in land-saving technologies that would allow more productive agriculture to develop. Instead, they would be trapped in a vicious circle of reducing fallows and declining yields. With hindsight, it can be seen that this analysis, which appeared to have ample circumstantial evidence to support it in the shape of an extraordinary rapid rate of land clearance, lacked firm evidence on four critical points:

- It was not demonstrated that exhaustion was a problem in the economic sense that yields were driven below the level at which it was profitable to crop. Evidence that agriculture could be sustained at low yields for long periods was ignored.
- The fact that farmers could and did fight to maintain tenure when it was important, as over gum arabic gardens, was ignored in the general presumption that tenure was a problem.
- At a time when the provision of borehole water supplies had radically increased the amount of land easily accessible to cultivation, it was not clearly demonstrated that population pressure had reached a level that was driving cultivation intensities upwards.
- Economic factors behind the explosive growth in cropping were not

considered, notably the profitability of groundnut and gum arabic production.

Despite these gaps in the argument, there remains to this day a belief, backed by substantial development efforts, that the establishment of secure title to land will in itself bring about more intensive agriculture on the *goz*. A report written by retired World Bank staff of the very division that had been responsible for the whole programme acknowledged in 1988 that the WSDC land management programmes were probably in a 'blind alley.' Despite this Pauline conversion, or perhaps because of it, the advice was rejected.

Land Tenure and the Value of Land

The value of land is the crucial link between the Prisoners' Dilemma of the free access resource and the paradise of the Coase Outcome. The value of land in Darfur is low and the lack of negotiations over reductions in livestock numbers and the relative weaknesses of most forms of land tenure are a direct result of that fact. Tenure, or the lack of it, is a symptom not a cause.

Land may have a low value because it is productive but abundant or because it is non-productive. For Darfur, it would seem that both are true. With poor soils, low rainfall and restricted links to markets, farming in Darfur is generally unproductive. At the same time there remain large areas of relatively unused land, so supply is abundant.

Traditional land tenure is summed up as follows: 'Within the village lands each villager has the right to cultivate. If he leaves the village the land occupied by him is allotted to someone else. There is no inheritance according to Mohammedan law. Land in excess of the requirements of the village may be alloted to strangers. The area allotted to a man is supposed to be no more than he can work (at Kifayat Yad)' . . . 'Gum gardens fall into two classes, those within the village boundaries and those outside them. A villager has the right to tap the trees which spring up on the plot of ground which he has abandoned. A short absence does not deprive him of the right to tap these trees. It is not unknown for a villager to pay a due to a shaykh for the privilege of tapping but a stranger is required to do so. Gum gardens outside the boundaries of the village are regarded by custom to be at the disposal of the tribal chief who as the agent of the government is entitled to collect these dues from tappers.' (Tothill, 1948)

As already mentioned, the ability to maintain a right to gum arabic meant that there was at least one way that farmers could retain control of their fallows despite the principle that tenure was communal. Added to that, once a sheikh had allocated land he had no right to withdraw the allocation later. Only if the land was clearly abandoned did it return to the common pool. Ownership of baobab trees, the crucial source of water, also conferred a form of ownership of the land and according to some reports the sheikhs allocated a complete package to each household, including baobabs, a gum garden and a site to build a house as well as cropland. Under the Condominium a register of the baobabs was kept in Kordofan (Davies, 1957).

Under the Fur Sultans a system developed called Hakura. This was the system of land allocation under the sultans, which paralleled European feudalism in that high officials of the Fur state were allocated estates (*hakura*) not to farm themselves but to administer. The sultan rewarded his men by allotting them the right to levy taxes, legal fees and labour dues on the estate. The Lord of the Hakura (*ar sid al hakura*) usually delegated most of his powers in turn to agents who became in effect the land sheikhs (*ar shaykh al ard*). The latter allocated the right to cultivate to the farmers whose title Lord of the Axe (*ar sid al fas*) illustrated how their tenure was established by the act of marking the trees for cutting and clearing. Once a farmer had laid claim to his land in this way he could subdivide it among his family or even sublet to others. What he could not do was transfer his rights to others (Hamza, 1979).

The *hakura* were granted to the great lords of Darfur in written documents. Many of these have been preserved and are still presented in the courts when disputes over land arise (O'Fahey & Abu Salim, 1983). The result is that 'contemporary systems of land tenure in Darfur and Kordofan are deeply rooted in the Hakura system' . . . 'By the nineteenth century much of the most desirable land west of Jebel Marra and around El Fasher had been parcelled into Hawakir.' Further south, among the Baggara Arabs a different form, the Hakura al 'Urban or Arab Hakura, was supposed to be in force. Under this the tribal chiefs were supposed to collect the dues, but because the sultan was never able to establish great control over the Baggara and because their wealth lay in livestock rather than cultivation, the same formal land tenure system did not take root (Hamza, 1979).

With the overthrow of the Fur sultanate, *zakat* and the other traditional forms of taxation were abolished, at least as far as government was concerned. This took away the feudal elements of the tenure system and many *hakura* owners and their land sheikhs slipped back to being merely village leaders, although they retained their role in the allocation of land rights and their power to do this was generally respected. During the 1960s and 1970s, however, various attacks were made on the system of Native Administration which had been built up under the Condominium. The land sheikhs formed a part of this and their position was correspondingly weakened.

Among the Fur, two classes of land were identified: *'ard al 'aysh* or millet land and the terraced *'ard al qamih* or wheat land of Jebel Marra. The latter was in all practical respects owned and it could be abandoned for quite long periods without losing a claim to it. A 1966 case saw the owner's right enforced after eight years. It could also be inherited (Hamza, 1979).

In principle, the farmer's right to rainfed land, *'ard al 'aysh*, lapsed after three years' absence. In fact there were elements of ownership even here. It was common, for example, to make gifts and it could even be 'sold' under the guise of compensation payments for clearing or planting hashab. It could be maintained in fallow by continuing to mark the trees or by weeding. 'Strong evidence is needed to rebut a presumption that the holder intends to return.' An illustration of the ways in which a right could be maintained was a case of a woman whose husband had given her half their land when they divorced. She did not cultivate it but she had hashab growing in it and she informed the sheikh of her intention to return. She even offered to continue to pay him dues in her absence. When she did return to tap the hashab and her husband tried to stop her he was overruled (Hamza, 1979).

In the modern era much of the old communal tenure system has become irrelevant. Gum arabic gardens have become private property and baobab trees have been replaced by boreholes. While the concept that land is allocated through the sheikh and that he may reallocate it after three years' absence is still acknowledged, it is admitted that even cropland has become *shibh wurathiah*, that is to say 'more or less heritable'. Many farmers in the old-established *goz* farming areas are able to hold on to extensive blocks of fallow in one or even two neighbouring village areas for as much as seven or ten years. Provided that they do not leave the area for good they run no risk of losing that land. An indication of the move towards retaining fallow is that many of the cases now coming before the courts in the area relate to attempts to return to land. (The speed of modern communications is an important factor that has greatly increased the ability of farmers who travel to make sure that they do not lose their rights to land in their home village.) These changes almost exactly match those described by Boserup as part of the process of increasing frequency of cropping (Boserup, 1965).

The relative abundance of land is shown most clearly in surveys of tenure which have shown that the largest single class of land was acquired by uncontrolled clearance from virgin bush. This was true in both the wider regions of WSDC area, where 46 per cent of fields were 'cleared from bush without permission', and the more intensive basement wadis of the JMRDP area. Even there, where agriculture is much longer established, 34 per cent was described as 'Free gift/cleared from bush'. Inheritance is the next most important class in most areas followed by free gifts or loans. Only in one part of south Darfur, the Goz Ma'aliya, is formal allocation by the sheikh still important. Perhaps it is significant that this is the heartland of commercial groundnut production. With the exception of land under dry season irrigation and the small amount of land rented on government mechanized schemes, rental is rare, no more than 5 per cent of all land, while purchase of rainfed crop land is even rarer (WSDC, 1985).

Conclusion

The evidence suggests that the emphasis on population growth and environmental decline was mistaken in almost every respect. There was ample circumstantial evidence of increasing pressure on both the cropland and the rangeland of Darfur, but this was misleading and it diverted attention from the need to establish three facts. The first was that an absence of formal land tenure was an obstacle to better farming practice and that the traditional support for communal access to rangeland prevented destocking. The second was that the cropland actually was overcultivated and the rangeland overstocked. The third was that more careful management of either cropland or rangeland would result in higher production.

As far as the first is concerned, farmers can and do win tenure, if it is worth it, and they can even enclose rangeland, if it is worth it. For the second, enormous efforts to count cattle numbers and estimate carrying capacities have failed to show that the range is overstocked, in any practical sense that production is lower than it would be if numbers were reduced. Nor has it been shown that the range is in terminal decline. Equally great efforts to measure overcultivation in south Darfur have merely established that cultivation intensity has actually gone down. The introduction of boreholes has effectively reduced the pressure on land, even if only temporarily. For the third, agricultural research has relatively little to offer while livestock research has barely got off the ground.

Low productivity has universally been confused with declining productivity. Even if it is declining, no viable technical defence has been identified. Given the limited opportunities available to the people of Darfur, there would be no equitable alternative to allowing them to continue to 'mine' the region until such a defence were identified. It has been suggested, for example, that cultivation cannot be sustained in areas with rainfall below an 'agronomic dry limit' of at least 500 millimetres without causing desertification. Even if that were correct, a ban on cultivation beyond that limit cannot be justified; a ban which 'would deprive the inhabitants of that zone of the basis of their existence. It would be unthinkable as long as no real alternatives can be offered' (Ibrahim, 1984). Although it is not central to the argument, it would in any case be beyond the capacity of the Sudanese state to implement such a rule.

There is no firm evidence that the expansion of either livestock herds or cropping in Darfur has gone significantly beyond the first of Lipton's four phases in the Tragedy of the Commons, in which expansion by any one individual does not affect the rest of the community at all. It may even be that the individual's expansion actually helps the community in some cases. Extending the cropped area has strong positive externalities, for example, in that it drives back the frontier of pests and diseases harboured in uncleared land. It seems highly unlikely that the third phase, in which communal losses are greater than individual gains but not by enough to cover the transactions costs of social management, will be reached in the near future. Once again, therefore, the conclusion is that aid-financed development strategies are 'anticipatory' and attempting to tackle tomorrow's problems, not today's.

The impact of trade on the resource endowment must be underlined. Export demand for gum arabic led to tenure in hashab trees and tenure in cropland is clearly related to quality. Irrigable land is clearly owned and customary ownership of rainfed land is most formally expressed in the major groundnut growing area. For this reason, the economic compression that has stifled development over recent years will also stifle developments in tenture.

The belief in the perils of overstocking and overcultivation has shown the most extraordinary persistence in the face of a signal lack of convincing evidence. Soil erosion became an issue in East Africa as early as the 1930s and in Sudan a Soil Conservation Committee was set up in 1942. This was followed by a Rural Water Supplies and Soil Conservation Board complete with five-year plan and executive staff. As early as 1955, however, the perennial complaint was raised that 'the recommendations of the committee were abandoned due to the circumstances of time and to the persuasive [*sic*: pervasive ?] influence of engineers' (Adams, 1982).

In Darfur, the strategies of the 1980s were already being tried 30 years and more earlier. Without significant success. In 1950 a co-ordinated pilot range programme in Rizeiqat territory was proposed and implemented. This involved fire-lines and controlled access to water supplies enforced by the leadership of the tribe and it was based on grazing improvements, 'with more popular measures being used as a lever to gain the acceptance of less popular ones' (Adams, 1982). In all essentials this was exactly the same programme as was being proposed in 1976 and, on a much reduced scale, implemented in the 1980s in the Bani Halba area south-west of Nyala.

Various reasons were given for the scheme's failure, but these begged the central question. Why were the Rizeiqat, one of the most powerful and cohesive tribes in Sudan, unable to carry out for themselves any part of the programme without the government encouragement that evaporated after 1956, despite the fact that the 'scheme enjoyed the full support of the Rizeiqat'? (Adams, 1982). Just as in the 1980s, the participants' support for the scheme did not remotely match their stated enthusiasm for it. In both cases the suspicion occurs that enthusiasm for the scheme reflected its potential as a weapon in local political competition, not any great belief in its technical merits.

Water supply was another never-ending debate. 'Despite the handful of technical staff involved and the close contact they maintained, there appears to have been little agreement on the purpose of, or the necessity for, a water supply programme for cattle in southern Darfur. Differences of opinion between the Water Supplies and Soil Conservation Board and the Veterinary Section and the Range Section were to recur in the post-Independence era.' . . . 'Accurate information on numbers of animals, seasonal occupance and movements, pasture resources and carrying capacity was not available. This gave the narrow professional interests involved too much room for manoeuvre.' . . . 'After independence, differences of opinion between engineers and land-use specialists became increasingly disruptive to planned change in Western Sudan . . . There was a general absence of practical solutions to the problems of over-stocking and over-cultivation. As a result the relatively straightforward engineering functions of water supply gained priority over land-use planning which required consultation with local people as well as with other departments' (Adams, 1982).

This description appears to match exactly Chambers's ideas of biases and barriers between professional cultures compounded by inadequate knowledge and a lack of consideration for local people's needs. Unfortunately, 15 years of effort to remove such obstacles have not resulted in any apparent advance in understanding, let alone in any development technologies that have proved their worth in action. With hindsight, it is clear that the inability of the different professional interests to agree reflected the fact that the problem under discussion was not relevant. If the 'pervasive influence of engineers' usually won the argument it was because the non-engineers were repeatedly unable to make their case in any concrete way. It should be added that the most pressing expression of local people's requirements took the form of ever more frequent demands for more boreholes to be drilled. Rural People's Knowledge seemed firmly on the side of the engineers.

The engineers prevailed and two major water supply programmes were carried out. In the 1950s *hafirs*, cisterns to collect rainwater, were dug and a major programme of borehole drilling started at the end of the 1960s. The engineers' justification lies in the fact that the borehole wateryard is now a central and vital service to the majority of the people in areas where it would be quite impossible to support the same population without them and south Darfur was enabled to absorb considerable numbers of people from the north without any increase in the cultivation intensity.

What lies behind the power of 'overgrazing', 'overcultivation' and conservation more generally in development thought? Why is it that these ideas, which are attractive and logically consistent but are not supported by the evidence, have proved so persistent? Why have they been considered adequate to justify large aid-financed investments despite the lack of evidence and, latterly, despite a consistent record of failure?

The answer seems to be that in both the colonial and aid eras, a consensus based on superficial observation and elegant theory dominated because it matched the concerns of the western world, regardless of an evident clash with local people's needs as actually expressed in what the local people did. The dominance of western concerns is visible as early as the 1930s. 'Anderson interprets this sequence of growing sensitivity to overstocking and environmental problems in relation to ecological, political and economic factors. A general run of dry years 1926–36 in East Africa; *the impact at this time of the Dust Bowl of North America on the training of generations of agricultural officers worldwide*; the Depression, the growth of African population and the resulting exacerbated competition between white settlers and African producers for both land and markets, all contributed' (Homewood & Rogers in Anderson & Grove, 1987, my italics). A modern version of the same statement would read: 'a prolonged run of dry years and very dry years in the Sahel; the impact at this time of green politics in the western world; an Africa-wide depression, the growth of African population and the resulting exacerbated pressure of African aspirations'. In neither case does firm evidence of environmental degradation come into the equation.

But it is not just a First World bias that makes the Tragedy of the Commons thesis attractive. First and most important, it allows the problems of underdevelopment to be cast in a framework that attributes no blame. After all, the Tragedy is founded on rational economic behaviour; as in all true tragedies, everyone is a hero and no one a villain. Second, it is a fertile ground for academic research and high-technology measurement methods such as remote sensing. These are expensive and so help to 'move the money'. They also allow the 'outsider' to retain a role without any imputation of backwardness to the insiders. No one can be blamed for not knowing the high skills of satellite imaging and both parties can fruitfully co-operate in the transfer of the necessary skills. This happy dream becomes less rosy after a visit to some of the African 'Soil Conservation and Land Use' units where aerial photography equipment and early versions of false colour imagers to interpret Landsat scenes have been gathering dust for up to 15 years.

Most important of all, it has helped to justify expensive development programmes in areas where the scope for any form of aid was extremely limited. Conservation offers at least some intellectually respectable justification for moving the money in regions where the likely development return in hard physical output was small but where the people were among the very poorest and consequently the most deserving of all for aid. The dilemma that aid should not be seen as charity but rather as a source of high rates of return and of growth is particularly strong in environments that are ecologically poor and unproductive. The Tragedy of the Commons offered a way out of that dilemma by seeming to make it possible that the low levels of production were 'correctable' rather than inherent.

Aid's short attention span has also contributed. The issues are extremely complex and no amount of technology can substitute for long experience. The earlier colonial concerns with environmental issues might have developed under the pressure of experience into a more fruitful understanding. After independence they were rejected, ostensibly because all aspects of the colonial legacy were rejected at that time. After ten or twenty years they were picked up again as the African nations became more dependent on the west once again. The result was that the colonial prescription was in some ways fossilized. It is only now after some twenty years of re-applying it that the thought even begins to occur that perhaps the newly independent African nations did right to reject it. Their reasons were mostly political, perhaps, but they could also recognize that the conservation policies of their colonial masters had shown little in the way of tangible results – a statement that remains true of the 'new conservationism' today. In short, some development ideas can be so attractive that they will be put into practice well before the evidence to support them is adequate, and their momentum can be so great that they remain current long after evidence to suggest that they are not working becomes compelling.

In Lipton's model, population growth leads first into and then ultimately out of the Tragedy of the Commons. That happens in Phase 4, when 'losses exceed gains enough that the light-grazing solution produces so much more total herd output than the heavy-grazing solution that the difference suffices to pay the cost of social institutions to ensure the light-grazing solution.' Lipton explicitly rejects, however, the idea that the answer is 'on Boserup lines, more population growth into Phase 4'. His grounds for doing so are partly that, even in Phase 4, it might be impossible to police free riders, which is to say that the social institutions will fail even when they can be paid for, and partly that there might be some catastrophic 'threshold' that the system would fall over before the institutions began to take effect. In other words the degradation caused before Phase 4 became fully operational would be irreversible or extremely costly to repair. He acknowledges that such 'thresholds' might not be very common and his first argument also depends on rather special cases.

Almost since the beginning of the colonial era, Machakos district in Kenya has been considered an area vulnerable to overpopulation and environmental degradation. A very important recent study of environmental change since the 1930s nevertheless concluded that 'the general Boserupian hypothesis has been validated in Machakos but there is a difficult early stage in population growth when natural resources come under acute pressure. Continuing population growth, in association with market development, has generated new technologies which have supported both increased productivity and improved conservation of the land and water resources.' (Boserup herself predicted that 'difficult early stage'.) High value cash crops sold to urban and export markets played an important role in raising productivity and in generating local demand for consumer goods and services. Transport was also important but even 'the trunk routes which from the beginning of the century traversed an area of low population density did not stimulate the growth of urban centres until population growth pushed settlement in their vicinity in the 1970s.' One last crucial point from the study was that 'policies that raise farm-gate prices are probably the single most important action required from governments that want to encourage soil and water conservation and the maintenance of the productivity of the agricultural resource base' (Tiffen, 1992). The evidence from Darfur matches this analysis word for word. The only possible conclusion is that the problems of conservation and development as a whole would indeed be best tackled by growing into and then through the problem, exactly on the Boserup model. It should be remembered that the American Dust Bowl did not greatly hinder the progress of what is now the richest economy in the world. On the contrary, a great deal of modern land-use technology springs from the experience that was gained in dealing with the problems of that era. Without minimizing the human misery of the Dust Bowl during the Depression, the ecological degradation was not irreversible and the process of rehabilitation itself paid big rewards in the lessons learnt. In short, real answers need real questions and it only by 'growing into' the problems that those questions can be put.

5· STATE WITHOUT ROOTS

> 'The real danger posed by state socialism in a society with fragile institutions is not a danger of making the government too strong but the risk of making it more conspicuously ineffectual.' Ali Mazrui (Clapham, 1991)

In 1983, Sudan was receiving $35 per capita in aid, compared with $19 for the whole of sub-Saharan Africa. By 1989, Sudan's arrears in debt repayments to the IMF alone were over $1 billion. Total debt was many times greater. The civil war between the north and south of the country flared up again in 1983 and eight years later, in 1991, there seemed little or no hope of a settlement. Even within the Muslim north of the country, political change seemed always to mean no change. Whatever the regime, the state appeared to lack all capacity to deal with any one of the problems facing it. A series of natural disasters such as drought and flood only emphasized this incapacity. There was a stark contrast with the high hopes at independence in 1956, when the Sudan's political problems were obvious but the economy was strong and government revenues were both high and more broadly based than in most other African countries. 'Few who had witnessed the Sudan's independence had predicted an easy future, but few too had foreseen such a grim one' (Daly, 1991).

There were many continuities between the colonial and independence eras. The most important was the extent of state involvement in the economy. Despite lip-service to laissez-faire, the colonial state had a direct stake in all major enterprises: irrigation, railways, hotels and others. By the late 1930s, the British Governor of Equatoria was able to argue with all seriousness that Sudan was 'a country where state socialism is practicable and to some extent actual' (Daly, 1985). To a considerable degree, however, the government had no choice. Direct taxation was both difficult and for a newly established, conquering state, politically very risky. Indirect taxation was squeezed, through the sugar monopoly for example, but it was only through direct investment that government could really expand its revenue base. If the post-independence state was interventionist, then it had ample precedent from the Condominium period and a ready-made base from which to start.

The largest and most famous of all the direct investments made by the colonial state was the Gezira irrigation scheme. Even before the First World War, the government of Sudan was lobbying in England for loans to establish the scheme in the peninsula (ar Gezira) between the White and Blue Niles. Although delayed by the war, the scheme went ahead immediately after it and was inaugurated in 1925. The Gezira was founded on cotton, and it was the Lancashire cotton industry which had provided much of the political and financial backing in the United Kingdom. After early success, blackarm disease, leaf curl and poor weather coincided disastrously with the 1930s Depression. For many years after that the national economy was hampered by pressure to pay off the debts incurred in building the Gezira.

There were also important differences. One was financial discipline. Like the independent Sudan, the colonial government was almost always dependent on foreign subventions but it was also under constant and intense pressure to reduce them. It had its own strong incentives to do so, as the only way to escape the interference of the twin colonial powers: Egypt and Britain. The result was that the colonial financial secretaries were bywords for parsimony; men who would 'count the knives and forks'. In addition, the modern tricks of deficit finance had yet to be invented. The contrast with the independence era is acute. If, however, the colonial state had survived into the 1960s, it might well have taken up the cheap capital that was offered and the respectable advice of the economists of that time – to increase investment and diversify away from export crops – just as eagerly as the independent Sudanese government did. As early as the 1930s there was a significant minority in the Sudan Political Service, the élite of British colonial administrators, advocating very similar policies (Daly, 1991).

The most important discontinuity, however, concerns performance. For all its failings and despite a number of spectacular setbacks, the colonial state did preside over a degree of development in Sudan. It may have been inequitable, it may have been slower than it should have been, but the overall trend was upwards: in health, in wealth and in education. The contrast with all except the very earliest years of the independence era is marked. This need not disguise the many faults of colonialism, nor the fact that its successes had much to do with plain luck. The fact, for example, that independence fell just after the Korean war boom in markets for cotton meant that the British left on an economic high-point. 'Ironically and significantly, the post-war boom had already run its course on the eve of the Sudanese self-government in 1953, and a legacy of rising expectations was left to the post-independence regime' (Daly, 1991).

Even the rainfall seems to have been on the side of the Condominium. Out of 35 years since independence, total rainfall was above average in only ten, compared with 33 out of 53 in the colonial period; the ratio of good to bad years was almost exactly reversed (Figure 4.1). The Sudanese blamed the 1984 drought on the Numeiri regime and similar thoughts were being voiced about Omar El Bashir in 1991. If rainfall is truly the measure of political legitimacy then it seems clear who are God's chosen rulers for the Sudan; and it is neither Structural Adjustment nor the Islamic Front.

Spending the Reserves

The relationship embodied in the Anglo-Egyptian Condominium of Sudan was so extraordinary that it was bound to collapse as soon as Britain's control over Egypt was weakened or there was serious opposition within the Sudan; an opposition which would find it easy to exploit the divisions between the Co-Domini. By the end of the 1940s, events were moving rapidly on both these fronts and Sudan became the first colonial African state to win independence on Flag Day, 1 January 1956 (Daly, 1991).

The Second World War had already seen a recovery in the Sudanese economy, stimulated by the needs of the British armies in Egypt. The post-war boom was even greater. 'A regular but none the less paradoxical feature of Gezira economics was that production seemed always to vary with price. Both withered in 1931; both shot up in 1951.' Between 1946 and 1951 cotton yields doubled: from 3.4 *kantars* per *feddan* to 6.8 (Henderson, 1965). The result was that government revenue in 1951/2 was ten times that of the pre-war period and three times that of only three years before. After the long years of economy during the depression, the government's surplus was £S3 million greater than its total expenditure. The political pressures to unleash the economy were only increased by the knowledge that government had built up large reserves during the bad years. Once the Gezira debts were paid off, as they soon were, the pressure to spend this 'embarrassment of riches' was impossible to resist (Daly, 1991). As a result, a more liberal approach to development was already under way some years before independence.

More ominously, several newly powerful interest groups proved able to force government to give in over pay and taxation during the same period.

The first five-year development programme was set in progress in 1946. The second, starting in 1951, was considerably more ambitious, reflecting the rapid increase in revenues. Expenditure on the two programmes together totalled £S50 million: between a fifth and a quarter of total government expenditure annually. Rehabilitation was necessary to make up for repair and maintenance that had been postponed during the war. Nevertheless, the major part of this expenditure was on new developments. Much was concentrated on the towns and the more developed areas of riverine Sudan and on productive 'sure bets', such as further expansion of cotton and the railways. To some this is evidence of a missed opportunity: 'not enough [was spent] on experimentation. Almost no attention was paid to developing an industrial sector' (Daly, 1991). Indeed, almost all the themes of later development debates are evident in this, the most early period in which a planned development effort was undertaken: exports versus import substitution, saving versus consumption, urban versus rural, modern versus traditional, and so on.

But in fact the government had little choice. The balance of expenditure was already being determined by political considerations, by the need to buy off powerful groups: the provision of better than average social services to the Gezira in order to ensure a 'satisfied tenantry', for example. And satisfied the tenant certainly should have been. In 1951, the profit per tenancy was £S800 and a British satirist wrote:

> Half-starved tenant in his Standard Vanguard
> Mowing down a passing herd of tick-thick goats,
> With a cargo of scent bottles, tooth sticks, prayer-mats,
> Petitions to the Governor and Ten Pound Notes.
> ('Masefield in the Gezira', quoted in Henderson, 1965)

Government attempts to maintain saving, through increased import and export duties and staggered payments to Gezira tenants, failed in the face of this pressure to consume. Private savings were equally deficient and signs of impending economic problems made a rapid appearance. The cost of living index, from a base of 100 in 1938, reached 307 in 1949 – an inflation of 11 per cent per annum. In 1951 the index for low-paid Sudanese rose by 29 per cent in that one year alone. Between 1946 and 1955, imports rose from £S11.4 million to £S 48.8 million:

17.5 per cent per annum. Much of this increase went on consumer goods. Sugar accounted for up to 9 per cent of the import bill, coffee, tea and tobacco were also important, but the largest item of all was textiles. All these commodities were, in theory at least, capable of being produced in Sudan, possibly marking a missed opportunity for import substitution when 'demand was incessant and the government awash with money to invest' (Daly, 1991).

Government was not awash with money for long. Its hard-won position of financial ease was rapidly eroded. One particularly ominous sign was the consolidation in 1950 of cost of living allowances for government employees into their basic pay and, hence, into their pensions. Inflation was so rapid that an adjustment was inevitable, but the close interaction between government service pay and nationalist politics set a pattern that was to be repeated many times in the future. Heavy development expenditure was another factor. From 1955 onwards, the development schemes planned 'depended not only on large anticipated [revenue] surpluses but on £E 45 million [Egyptian pounds] in foreign loans or grants.' Government foreign exchange reserves fell in every year after 1951 and 'by 1955 the Sudanese public were living on credit.' The last factor was the end of the post-war boom itself. The value of cotton exports peaked in 1951 and did not reach the same level until 1968 (Daly, 1991).

Also significant was the first of many futile attempts to fight international markets in defence of those expectations. By 1956, the Sudan Gezira Board was already in difficulties over marketing the cotton crop. By abandoning its traditional UK buyer in favour of auctioning the crop and by setting unrealistic reserve prices, it failed to sell an increasing proportion of the cotton. By 1958, it had the equivalent of the whole season's crop unsold and this was in a year when production had not been especially high (Henderson, 1965).

Two important private sector activities expanded shortly after independence: irrigated pump schemes and mechanized farms. Pump schemes rose from 244 in 1939 to 1,331 in 1954 (Barnett & Abdelkarim, 1988). As a result, 27 per cent of the national cotton acreage in 1956 was in private schemes, which held this share until the late 1960s, keeping pace with a considerable expansion of the public sector acreage after independence (Beshai, 1976). The government introduced tractors to grow sorghum on the rainlands at the end of the Second World War and the area planted expanded very rapidly. By 1956, 388,000 *feddan*s were under cultivation and this expansion has continued ever since. The area in 1973/4 was 3,186,000 *feddans*: a growth rate of about 14 per cent per annum for nearly two decades (Lees & Brooks, 1977). By 1985 it had reached around 9 million (ILO, 1987).

State patronage was an important element in both activities. Land rents were low and credit was offered. After the cotton boom, the foreign commercial banks became relatively reluctant to finance pump schemes and the Agricultural Bank was established to fill the gap. Government did the land clearance for the mechanized farms and here too finance was provided through the Agricultural Bank (Mahmoud, 1984).

Breadbasket to Basket Case

If the pattern of the problems to come was set immediately after independence or even somewhat before, the major acceleration came in the mid-1960s. Figure 5.1 shows the budgetary position from 1961 onwards. At no stage was government out of deficit, although it briefly came close in the early 1970s. Initially, the deficit was linked to development expenditure and it rose to a peak in relation to GDP surprisingly early, in the 1960s. It was not to go as high again for another 15 years. At this stage, current expenditure was mostly kept well within the bounds of revenue. The turning-point came in 1978/79 when current expenditure exploded. Spending on development, however inefficient, did at least offer a hope of a return in the future. From 1978 even the hope was gone. Development expenditure relative to GDP never returned to the level of 1963/64.

For almost all the period, the state's share of the economy was growing. During the 1960s there was considerable public investment in new irrigation schemes and many other sectors; investments which should have at least maintained government's non-tax revenues. Instead, an 'increasing share of the surpluses generated on the new as well as the existing schemes drifted away from the control of the state sector' (Brown, 1990: Ch 3). The élite, the 'indigenous agricultural entrepreneurs', were major beneficiaries, but other powerful groups also gained: notably the tenants on the irrigation schemes and organized labour in the government services.

The May revolution of 1969 brought Ja'afar Numeiri to power. Initially there was a fairly determined effort to raise government revenue. There was widespread nationalization, including the entire banking system. Other measures included dual exchange rates, which was in effect another indirect tax on cotton and other exports, substantial extra levies and excise duties, and increased direct taxes (ILO, 1976: Ch 13).

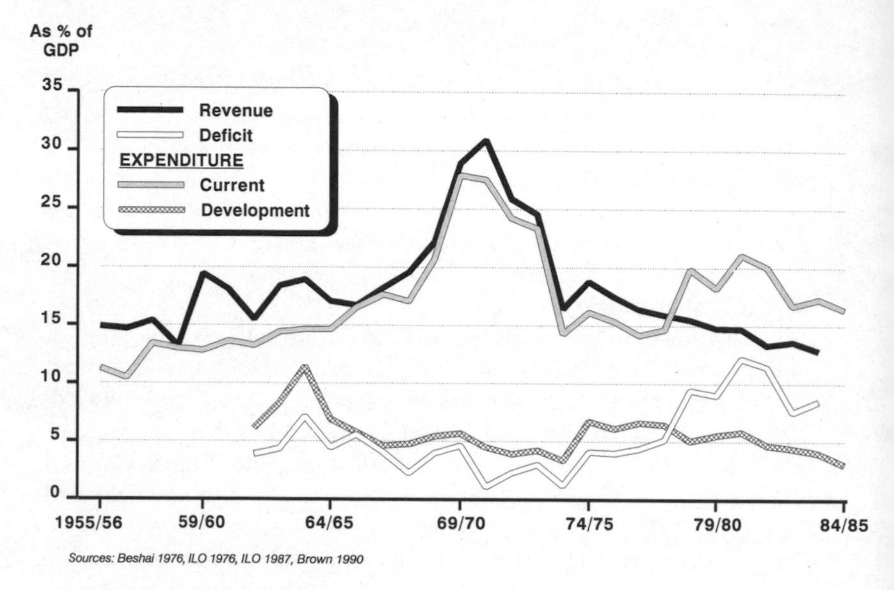

Figure 5.1 Government of Sudan, Revenue, Deficit & Expenditure – 1955/56 to 1984/85

It was significant that the solution was to raise revenue despite the fact that the budgetary problem had arisen from a rapid expansion in expenditure. Despite some reduction in the fiscal deficit, by far the larger part of the revenue increase was absorbed by higher current expenditure (Figure 5.1).

And even that minor fiscal improvement was not maintained, being 'politically unsustainable'. The IMF had to be called in for the fourth time in 1972. Shortly afterwards, the rise of OPEC set off a surge of petrodollar investment in Sudan, to turn its supposedly limitless natural resources into the breadbasket of the Arab world. Its true effect was to postpone the day of reckoning. The ' "breadbasket" funds perhaps offered only temporary respite to the regime, from the impending fiscal crisis and balance of payments crisis that was further exacerbated by the external shock of the 1973/74 oil price hike.' Both the beginning and the end of this breadbasket era were astonishingly rapid. The peak came in 1974, when actual disbursements of foreign borrowings rose to $460 million: an increase of more than 300 per cent over the previous year.

Only three years later it was all over. Between 1974 and 1977, when disbursements declined again, nearly $2.5 billion had been borrowed (Brown, 1990: Ch 3).

The short life of the breadbasket reflected the lenders' rapid realization that the projects were turning out far more expensive and slow to implement than had been hoped. A shortage of complementary local resources and heavy cost overruns led to a mounting backlog of unfinished and non-operational projects. Direct corruption also took its toll of both the money and the lenders' patience. The effect on government's own finances was disastrous. It had devoted most of its own investment resources to the breadbasket schemes, at the expense of its principal revenue base: the older agricultural schemes and other established sectors of the economy. Unlike the previous decade, import duties and other consumption taxes did not make up for the decline in revenues from export producing schemes and from export duties.

The reasons for the decline in export revenues, especially from cotton, were much the same in both the 1960s and 1970s; both areas and yields fell, not because of any change in world markets but because of increasing disincentives inside Sudan. Internationally, the terms of trade for Sudan's long-staple cotton remained relatively steady till after 1978. Domestically, on the other hand, the tenant's share of the cotton profit, raised to 50 per cent in the 1960s, was reduced to 40 per cent again. The multiple exchange rate system imposed a further implicit tax on cotton. The fact that all the costs of the irrigation schemes were charged to the cotton crop alone acted not only as a disincentive but as an increasing one; as less of the crop was grown, the greater the costs to be borne by the cotton area that was left, making the disincentive even greater. By 1978, these pressures had reduced cotton to only 30 per cent of the cropped area on the Gezira, down from 40 per cent a decade earlier and nearly 60 per cent at independence (Brown, 1990: Ch 3).

As early as 1976, Sudan had begun to default on debt service payments and by late 1979 the country was $1.2 billion in arrears: 150 per cent of total export earnings. The breadbasket funds inevitably dried up and government was forced to borrow more and more from the Sudan's own banking system to meet its deficit. Government financing from the Central Bank leapt from £S4 million in 1972/72 to £S173 million in 1977/78. Money supply grew through the 1970s at around 30 per cent per annum and inflation followed at 20 per cent. Exports were down from 16 per cent of GDP in 1970/71 to 8 per cent in 1977/78 (Brown, 1990: Ch 3).

In the real economy, the list of depressing statistics is endless. Between 1967 and 1978, real household expenditure in Greater Khartoum declined by a third. For cotton, 'In international markets the view is of a disorganised and unreliable Sudanese cotton marketing policy.' In 1971, Sudan had half the world's trade in sesame. By 1983, it only had a quarter. For gum arabic, where Sudan had 80 per cent of world trade, it 'took years to recapture markets lost [to substitutes] when a high export price was set for the 1974–75 crop.' In 1972, three million tons of goods were moved on the railways. In the 1980s it was one million tons per year. Rising oil prices should have given the railways a cost advantage, but road transport's share of freight traffic rose from one-third in 1969 to two-thirds in the 1980s (ILO, 1987). 'The one major new cotton scheme of the 1970s, the Rahad scheme on the Blue Nile financed with World Bank support, proved in need of rehabilitation virtually as soon as it was completed' (Woodward, 1990).

Adjustment?

Since the late 1970s, the debate about development in Africa has been dominated by the policies summed up as Structural Adjustment. This title, with its implications of some deep-rooted structural problem, deliberately obscured the central point: that Africa's problem lay principally within government. By 1978 the Sudan was, on every possible measure, a classic case for the Structural Adjustment treatment. High foreign debt, declining government revenue, ballooning government expenditure and a whole range of previously successful export crops in rapid decline. Shifts in the terms of trade, notably the second oil shock of 1978, must have had some effect, but it was impossible not to conclude that Sudan's problems sprang from bad domestic policy and outright bad management.

The distinction between policy and management is important. Foreign debt was a good example. As a matter of policy, the volume of debt taken on by the Sudan is incredible enough, but it is the lack of control that is truly shocking. Virtually any government agency was entitled to organize a foreign loan and so commit the Sudan to repayment without consultation. The result was that the Sudan was 'unable to provide the organizations monitoring its external debt with an adequate list of its creditors, let alone with reliable information on the magnitudes and terms of its borrowings' (Khalid, quoted in Brown, 1990: Ch 1). A debt that was estimated to be $2 billion in 1978 was revised upwards, after investigation by foreign consultants, to $7 billion in 1982 (Brown, 1990:

Ch 1). That it took four years for this fact to even emerge says something about the utter lack of management.

From 1978 to 1984, the Sudan, the IMF and the Sudan's creditors represented in the Paris Club were almost never out of negotiation over debt rescheduling. Five separate agreements were reached. Five separate agreements were suspended, terminated or superseded by the one that came after. A sixth was under negotiation in 1984, but the Sudan was by that time not even able to meet its obligations to the IMF. The failure of these agreements was matched by continued deterioration in the Sudanese economy. In 1978, the current account balance of payments deficit was 7 per cent of GDP and the nominal debt service ratio was 14 per cent. By 1982 an 'imbalance' had turned to bankruptcy. The current account deficit had more than doubled, to 17 per cent of GDP, and the debt service ratio was over 150 per cent. For the people of Sudan, the adjustment years saw per capita income drop from $526 in 1978 to $330 in 1987 (Brown, 1990: Ch 6).

There are two possible interpretations of the dismal performance of the reforms laid down in the IMF agreements; either the adjustment policies were wrong, presumably because the analysis of the problem was also wrong, or they were not applied. On all counts, the evidence points to the second conclusion. The relatively limited devaluations were undermined by the multiple exchange rate system, which was not abolished despite that being a condition of the IMF agreements. By 1984, the exchange rate regime had 'if anything, become more discriminatory and administratively cumbersome and offered those in privileged positions enormous scope for financial gain through illegal dealings in this complicated market' (Brown, 1990: Ch 4).

Most important of all, however, was the fact that the domestic policy changes required to match the devaluations were never implemented, with the result that nominal depreciations of the Sudanese pound barely kept pace with the domestic rate of inflation. By 1984, the real value of the Sudanese pound at official rates was back to, or even above the 1978 level. The cause was not hard to find. Without exception, the fiscal and monetary statistics did not just miss their adjustment targets, they went in the opposite direction. The budget deficit was supposed to be eliminated by 1984. It increased. Money supply was supposed to grow at 16 per cent per annum. It was closer to 30 per cent. Central government's domestic bank borrowing rose at 38 per cent per annum. Even this was not enough to cover the budget deficit. The gap was filled from overseas. 'Effectively, there had been a movement away from domestic borrowing to foreign financing of the government's budgetary deficit, associated with the IMF Extended Fund Facility and increased foreign lending that this unleashed' (Brown, 1990: Ch 4).

As Figure 5.1 shows, this failure did not even reflect a determination on the part of the Sudanese government to maintain a higher level of investment than was compatible with adjustment. Instead it was the result of a huge loss of control over recurrent expenditure, which rose above revenue for the first time since independence, although it had been close to doing so for a long time. A major factor had been the Job Employment and Classification Scheme, implemented at IMF/World Bank instigation in 1978. Far from achieving any rationalization of public sector employment, this led to a large increase in public sector pay (Brown, 1990: Ch 4). Numbers in public service also rose as fast, if not faster than ever. Between 1978 and 1985, central government employees alone increased from 274,941 to 338,354: a rise of over one-fifth for a government supposedly in dire financial difficulties (ILO, 1987: Ch 7).

Nor did the expansion of recurrent expenditure meet valid social needs that might have justified government's failure to take the adjustment medicine. The service government offered deteriorated almost as fast as the numbers employed increased. This combination, of swelling numbers providing a worsening service – this bureaucratic stagflation – saw a growing imbalance between clerical and productive staff. The numbers of white-collar, pensionable employees grew fastest, especially in the parastatal corporations and institutions. Nearly one-third of employees in these supposedly productive organizations were in classified, pensionable posts. A UNIDO survey of 1981/2 'indicated that average value added per worker may be four times higher in private companies than in public establishments' (ILO, 1987: Ch 7).

The second factor behind the stagflation was a gross imbalance between expenditure on staff and expenditure on complementary costs: materials, fuel, maintenance, depreciation and so on. By 1985, even a relatively sympathetic observer such as the International Labour Organization could only conclude that, 'Deterioration has reached the point that there are serious doubts about the capacity of large areas of government administration to implement necessary policies.' This deterioration was leading to a process of 'creeping privatization' as user fees and contributions to running costs, not to mention outright bribes, became the norm for consumers of government services (ILO, 1987).

The impact of these developments in the public service only became obvious in the macro-economic variables, such as the budget deficiency,

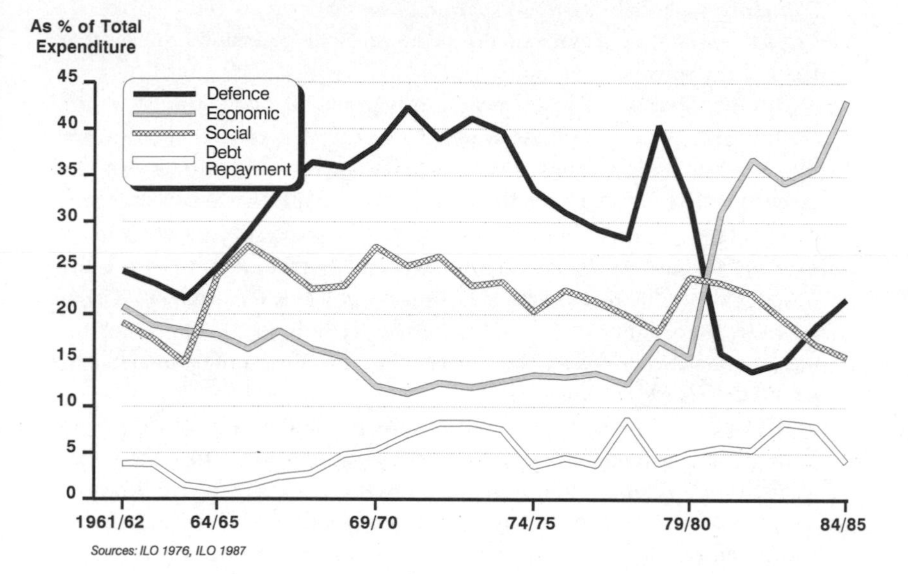

Figure 5.2 Government of Sudan, Current Expenditure by Sector

in the adjustment period. The process of stagflation in government service had started much earlier. 'While the Sudan Government was consistently increasing its employment during the 1960s, it was simultaneously reducing the availability of goods and services to accompany them' (ILO, 1976: Ch 13).

Defence expenditure and debt repayments are often seen as the primary causes of African governments' failure to control their budgets. Between 1964 and 1974 in Sudan, this was true to a degree. The civil war in the south inevitably raised defence expenditure, and debt service was rising well before the breadbasket period. Administration expenditures were also increasing (Figure 5.2). There was a sharp contrast in the Structural Adjustment period when the defence/administration share of government expenditure actually fell sharply, despite the rekindling civil war in southern Sudan. Debt repayment also remained a relatively unimportant item while expenditure on social services was steady. This time it was economic services that saw a big expansion, reflecting the impact of the World Bank-inspired Three Year Public Investment and

Agricultural Rehabilitation Programmes designed to reinvigorate the export production sectors of the economy and government's revenues from those sectors.

In other words, the investment funds provided under the Structural Adjustment programmes were spent exactly as intended, in the productive sectors. The continued miserable performance of exports and government revenues forces the further conclusion that those additional investments completely failed to achieve what was expected of them. As a result the decline in revenue, which had begun in the early 1970s, continued steadily throughout the adjustment years. By 1985/86, current revenues were down to 8 per cent of GDP, only half of government's current expenditure and 'far lower than in most other low income countries' (ILO, 1987: Ch 6).

All these factors were reflected in a major shift in the real economy. 'The general impression is of an economy failing to perform in its key agricultural sector while moving strongly into services where, however, the growth has been of a nature and composition hardly conducive to continued development and least of all to the well-being of those most in need.' The service sector of the economy, which had been slightly less important than primary production in 1973, was 55 per cent larger in 1986 (ILO, 1987: Ch 1).

To sum up, both halves of the Structural Adjustment programme for Sudan were abject failures. On the IMF side, the disciplines of exchange rate, monetary and fiscal reforms were utterly ineffective. On the World Bank side, the investments designed to restore the productive momentum of the economy had only one significant effect. They further undermined government's control over its budget. For the Sudanese economy, the outcome was wholly at odds with the rhetoric of both sides of the debate on Structural Adjustment. Far from it being a major turning-point – towards reform and a return to growth for its proponents, or towards misery and inequity according to its critics – Structural Adjustment was little more than a rearrangement of trends that had been under way since before independence: growing but increasingly ineffective public investment, repeated failures to control staff and other recurrent costs, a steady reduction in the quality of government services, only partly offset by a wider coverage, and a steady decline in government revenues.

The only difference between the three post-independence periods is in the way in which these trends were financed. Between 1956 and 1970, expanding investment and consumption were financed partly out of overseas lending but principally by reducing the surpluses of the last decade of the Condominium; surpluses which included government reserves and the profits of the productive economy. Taxation did not keep up with increasingly ambitious government services. Prices for commercial operations fell behind costs. The labour force, or in the irrigation schemes the tenants, were able to force larger and larger distributions in their favour. The élite invariably sought and gained compensation for their losses from these redistributions. In 1973, just as the scope for squeezing any more out of these surpluses was exhausted, the influx of breadbasket funds allowed the process to be prolonged. Finally, in 1978 when the more commercially-minded investors in the breadbasket lost patience, concessional funds provided under Structural Adjustment programmes took their place and so prolonged the process once again.

It has been suggested that the IMF, the World Bank and the rest of the aid community are, by their very nature, bound to be paper tigers, unable ever to actually wield the stick of leverage that they purport to carry. This seems all too evident in the Sudanese case. The very word 'adjustment' carries the idea that the both the problem to be tackled and the solutions required are temporary, and this is the weak point in the donor agencies' armour. Just as adjustment is temporary, so is the leverage. The Sudanese government, once it recognizes that fact, takes little risk in accepting loans, ostensibly to cover the costs of adjustment but in fact as the price of policy reform, and in failing to maintain reform afterwards. 'A temporary reward is a recipe for temporary liberalisation' (Collier, 1991).

The international agencies also have no defence against a government that claims adjustment reforms are 'politically unsustainable'. By presenting the 1982 sugar price riots in Khartoum as more disastrous than they really were, the Sudan government was able to persuade the IMF to renegotiate yet again 'having only shortly before suspended the Extended Fund Facility' (Brown, 1990: Ch 4). By the standards of more violent societies the damage done was slight, just as the rise in the price of sugar was slight compared to what was to happen later without provoking a riot. In short, the Sudanese government had more leverage over the IMF, the World Bank and the rest of the aid agencies than vice versa.

If government held the whip hand in its dealings with the aid community, it was increasingly unable to control its own people in order to regain budgetary and economic control. Many of the central features have already been described: the failure to resist the demands of tenants on the irrigation schemes, the loss of control over civil service pay, diminishing returns from state enterprises reflecting a similar inability to resist the demands of the work-force and subsidies to the mechanized farm sector are just some examples. Many others could be added. Ironically, the colonial state had paved the way for much of this because the machinery of that state was turned inside out. A system that had developed out of the need to raise government revenue was converted into a mechanism for distributing government benefits. The government sugar monopoly, established as a means of taxation, became a system for the provision of subsidized sugar rations. As time went by, more and more commodities were added to the ration list. By 1989, even the one consumer good that the Sudanese private sector had proved more than capable of producing in abundance, edible oil, became a rationed good for a while. Condominium civil servants were given subsidized housing or cheap loans to build their own. This perquisite, combined with the government control over the distribution of land also inherited from the colonial state, led naturally into civil servants' participation in real estate speculation after independence. 'Civil servants in government housing found it easy to raise loans and join in.' Education under the Condominium was concentrated on the needs of the government services. This led to events like the 'distribution of jobs to hundreds of graduates before the 1968 elections in an effort to boost the Unionist vote' (Woodward, 1990).

All the above may be grouped under the heading of policy-based patronage as opposed to management-based patronage. Although the driving force was to buy political acquiescence with benefits, those benefits were distributed through legitimate channels and by the implementation of policies which may have been mistaken, but were neither illegal nor dishonest. Management-based patronage, which was just as widespread, ranged from legal 'inefficiencies', such as the appeasement of employees by lax discipline and overmanning, through to many kinds of outright corruption. Here, too, the colonial institutions of economic control provided much of the machinery, especially licences. In commerce, 'The acquisition of licences has been the top entrepreneurial concern.' There was widespread 'pseudo-investment' to qualify for licences (ILO, 1987: Ch 4). The supply of subsidized commodities also created shortages and wide scope for patronage and speculation. There has rarely been a time in Sudan when there have not been rumours of vast warehouses full of basic consumer commodities such as tomato paste and sugar.

It has been suggested that what would be considered corruption in the modern world is more leniently viewed at all levels of Sudanese society. Within the tribes of western Sudan, respect for government does not depend on its honesty but on its power. The word *haramy*, which is derived from the religious term for 'sin' and is used for all forms of dishonesty, sums up the attitude. 'It is not a bad thing to be Haramy and to use what power you have to try to effect transfers of wealth to your own person.' . . . 'Nazirs [tribal leaders] are Haramy, the [colonial] Government is too.' At the same time, accusations of dishonesty are legitimate ammunition in political struggles over tribal leadership. Under the Condominium, charges of corruption against members of the Native Administration, especially over the distribution of rationed sugar, were a favourite weapon by those intriguing for posts in the same administration (Cunnison, 1966: Ch 8). In national politics the pattern was almost exactly the same. Frequent resort to accusations of corruption as a political weapon only served to obscure what seemed to be a widespread, albeit covert, consensus that it is not particularly dishonest. Some have even argued that corruption has almost become an institution, the 'Fifth Factor of Production' (Kameir & Kursany, 1985).

Apparent political differences within the élite were misleading. Under the military regime, both the son of the spiritual leader of the National Unionist Party and three members of the Islamic Charter Front, the Muslim Brothers' political party, were on the board of the same corporation (Kameir & Kursany, 1985). In the democratic coalition government formed in May 1988, 18 ministers out of a total of 25 'had served as national or regional ministers under Numeiri'. 'Northern Sudan's healing social relations at the elite level once more assured that there was little by way of a purge in most ministries, and it soon became clear [after the 1985 coup] that a general return to the old corrupt ways was taking place' (Woodward, 1990).

To explain these patterns, some argue that the colonial legacy has irrevocably distorted Sudanese society. Divide and rule has created a pattern of meaningless competition over the spoils of the state. Others lay the blame on the 'hurried transformation of the state into a series of service-orientated ministries' at independence, which gave rise to 'the symptoms of an "overdeveloped" and "soft" Third World state'. Yet another view emphasizes the Numeiri era, 'that transformed an inert party system into one of Africa's longer running personal, clientilistic regimes . . . ultimately, in seeking to deconstruct what had been central to political life hitherto, it created little of lasting substance as a replacement. Whereas the liberal-democratic system had rested on relatively stable, if selective social bases in northern Sudan, in moving away from those, Numeiri had turned towards new ideological and institutional forms, and in doing so he showed up the grave problems inherent in such attempts' (Woodward, 1990).

One feature is evident throughout. Patronage in Sudan is not the prerogative of a small, all-powerful élite who are exploiting a position of unchallenged political power to their own benefit. On the contrary, patronage is the only way of maintaining a very weak form of political power. The management of patronage is the fundamental skill of politics, a skill practised by everyone from the tribal sheikh to the president. Even before independence, 'the loyalty of southern MPs depended on subsidies' (Daly, 1991). It was for this reason that the impact of outside intervention, whether it was the commercial lending of the breadbasket or the Structural Adjustment package, was very different from that planned. 'The importance of the Gulf Arab states' money in the end lay less in its contribution to Sudan's economic development than in the resources it provided for the exercise of clientilist politics' (Woodward, 1990). 'Access to these [breadbasket] funds and the lucrative contracts associated with them was enjoyed by a relatively wide group of well-placed senior civil servants, politicians and others who the Nimeiry government depended on for its support' (Brown, 1990: Ch 3). And if government appeased the élite through the allocation of commodity aid, import licences and the like, it appeased its workforce through continued wage drift and it appeased the general public, albeit less generously, through subsidies.

If the state depended on patronage for its survival then it depended on foreign money to finance that patronage. As early as 1976, 'The state, although not the subsistence sector of the economy, is dependent on outside support for survival' (J. Waterbury, quoted in Woodward, 1990). By 1983/84, 79 per cent of the deficit was funded externally (Brown, 1990: Ch 4). Commodity aid was particularly important. In the 1985/86 budget, it was planned that commodity aid would finance half the total deficit (ILO, 1987: Ch 6). The Sudan had moved full circle from the early years of the Condominium, when the state was equally dependent on external finance, from Egypt, for its survival.

If, however, the state was dependent on foreign money to finance its patronage, it was quite unable to accept the reforming conditions that were supposed to be attached to that money. To do so would destroy the very same patronage. The fact, for example, that the exchange rate was so critical to the system of patronage played a major part in the government's unwillingness, inability even, to implement the central policy of the whole adjustment programme: 'maintaining a multiple exchange rate system plays an important role in deciding who is to enjoy privileged access to such resources (Brown, 1990: Ch 4).

Brain Drain and Capital Flight

In 1986, the real value of the minimum wage in Sudan was only 16 per cent of what it had been in 1970. Driven by the growing poverty of Sudan and drawn by the wealth of OPEC, every Sudanese now dreams of migration. And, because they are hard-working, skilled, pleasant, Arabic-speaking Muslims, the Sudanese are in demand. In 1986 it was estimated that two-thirds of Sudan's professional and skilled work-force was overseas, predominantly in the oil exporting states of the Arabian peninsula (ILO, 1987: Ch 9). There have been various estimates of the numbers of Sudanese nationals working abroad: 45,000 in 1979 up to 200,000 or even 500,000 by 1983. In the mid-1980s, 350,000 was a conservative estimate. And the result was that 'Sudan's recorded and unrecorded remittances together would have been sufficient to support three times the value of officially recorded imports' (Brown, 1990: Ch 6).

These estimates raise a whole flock of questions about what is happening in the Sudanese economy. Why, if these vast sums are remitted, can Sudan not pay for its imports and why is the supply of imports so restricted? Why is the real value of the Sudanese pound under constant pressure? Why does inflation continue to run at high levels? Why do government revenues continue to decline? According to Brown, the answer lies in grossly distorted markets that allow the extraction of very high 'rents' which are then lost in capital flight. Sudan's balance of payment problems therefore spring not from excess demand for imports, reflected in the current account, but in excess demand for foreign assets on the capital account. After the coup in 1985, it was estimated that some $15 billion of capital had been exported from Sudan between 1978 and 1986: as much as a quarter or even a half of all capital exports from sub-Saharan Africa. 'The estimated unrecorded export of capital from Sudan in 1983/84 comes to $2.6 billion, or more than twice the level of the country's net foreign borrowing in that year.' . . . 'In reality Sudan is a net exporter of capital' and 'Sudan ceases to be a net debtor in that the estimated value of its privately held foreign assets far exceeds the recorded value of its publicly held foreign debts' (Brown, 1990: Ch 6). The extraordinary nature of this conclusion bears underlining; the biggest debtor of the international community in Africa, the country with the largest single outstanding debt to the IMF, is in fact a net exporter of capital.

Regional Government

The patterns of bureaucratic stagflation were matched at the regional and lower levels. Devolution policies made the situation worse rather than better. 'The Peoples Local Government act of 1971 vested responsibility for administering all central government services except the judiciary, defence, communications, foreign affairs and banking in the People's Executive Councils at provincial level' (Davey, 1976). This was not accompanied by recognition of the extra cost. The number of rural councils was increased from 86 to 500, but the Ministry of Local Government explicitly instructed that the new system of People's Local Government should not involve the national government in any increased financial burden. In 1981, there was once again 'no radical reappraisal of National/Sub-National financial distribution with the implementation of regionalism' (Shepherd *et al.*, 1987: Ch 6).

The result was that while it was burdened with ever-increasing responsibilities, local government's share of total government expenditure actually decreased. In 1955, local government spent one-third of all government expenditure. By 1967, that share had been halved, to only 17 per cent. On the revenue side of the account, local government was more or less self-sufficient in 1955. By 1966/67, it received nearly 80 per cent of its resources as a grant from the centre (Howell, 1974). Both in share of expenditure and the degree of dependence on central government grants, the pattern set in the mid-1960s continued into the 1980s, when even the Gezira, the most productive province of all, drew 72 per cent of its budget from the centre (Shepherd *et al.*, 1987: Ch 6). Darfur drew over 90 per cent.

Financial dependence undermined the whole concept of devolution. Local budgets were increasingly liable to savage cuts as a result of the national government's own financial difficulties (Davey, 1976). In the end, the whole budgetary process became nearly meaningless. By the mid-1980s, financial control had collapsed to such an extent that national Ministry of Finance officials had no information on Darfur regional expenditure except the amount paid as central government grant each year. Regional accounts had not been audited for some eight years. In

Kordofan it was concluded that 'The concept of the finance of an operating Department or Agency being the means of its achieving some programmed objectives [was], to say the least, obscured' (Shepherd *et al.*, 1987: Ch 6).

Local councils also failed to live up to their new responsibilities. It made political sense to avoid raising local taxes by pressing central government for increased aid and 'For many of the councillors, "participation" involved, above all, the opportunity to make demands on the Government, as well as the higher councils' (Howell, 1974).

Government budgets in Sudan are divided into three chapters. Chapter One is for wages and salaries, Chapter Two for running costs and Chapter Three (a) for repair and maintenance. Chapter Three (b) is for 'development' funds and is the channel for foreign aid money for regional projects and for matching central government funds. However, large projects like the two integrated development projects in south Darfur are financed directly from Khartoum and outside regional government's responsibility – a particularly fruitful source of jealousy and noncooperation.

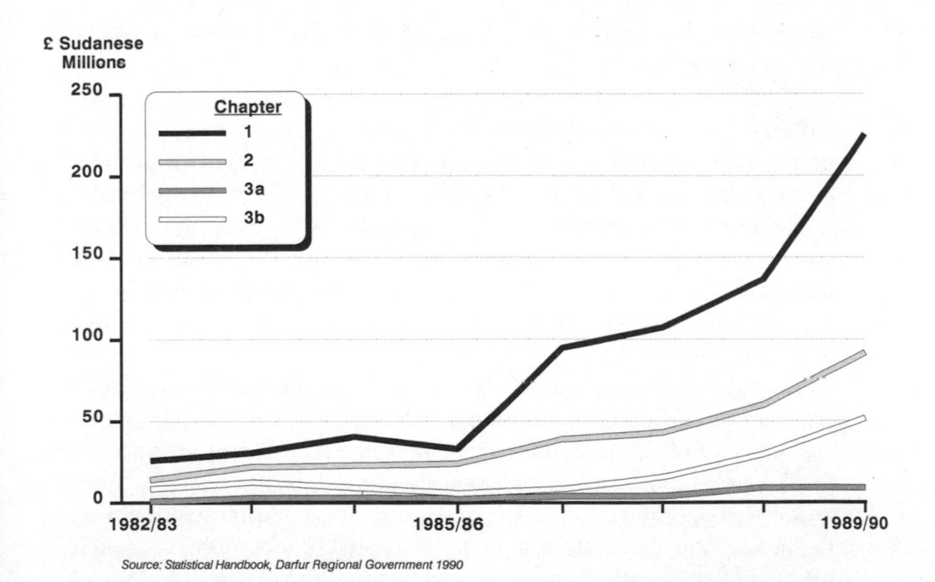

Figure 5.3 Darfur Regional Government, Budget by Chapters of Expenditure

Figure 5.3 graphs the four budget headings for the period 1982/83 to 1989/90. The acceleration of Chapter One after 1985–6 is most striking, but the desperate inadequacy of Chapter Three, for repair and maintenance, tells the most important part of the story. It should be emphasized that these are budget figures. Actual expenditures are not known. Any shortfall in receipts or overspends on staff had to be met by raiding Chapters Two and Three. In 1985 the regional government was in the process of trying to bring the payroll back under control. At the time it appeared that the number of staff was as much as 7.5 per cent over budget and that a further 12 per cent were being paid at grades higher than those shown in the budget, which explains the jump in Chapter One for 1986/87. Unfortunately, any improvement in control was temporary as the continued acceleration of Chapter One shows.

These figures do not mean that staff were overpaid. By the early 1980s government pay rates were deeply unattractive. They do not even necessarily mean that the regional government was overstaffed relative to its ambitious responsibilities, although the ratio of one state employee for well under 200 people seems very high in an area where very many inhabitants neither receive anything from nor give anything to the state. Above all, it must be stressed that these budget figures are no indication that the regional government actually received anything like the sums planned, 'money frequently being unavailable despite its formal authorisation (Shepherd *et al.*, 1987: Ch 6).

Although they are not supposed to be, the expenditure chapters are closely linked to the revenue sources. The size of the central government grant to the region is almost entirely determined by the Chapter One requirement. 'In view of the inflexible character of salary payments this is not surprising. Scales are set down nationally, and the reduction of staff to any radical extent is politically and socially inadmissible, offering little room for manoeuvre' (Shepherd *et al.*, 1987: Ch 6). Chapters Two and Three (a) are left dependent on local revenue and they are the first to suffer when central government is looking for economies. Chapter Three (b), on the other hand, is protected by the fact that if central government reduces its contribution the matching foreign aid funds may also be reduced. Because these development expenditures are intended for the creation of new capital assets they automatically create yet more burdens on Chapters Two and Three (a) in future years. At least, they do if they are spent as intended, on capital works. Where possible they are often diverted either to running costs or to maintenance. Given the 'admitted value of development expenditures from which recurrent activities can discreetly withdraw resources' . . . 'any project is desirable, however poorly conceived and whatever the scepticism of the Sudanese counterparts' (Shepherd *et al.*, 1987: Ch 6).

The shortage of operating finance means that departments become obsessed with any possible form of revenue-raising activity. Schools, hospitals and veterinary services make more or less explicit charges for their services, on the often valid excuse that they cannot operate without them. The National Water Authority undertakes private contracts for drilling boreholes, the Range and Pasture Administration grows fodder, the Veterinary Department organizes cheesemaking and chicken farms. These operations are almost never profitable. No allowance is made for depreciation and wear and tear on the equipment used. The labour is drawn from underemployed staff already on the payroll. Fuel and other inputs are diverted from other purposes. Vets making cheese, for example, buy milk for cheesemaking with an official allocation of scarce sugar. In effect this converts the sugar to its black market value and realizes that value for the department.

The charitable interpretation is that these activities raise revenue for the department's other operations. In many cases, however, they serve instead to convert what little is left for Chapter Two expenditure into additional staff benefits. Government departments sell each other the produce from their various farms and other activities at much below the market price. The staff employed in those activities are paid overtime and extra 'incentives' out of the revenue and so on. Once again it should be emphasized that this activity reflects the absolute inadequacy of government pay at every level. Corruption is not so much exploitation by officialdom. Instead it is a mechanism by which inadequate government salaries are brought somewhat closer to the market rate.

It seems senseless to consider increasing revenue after a decade in which Darfur faced famine twice. Nor are the figures available to make confident estimates of regional income and the potential for increased taxation. Nevertheless, some approximations give surprising results. For example, a JMRDP survey for 1988 recorded an average household cash income of over £S3,000 (JMRDP Wet Season Survey, 1988), which did not include the important contribution of subsistence production. This income was matched by annual cash expenditures of very much the same. The Jebel Marra area is undoubtedly better off then many other parts of the region, but it would be reasonable to assume that the average household income for the whole region is around £S1,500 except in drought years. There were 639,000 households in Darfur at the 1983 census, which would indicate some 740,000 in 1988. Taking these very broad estimates, cash income for the region as a whole would be £S1,110 million. If regional government could raise only 5 per cent of that it would receive £S55 million, nearly four times its budgeted revenue for 1988/89 and 27 per cent of its budgeted expenditure for that year.

When attempts are made to raise tax revenues they do have an effect. Levels of collection by the area councils in Kordofan in 1981/82 were 102 per cent of budget. 'In contrast the recorded collection of income from projects and services by Departments was grossly below target, only £S988,628 being realised of £S4,796,650 [budgeted]' (Shepherd *et al.*, 1986: Ch 6). The reason behind this nonsensical over-estimation of their revenue potential is the department's knowledge that it might strengthen its case for larger allocations of fuel and so on.

It is difficult for anyone who has not attempted to find out something about local administration in rural Sudan to comprehend the extent of the collapse in management, especially in financial management. 'Bad as [the approved budget record] might seem, reconstruction of actual expenditures is far more difficult. Records are very poor if not totally missing. Discrepancies between disbursement requests and actual payments about and the intended use of disbursed funds is usually difficult to ascertain. Finally, it is all but impossible to examine actual uses of funds once they are disbursed to the line ministries and operating departments.' This collapse does not reflect any concentrated effort to divert funds or to cover up abuse. It springs from a total breakdown of basic management disciplines, partly because of poor pay but more importantly because there is no political interest whatsoever in maintaining it. There is an 'apparent absence of political influence and intervention in the recurrent budget preparation, a process confined to routine public service action and interaction' (Shepherd *et al.*, 1987: Ch 6). This observation points to a very important conclusion: that the modern Sudanese politician has next to no interest in the day-to-day business of government.

The Administration

Since the early colonial period, administrative developments in Sudan have run on two tracks. One employed traditional groupings – the religious sects and the tribes – as agents of the administration. The other created a bureaucratic machinery dealing with the members of society directly, as individuals not as members of any particular group.

This machinery was supposed to be subordinate to a matching democratic framework of elected councils. The dilemma of the state, in the post-colonial as much as in the colonial era, has been how to strike a balance between the two.

The colonial government was perceived, not altogether fairly, as having overemphasized the first track. Partly in reaction, post-colonial regimes have regarded the traditional leadership with suspicion and attempted to reduce their role. Despite this, the traditional groupings have survived and retained their political force. The more modern elements of bureaucratic administration and participatory representation have repeatedly failed to escape the influence of the traditional or to deliver the improved services that they were supposed to offer. The traditional system cannot, however, stand on its own. Tribal leaders can only function if their powers are clearly delegated from a higher, independent and dominant authority. The colonial state was able to harness the traditional groupings because it stood above them and controlled them from a neutral position. In this way it created what was known as the Native Administration from the tribal leadership of northern Sudan. When, however, the Condominium government attempted to promote the most dominant traditional rulers as the controllers and arbiters of the Native Administration, under the doctrine of Indirect Rule, it failed (Daly, 1986).

Elected councils were the alternative to Indirect Rulers. In 1948, Dr Marshall, City Treasurer of Coventry in the English Midlands, was commissioned to draw up recommendations for future development of local government in Sudan. Marshall was looking for a system that would not 'confuse administration of local services with the "cross currents of national politics" ' (Daly, 1991). It took only two years after independence for this dream to collapse with the end of the first democratic government. By that time it had become all too clear that national and local politics are inextricably entwined in Sudan. After the 1958 coup, 'The absence of "sound democratic institutions" at provincial level had been blamed by the President for the failure of parliamentary institutions' (Henderson, 1965). Two attempts were made after independence to tackle the issue of local government, under the military governments of Abboud and Numeiri. The latter tried a socialist/one-party approach through the Sudan Socialist Union. Neither had any greater success (Woodward, 1990).

In this sense, both the colonial and post-colonial states failed at the same hurdle: the creation of a sovereign and independent power that could oversee, direct and discipline the lower levels of social organization. Just like the majority of Indirect Rulers, neither a modern bureaucracy nor democratically elected councils nor a monopoly ruling party have been able to achieve sufficient independence from the religious sects, from the tribes, from the unions and from the Gezira tenants to be able to rule them. Without a such a sovereign ruler, the sects and the tribes have been unable to escape the tendency to pursue their particular interests at the expense of the greater good. Far from being unrepresentative, the government of Sudan has been all too representative in this sense, even under military regimes. 'The Sudan army, like the bureaucracy, has been not so much a detached institution as something of a mirror of Sudanese society' (Woodward, 1990).

The development of that military/bureaucratic mirror has been an important feature in Sudanese political history. The slow pace at which they opened the public service to Sudanese recruitment and the limited effort they put into developing modern education for potential candidates were major causes of resentment towards the British. Even in the later years of the Condominium they were accused of 'dreamy conservatism' for believing that 'ultimately the educated class may tend to merge with the class from which native authorities are drawn, and a nazir [tribal leader] and a bashkatib [government clerk] may wear the same Old School Tie!' (Daly, 1991). If they were suspicious of the political problems that education was likely to cause them the British were, of course, well-advised to be so, but they were not effective in preventing it. The Graduates' Congress was the earliest body to force the Condominium government to recognize its right to make its views on independence and other issues known. Whether thanks to the colonial government or in spite of it, Sudan has one of the strongest cadres of capable and well-trained graduates of an African country.

Similarly, if it was a dream that the educated *effendia* should be drawn from and merge with the tribal leadership on the basis of the 'old school tie', then the dream has largely come true. One of the strongest personal relationships among Sudanese is that of 'colleagues' at secondary school and at university, a relationship that often seems regrettably stronger than any loyalty to the greater good, when it comes to staff discipline for example. Similarly, Sudan may be a society without a strong feeling of class, as is sometimes suggested, but the closest the Sudanese come to snobbery is over the issue of educational qualifications. On one occasion at a tribal peace conference in south Darfur, the leadership of one side opened the conference by complaining that they had not been given time to summon their educated sons back to match the graduates in the other side's delegation (M. H. Mukhtar, personal communication). Weak as it is in so many other respects, one of the strengths of the modern bureaucracy is the high proportion of qualified staff drawn from the local community. Sons of the Native Administration can and do end up as regional governors, as director-generals on multi-million-dollar projects, as World Bank officials and so on. The chances even seem to have been well distributed. Even in the middle of a major tribal battle such as that between the Fur and the Arabs, projects such as the JMRDP can maintain a capable staff of qualified graduates in which both sides are well represented and continue to work together. It is not necessarily easy, but the fact that it can happen at all reflects the strength of the educated élite that was created.

If it is correct that the key factor behind the travails of the Sudan is the lack of a sovereign power capable of standing above the fray, then the only obvious source of such a power within the country is this educated élite. Yet its members seem resolutely uninterested in taking up the role effectively. Corruption is not the issue. A corrupt élite might not be perfectly efficient because it would wish to raise taxation and to make all the little revenue-earning schemes of the rural Sudanese bureaucrat as profitable as possible. Given the total collapse of accounting mechanisms, there is little to stand between them and the diversion of any greater revenues to themselves. There are many more corrupt Third World states than Sudan which have vibrant and progressive economies. By all reports Indonesia has more or less institutionalized corruption without obvious direct economic damage. Rampant patronage has not hindered Japan or, more recently, Thailand. A key difference lies in the approach to work. The Sudan government's employees do not steal its money. Instead they cheat it by not doing the work they are paid to do. One obvious reason for this is that the government does not have any money to steal, once it has paid the salaries.

How has this situation arisen? After all, the bureaucracy inherited much of the status of their colonial predecessors. To return to the concepts of Chapter 1, was this not an adequate incentive to seek out and to raise their X-efficiency? The answer appears to be that it never had the chance because graduate status was rapidly devalued. In many ways, it was the graduates' very success in winning a share of political power as a separate entity – they have their own parliamentary constituencies and powerful unions – that led to their economic downfall. Appeasement of the graduates has been a common theme of Sudanese politics and it was that appeasement that devalued their economic worth. Between independence in 1956/57 and 1968/69, the number of central government classified posts, which is to say in the middle and higher grades, rose from 15,868 to 39,769. The pressure to 'jobs for the boys' was such that there was a 'distribution of jobs to hundreds of graduates before the 1968 elections in an effort to boost the Unionist vote' (Woodward, 1990). The strength of these forces may be seen in the failure of the Job Employment and Classification Scheme.

In 1989, the position of the graduate was so devalued that a Khartoum University graduate with a UK Master of Science degree and five years' experience working in an aid-financed corporation, where pay was higher than in the government mainstream, was paid the equivalent of only £40 sterling a month, valued at the official rate of exchange. At the black-market rates, which actually determined his cost of living, it was worth much less. There was no one on the project, from the director-general downwards, who could realistically survive without some other source of income: onion farming, livestock herding and so on. In order to keep any staff at all, management spends more and more time devising ways to boost pay: overtime, special incentives, staff co-operatives selling rationed goods at cheap official prices, use of project facilities and so on. Some of these indirect benefits are even institutional at the national level. Accounts departments are paid an 'incentive' by the Ministry of Finance and Economic Planning if they submit their accounts on time, or at all.

To sum up, when planning work as little attention is paid to ensuring that the staff resources are available to carry out a properly conceived programme as there is to ensuring that adequate funds are available. The concept of the staff of an operating department being the means of its achieving some programme's objectives is just as obscured as is the concept of its finance being that means. If an attractive job on a project is on offer, secondment is never refused; if a long training course overseas comes up in the middle of a heavy project work-programme, permission is always granted; and if there is a job overseas with the UN or in Saudi Arabia, leave without pay is always agreed.

Political Entrepreneurship

One of the most disorienting things for an outsider working inside the Sudanese government system is the lack of any evident urgency when facing the extraordinary chaos and lack of control. Individually, most of those involved in government know full well the extent to which the system has crumbled. Many can discuss in detail what is happening and why. The overwhelming consensus clearly is, however, that nothing can be done about it. A conference on local government held in Nyala in 1976 led to no improvement. Aid-financed regional planning units in both Darfur and Kordofan have no obvious effect on the central issues of budget and control. Instead they have been used as co-ordinators of aid-financed programmes and as a means to attract more aid. Even at the national level, the most glaring of problems are only ever confronted when donor finance is provided and it soon becomes clear that there is no sincere intention to tackle the problem identified, merely a sincere desire for the foreign funds. The perversion of the Job Employment and Classification Scheme was an extreme example of this pattern. Why are the politicians and bureaucrats so uninterested in addressing these problems?

Political development can be described in terms of political entrepreneurship. As populations grow and as technology changes, so the institutions of ownership and financial and market institutions must also change. These institutional changes involve costs and 'political entrepreneurs' are needed to negotiate and enforce the new arrangements in return for benefits to themselves (Hayami & Kikuchi, 1981: Ch 1). The Sudan is suffering from an acute failure of political entrepreneurship.

In recent years, Darfur has seen increasing levels of tribal unrest. The standard explanation is that it reflects pressure on the land and competition for resources. The truth is, on the contrary, that it springs from a failure to find a neutral sovereign power in an area of loose social structure and considerable ethnic diversity: a political failure pure and simple. Certainly there is some competition for resources, but nothing unusual. In a more densely populated area it would be greater. The critical question is not why there is competition but why the mechanisms to deal with it are so defective. Why do no political entrepreneurs come forward to offer a solution?

Race and tribe might seem a plausible answer. Darfur is ethnically diverse and Islam is the only only truly common factor. On the other hand, tribal and even racial boundaries can only be described as porous. Individuals, groups and even whole clans drift from one tribe to another as best suits their circumstances. Despite the strong preference for cousin-marriages, cross-tribal marriages are frequent. In this sense the division between Arab and non-Arab is a tribal boundary, not greatly different from that between one Arab tribe and another. 'Such mobility suggests that tribal labels have only a limited ethnic content or stability and that mainly political mechanisms accounted for the preservation of territorially defined groups in an area of open frontiers. Changes in political allegiance were later legitimised by changes in one's ancestors' (O'Fahey, 1980: Ch 1). The economic content of tribe is also weak. Even though Baggara means cattlemen, at least one of the major Baggara Arab tribes, the Habbania, were described by Gleichen as principally farmers as early as 1905. More recently some non-Arab Fur have taken up nomadic cattle management while the non-Arab Zaghawa are large cattle- and camel-owners (Haaland in Cunnison & James, 1972).

It is easy to conclude that as the idea of the tribe has neither ethnic nor economic content, it is not important; a conclusion that was particularly welcome in the post-independence era of reaction against all things colonial. Yet the survival of the traditional leadership and the continued conflict over tribal boundaries show the opposite. Ibn Khaldun, the great Arab philosopher of the 14th century, stated that 'Kinship only serves a function when blood ties lead to actual co-operation and mutual aid in danger – other degrees of kinship being insignificant . . . For although kinship is natural and objective it is also imaginary' (Issawi, 1950). Studies of Sudanese tribes such as the Humr and the Rufa'a al Hoi confirm the functionality of the tribal system, especially in the restraint of internal disorder. 'From the number of clusters making up the camp a leader emerges. His role is mediating the disputes between his camp members through the help of his elders, as well as representing the camp to the rest of the tribe and its ruling elite' (Ahmad, 1974). The flexibility and severe practicality of the arrangements are most clear in the blood money arrangements among the Humr. Blood money obligations are not fixed, so much for the close family and so much for more distant relatives, for example. On the contrary they are negotiable. 'Relations between groups within omodiya or lineage are stated in formal terms by agreement or refusal to cooperate in payment and receipt of blood-money.' Even among relatives, bad feeling may lead to a refusal to co-operate in blood money payments while 'commonly a minor lineage seeks Book (ar *kitab*) allies outside the omodiya to relieve the heavy obligations if one of its men should kill' (Cunnison, 1966: Ch 10). Kinship is indeed 'imaginary'.

Clearly, then, traditional leaders of Darfur are active and effective political entrepreneurs, competing at every level for supporters and the benefits while providing services of arbitration and conciliation. Tribesmen, for their part, shop around quite actively for the best leader. The same is just as true at the regional and national levels, where the leaders of the religious sects or *tariqas* provide the same services of conciliation and arbitration to their followers. From their foundations in the late 18th century, the *tariqas* have served as channels for political and economic expression as well as for worship. One of the two most important, the Ansar, sprang out of the Mahdist movement which won much of its support from traders resentful of Egyptian rule. The other, the Khatmiya, was linked to that rule. They are now each associated with one of the two largest modern political parties.

If political entrepreneurship exists at so many sub-national levels, then why does it fail so miserably at the national? The answer is that it does not pay at that level. Sudan is not a rich country and the benefits of negotiating new economic arrangements will initially be small and difficult to achieve. Small especially when compared to the much easier pickings to be made from negotiating yet another deal with a soft-hearted overseas donor. And the process is self-reinforcing. By failing to tackle the problems of inflation and bureaucratic stagflation, the state weakens the economy, and with it the likely rewards from any reform, still further.

By way of conclusion, one revealing example serves to illustrate how the Sudanese state has managed to avoid any realistic negotiations over resources with any of its citizens. Following the October revolution of 1964, tension between the irrigation scheme licensees and their tenants increased. Government, under pressure from the tenants, first raised their share of profits from 40 to 50 per cent and then, in 1968, nationalized the pump schemes under the Agrarian Reform Act. This was ostensibly in response to the tenants' accusations against the scheme operators. Nevertheless, the blow for the latter was considerably softened. They were paid compensation, although many of their licences had nearly expired, and their debts were taken over by the new government corporations. It has been suggested that the scheme operators were allowed to escape just at the point when falling prices meant that irrigated cotton was no longer profitable (Mahmoud, 1984), although overall, the evidence does not support this. There was no clear decline in either the commodity or the income terms of trade for cotton in the 1960s (Beshai, 1976).

The true reason cotton was becoming unprofitable was the way the tenants were winning a greater share. Not only had government increased the tenants' share of the profits on the cotton crop, they were also diverting their efforts to other crops. As all the overhead costs of the scheme were charged to cotton, those other crops were much more attractive to the tenant but not to the scheme operator. As their political strength grew, the tenants were increasingly able to disregard the stipulated cropping patterns and practices and the area under cotton on the Gezira dropped from 57 per cent in 1954/55 to 43 per cent in 1969/70 as a result. In the face of this competition from their tenants, the pump-scheme operators preferred to abandon irrigation and shift into mechanized farming on suitably attractive compensation. By doing this they preserved their political support among those same tenants at small cost to themselves. In mechanized farming, the seasonal labour force was never likely to develop the political strength of the irrigated tenants, so the operators were unlikely to face similar pressure again. This shift kept all groups more or less happy, at the expense of government taking over the thankless task of trying to maintain its share against the tenants' pressure, something it was manifestly failing to do on its own schemes.

Conclusion

The Sudanese state, that mirror of Sudanese society, has always operated within quite narrow limits in both colonial and independence periods. It had little room to change its policies and even if it had been able to, it is far from clear that it would have made much difference. There have, for example, been incessant accusations that the traditional sector and the outlying regions like Darfur have been systematically neglected as a result of 'urban bias', of 'intensive crop bias' and so on. As always, the veil of economic benefit is drawn over this essentially political charge. Traditional crops grown in the 'semisubsistence economy' contribute a large share of exports at very little cost in terms of imported inputs. For this reason, the argument goes, greater investment in that sector is bound to be profitable. Yet nothing has been done for the 'poor in the traditional sector, not even a foundation laid for the future' . . . 'Research in Sudan has shown huge potential for productivity increases by applying optimum sowing dates, higher yielding varieties, increasing crop densities' etc (ILO, 1987: Ch 3). This combines an economic non sequitur, that cheap exports of traditional crops guarantee high returns to investment in that sector, with outright ignorance of the state of research, which had shown barely any potential at all.

If there was no scope for changes in policy and if such changes would have made little difference, how did Sudan reach a state of relative prosperity in the post-war years and of abject poverty in the late 1980s? The answer is administration and management. The simple truth is that policies did not fail in Sudan because they were the wrong policies, but because they were implemented in the most wretched manner. It was not just the liberalizing reforms of Structural Adjustment that met this fate. The post-colonial drive for industrialization, the breadbasket investments, integrated rural development and many others have gone the same way.

Management also failed in another aspect that was particularly critical for an economy like the Sudan's: absorbing shocks. While there has been no consistent adverse movement in Sudan's terms of trade, the year on year fluctuations have been extraordinary. Some of the other shocks that have hit the Sudanese economy make even the two oil shocks of the 1970s seem relatively insignificant: wartime booms in livestock and grain, post-war booms in cotton, post-boom crashes in cotton, and all compounded by the highly unreliable climate and by pests and disease of a ferocity that Europe has not experienced since the days of the potato blight and phylloxera. No policy can prevent these vents; they have to be managed. Decisions have to be taken at the time and executed with expedition. And those who do it will receive little credit. The colonial financial secretaries who built up reserves to soften the blow of fluctuations in cotton prices were universally damned for parsimony. And their reserves were dissipated with speed once their political backing was lost.

Clearly, this applies with particular force with regard to famine. It is far from evident, given the appalling rains, that any state could have managed the famines of the 1980s successfully. The colonial state never succeeded in eliminating famine, in generally better circumstances, despite a body of experience and regulations imported from India to deal with it. Nevertheless, it is difficult to believe from their performance in the 1980s that any of the recent Sudanese regimes has either the capacity or the will to manage famine.

If management and implementation are the issue, rather than policy and analysis, then the ideas of X-efficiency discussed in Chapter 1 become central. Virtually every aspect of the Sudanese economy has been 'rehabilitated' with aid money: some, like the Gezira and Sudan Railways, more than once. It is no longer possible to believe that shortages of resources or technology are at issue. It is the absence of those pressures and incentives which generate productivity increases off an unchanged endowment of resources and technologies which explains the failure of Sudan.

The colonial legacy is important, but not for the reasons usually given. It was not because they perpetuated the struggle of sect and faction that the British left Sudan more vulnerable than they knew. Rather it was because they left an unbalanced state machinery which combined economic 'state socialism' with a 'light and thinly spread administrative structure': almost exactly the wrong balance for a nation as loosely integrated as the Sudan. The result has been that the independent Sudanese state has been unable to resist demands on its resources from virtually any group in society.

But then they were not really its own resources. For Sudan it is not so much the economy as the state that is 'outward-looking' and it has been able to play off its internal political supporters against its external financial supporters and so escape any discipline from either. In Chapter 1 it was argued that taxation was the critical link between ruler and ruled: in effect the roots of the state. By chance, the independent Sudanese state has never really had to develop those roots. From first to last it has been financed externally: from the inherited reserves of the Condominium, from the first aid era of the 1960s, from the breadbasket and lastly from Structural Adjustment.

6 THE POVERTY OF NATIONS

> 'Royal authority exists through the army, the army through money, money through taxes, taxes through cultivation, cultivation through justice . . . '
>
> Exhortation from Sultan's tax demand (O'Fahey, 1980)

Sudan since independence has been near enough catastrophic. Rainfall has been extremely unfavourable. The economy has declined. Security has deteriorated steadily, not merely in the south where the civil war has dragged on with few interruptions, but also more insidiously in the north of the country. Educated and energetic Sudanese have emigrated and taken their money with them. All this in spite of access to staggering sums of foreign capital, both borrowed and as outright aid, and in spite of a political system that was more representative and open than many.

Yet it was not the fault of the Sudanese people. If the Darfuri is any measure, they have grasped every genuine economic opportunity that has come their way with both hands. Many internal barriers to development have been identified: tribalism, communal land tenure or tradition in general. Those barriers turn out to be 'fictional'. This does not mean that they are not important. Some are key symbols in the way the Darfuri thinks about himself and his society. It does mean, however, that they are no obstacle to changes in that society. Where circumstances have justified a change, above all where they have made a change worth while, it has happened without difficulty.

If tradition is not a barrier, is it perhaps the rapid loss of tradition that has led to disaster? Has their enthusiasm for the exchange economy made the Darfuris vulnerable to its fluctuations? Have they given away a golden age of sustainable subsistence for the unreliable attractions of crash, imported consumer goods and export crops? Again, the answer is no. The current crisis certainly reflects a retreat from the money economy, from the wider opportunities of trade, but that retreat is not a willing one. On the contrary, Darfur is being driven out of the world economy. Declining standards of living reflect the loss of gains that it had won – hard won – from that economy, not the costs of joining it in the first place. Standards of living are, in fact, rapidly returning to those which prevailed during that imaginary golden age of subsistence.

Technology has had little to offer an economy that is being forced back into its subsistence shell. Aid has developed an enormous apparatus to identify and, above all, transfer technology – research, extension, training and so on. If technology has no market, that apparatus has no job. It is forced to pursue ever more complex and unfruitful topics as a result: topics with theoretical elegance but little relevance. The Tragedy of the Commons is only the most striking of the many blind alleys up which aid research has wandered, never to come out again. This persistence itself reflects the lack of more promising routes to follow.

Repeated injections of capital have been just as unsuccessful. Failed capital does not, however, wither away in the desert air. Instead it leaks into consumption. Which is clearly what has happened in Sudan. And Sudan did not even need to import capital. At several levels the Sudanese have more than they can usefully use. Farmers have substantial savings in the form of stored grain and livestock. Most importantly of all, the Sudan is a net exporter of capital at the national level.

If farmers store grain and herders keep large herds it is to insure against the unreliable climate. It is a commonplace for western investors that a secure portfolio of investments is a wide-ranging one. When it promotes supposedly more secure subsistence technologies, aid actually narrows the range and increases the farmer's exposure to the risks of climate, pest and disease. A far better insurance would be an investment outside Darfur, preferably outside Sudan – something amply demonstrated by the fact that any Sudanese who can takes his savings out of the country. The World Bank would achieve far more if, instead of injecting yet more capital into the Sudanese economy through the Sudanese government, it set up a deposit-taking branch in Nyala paying international real interest rates to individual Darfuri savers. This notion may see far-fetched and it is, but only in the sense that the political implications would be far-reaching and unpopular. If the Bank were to set up a shop full of First World technologies next door to its Nyala branch, then the Darfuri would have what he really needs: the widest possible choice between investing in new technologies in Darfur or putting his savings into the most secure and lucrative market there is, the world market.

Cultivation through Justice

The Sudanese are not to blame as individuals or as a society for the retreat from development. As a state, however, they are entirely to blame. For it is the Sudanese state that has stifled the economy by gross and persistent mismanagement. Corruption is a problem and misguided policy is a bigger one. But sheer day-to-day inefficiency has done most damage. This has not been the doing of any all-powerful and exploitative ruling class. On the contrary it is the result of the Sudanese state's inability to out-face any interest groups, however undeserving and unimportant. These problems have been exacerbated by a colonial inheritance of economic intervention and by socialist policies after independence. State intervention in the economy was not, however, so much the product of conscious policy as the inevitable result of the pressures that any government has to face, in a country as large as the Sudan with a society as loosely structured as the Sudanese. Those pressures were evident long before the establishment of the colonial state and they have still not lost their force.

Nowadays the word 'sovereignty' is used to describe the right of Third World governments to resist interference from abroad. This has distracted those governments from the older, more powerful and much more relevant meaning of the world; that sovereign power which meets 'the indispensable need that human beings have to surrender some of their natural rights to liberty to secure their lives against death and their property against plunder' (Gamble, 1981: 50). Hobbes's classic description of life when the sovereign has failed is hackneyed in Europe. It still retains all its brutal sting in Africa.

> In such condition, there is no place for industry, because the fruit thereof is uncertain: and consequently no Culture of the earth; no Navigation, nor use of commodities that may be imported by Sea; no commodious Building; no instruments of moving and removing such things as require much force; no Knowledge of the face of the earth; no account of Time; no Arts; no Letters; no Society . . . And the life of man, solitary, poor, nasty, brutish, and short. (Quoted in Gamble, 1981: 42)

Sovereignty in this older sense is fundamental to the problems of Sudan. The peculiar nature of colonial rule disguised the fact that sovereignty was undefined in Sudan until shortly before independence. The subsequent crisis has all revolved around the failure to achieve a definition once the colonial state was overthrown.

In 1989, the Jebel Marra Rural Development Project, which was financed by the European Development Fund and the central government of Sudan, had over half its fleet of Land Rovers commandeered by the police and army, who were trying to control widespread fighting between the Fur and a number of Arab groups. To many outsiders this action seemed to be yet another instance of repression by the Sudanese state, but that was the opposite of the truth. Some intervention between Fur and Arab was urgently needed and actively sought by responsible members of both groups. They certainly did not trust the security services, but they recognized that it was their job to intervene and that they were the only ones who could. For the same reason, the management of the JMRDP had no alternative but to comply with requests for vehicles. The restoration of law and order had to take precedence for the sake of the Project's own work as well as for the sake of the people of the area.

Even with the commandeered vehicles the security services continued to be ineffective and few of the fighters were apprehended. The fighting had several causes but the security services' inability to police the area, and to intervene before the violence ran out of control, was the single most important factor behind its spread and escalation.

These events provide several new perspectives. One is that the roots of the problem do not lie in a lack of balance between the government and the governed but more simply in the state's failure to deliver the services that form its primary obligation: law and order. Another is that technical or economic development takes second place to security and must always do so. 'Cultivation comes through justice.' A third is that the basic functions of the state have become hopelessly dependent on the crumbs from aid's table. Aid projects may or may not be successful but they nowadays command far greater material resources than the state itself. Following a spate of highway robbery, new police vehicles were not labelled 'Darfur Police Department' but 'Project Against Armed Robbery'. The most fundamental tasks of the administration have thus been turned into short-term projects. Policing has been reduced to crisis management, law and order returned to the age of the posse. The Arabic word for a posse is *faz'a* and it is a common Darfur experience to hear of villagers on a *faz'a* after their stolen cattle. Many of the outbreaks of violence in western Darfur have sprung from a clash between the *faz'a* and the first group they meet who can be plausibly suspected of involvement in the theft, innocent or otherwise.

The problem is not, then, state repression but rather state incapacity. Which is not to say that corruption and repression do not exist in Sudan. They are very evident, in southern Sudan in particular. Those abuses are, however, symptoms of weakness, not strength. The state lacks the financial resources, the political will and, especially, the managerial capabilities to control events, and without control the cruder weapons of terrorism are all that remain. The agents of the state itself are also uncontrolled and freer to abuse their position unchecked. Poor pay makes such abuse almost inevitable. For all these reasons the Sudanese state of the 1980s and 1990s shows strong elements of the 'minimal government' typical of the Ottoman empire in the 19th century: 'States may maltreat or murder their citizens when they can catch them but first they must catch them. In general, the less likely they are to catch them the more brutally they are prone to treat them when they do apprehend them on the principle that severity may compensate in deterrent terms for infrequency' (Yapp, 1987: 39). Even at rule by terror, the Sudanese state is ineffective by comparison with most other African and even some First World states. This, at least in part, reflects a genuine reluctance to use such methods, although southern Sudan, where racism weakens the consensus against violence, is an exception. However, it also reflects the fact that the state has proved incapable of forming and implementing successfully any coherent policy, even such a repugnant one as rule by repression.

Growth or Development?

To the west, where issues of sovereignty are more or less settled, development is synonymous with economic growth. There remains, however, the nagging problem of the 'residual', that growth which cannot be explained by increases in the stock of capital or by population growth. Economists abhor a theoretical vacuum, and this is a large one, but attempts to fill it have never been wholly convincing. To say that technological change improves the quality of capital and the skills of labour is no explanation. What after all causes technological change? This paradox led to the conclusion that 'Until recently, economics had little of interest to say about economic growth.' (*The Economist*, 4 January 1992). Which did little to reduce the economists' dominance of development aid.

One of the new theories claiming to add interest to what economics has to say about growth stands as an *ex post facto* validation of the modern aid prescription, with its doses of Human Resource Development. 'The new theory recognises that knowledge can raise the return on investment . . . Economics have to invest in knowledge in the same way that they invest in machines . . . Since past investment in capital may make it more profitable to accumulate knowledge, the new theory admits the possibility of a virtuous circle in which investment spurs knowledge and knowledge spurs investment' (Romer summarized in *The Economist*, 4 January 1992).

A second new approach comes to a different conclusion, maintaining that technology change and capital investment are not merely linked; they are indistinguishable. 'The rate of invention is determined by the rate of investment . . . inventions are best regarded as a form of investment and their volume depends on their expected profitability . . . The pace of scientific advance can thus be neglected in constructing a theory of economic growth . . . Research and development can be merged with other forms of investment' (Scott, 1989: Ch 5). This is tantamount to a justification for the old aid prescription; that capital expenditure is all that is required for development because that investment will on its own stimulate technological change.

However theoretically coherent, it is impossible to match these positive views of investment, in men as well as machines, with the reality in Sudan or in Africa generally; although it is safe to predict that this will not stand in the way of their being widely used to buttress the case for aid.

Scott makes a number of qualifications. In Africa these look far more important than his central conclusion. He explicitly excludes X-efficiency (148). He points out that although his model does not allow diminishing returns to the capital stock, 'one should allow for diminishing returns to the *rate of investment*' (his italics p xxxi). Finally, having dismissed, with some contempt, the whole concept of a residual in economic growth, he then falls back on something very similar. This is forced upon him by the evidence of a world-wide decline in growth rates after 1973. 'The principal problem that has to be overcome in returning to the rapid growth experienced after the war is that of readjusting expectations and aspirations. On the one hand, wage earners' expectations have to become sufficiently modest. On the other hand, businessmen's animal spirits have to recover.' In other words, growth is not explicable simply by the volume of investment after all. The new growth theories are clearly correct in one respect: that technological change is a response to the market. The Sudan experience demonstrates the logical extension; that without a market technology must fail. What the Sudan also shows, however, is that investment cannot make the market for technology on its own. There remains some unexplained factor that is capable of nullifying the impact of investment. Which is true even in the west. For all the vast gap between them, descriptions of the slackening in First World growth after 1973 could easily be applied to the Sudan: 'When all these changes, in the form of market distortions, disincentives, inflexibilities and uncertainties, are considered, it is tempting to speak of an emerging "arteriosclerosis" of the western economic systems accentuated by the resistance to change and the fights about income shares, by organised interest groups' (Lindbeck, quoted in Scott, 1989: 487). Short-term economic shocks – booms, busts and cyclical changes – interact with the 'expectations and aspirations' that drive this struggle over income shares. 'Expectations of rising real wages were coupled with expectations of a rising "social wage" – of better and better collectively provided services . . . These rising expectations collided with a lower ceiling imposed by worsening terms of trade in the early 1970s . . . The principal problem that has to be overcome is that of readjusting expectations and aspirations' (Scott, 1989: 522).

In Sudan, expectations and aspirations have been on a roller-coaster ride driven by booms and busts in cotton, groundnuts, cattle and gum arabic and by the various waves of imported capital. The powerful states of the western world have had difficulty enough 'readjusting'. It is hardly surprising that the much weaker Sudanese state, in both the late colonial and post-independence periods, failed in precisely this area. A similar thesis is that 'growth rates between countries can be partially explained by the differences in the strengths of "distributional coalitions" ' (Scott, 1989: 334). The statistical evidence that this is true for the west is said to be weak. For the Sudan, on the other hand, the telling phrase 'distributional coalition' serves to sum up the whole of the post-independence era. It is only a small exaggeration to say that the nation as a whole is one big 'distributional coalition'.

The conclusion must be that economic growth, residual and all, depends on wider developments in the social and political arena; something recognized in the modern aid emphasis on governance. That recognition is, however, only partial. The modern liberal tradition sees a healthy civil society – free markets, individualism and so on – as the natural order and as a beneficial one. Individuals in the market pursue their own interests, but this leads to the best result by the miracle of the 'hidden hand' of market economics. This model makes a lot of sense in the successful west, especially after the collapse of the communist alternative. If state intervention is still required, it is merely to minimize the less attractive side-effects of civil society. Aid, hesitant as always about interference in control, is all too willing to transfer this view of the world to Africa and accept the easy assumption that the benevolence of civil society will bring about good governance naturally and painlessly, through individualism, grass-roots associations and free markets.

That assumption puts the cart before the horse. 'A market is a highly precarious and artificial thing, since a basic security must exist; yet such security does not flow spontaneously from the interaction of the producers, nor can any individual producer ensure it. Only a centralised power which enjoys legitimacy and can enforce obedience can do that. The market in which exchange is free and equal, in which contracts are honoured, in which the fruits of economic activity are secure, in which money is universally acceptable as a store of value and as a means of payment, requires a strong and active state pledged to maintain all three. But it must be a state that is separated from the producers themselves and so not tied to any sectional interest' (Gamble, 1981). The last point bears emphasis: the more representative a state is, the more difficulties it will find in successfully refereeing civil society.

Nowadays, Adam Smith's great work *The Wealth of Nations*, reads like a first economics of civil society. At the time of writing it read far more like a manifesto of how such an economy should work if it ever came about. In the world Smith describes, life is nearly as 'nasty, brutish and short' as in that of Hobbes: 'It is not uncommon in the Highlands of Scotland for a mother who has borne twenty children not to have two alive . . . In the happiest and most fortunate period of them all [in England], how many disorders and misfortunes have occurred, which not only the impoverishment, but the total ruin of the country would have been expected from them? The fire and plague of London, the two Dutch wars, the disorders of the revolution, the war in Ireland, the four expensive French wars together with the two rebellions.' Markets in Smith's world were far from free. Grain prices were controlled and government intervention was widespread. Above all there were severe restraints on the movement of labour. International trade was equally restricted. Resentment of British controls on trade was a major factor behind the American revolution of 1776, the same year that *The Wealth of Nations* was published.

Nor was Smith impressed with the governance of his day. 'It is the highest impertinence and presumption in kings and ministers, to pretend to watch over the economy of private people . . . They are themselves always, and without any exception, the greatest spendthrifts in the society.' Unemployment among the over-educated is another of his targets. 'That unprosperous race of men commonly called men of letters . . . In every part of Europe the greater part of them have been educated for the Church . . . They have generally, therefore, been educated at the public expense, and their numbers are everywhere so great as commonly to reduce the price of their labour to a very paltry recompense.' Not a very gracious remark from an educated man, but then academics were ever so.

Yet despite all this, the processes of growth and development were already under way and sufficiently well established for Smith to be able to describe with utmost clarity how things ought to be well before they actually were. In his view, this was because the good sense and thrift of ordinary people was more powerful than any amount of government folly, was able to withstand the worst of natural and man-made disasters and was developing new skills and techniques despite the efforts of their supposedly educated betters:

> [The frugality and good conduct of individuals] is upon most occasions sufficient to compensate, not only the private prodigality and misconduct of individuals, but the public extravagance of government . . . Like the unknown principle of animal life, it frequently restores health and vigour to the constitution, in spite, not only of the disease, but of the absurd prescriptions of the doctor.

The Vent for Surplus

A whole range of anti-growth factors were present in Smith's world, but did not stop growth. Why is it that in Africa those same factors can stifle growth with so little difficulty? Why were the energies of individual citizens able to overcome all the follies of government in 18th-century Europe but not in Africa today?

Freedom is a common explanation for the explosive success of civil society because freedom released the powers of 'frugality and good conduct of individuals' in what has been called the 'bourgeois revolution'. Before that revolution, 'society was not made up of "individuals" enjoying a considerable degree of personal freedom, choice and mobility, but of families, tribes and clans – entities where the scope for individual freedom of action was more restricted.' It was only by breaking these traditional barriers that the free movement of land, labour and capital became possible and only then could all three be traded in the market and so shifted towards the most productive use. 'A major problem still remains over how the change was accomplished, how the obstacles were overcome and the tremendous power and authority of traditional relationships loosened' (Gamble, 1981).

Smith provides the answer to this latter question: the spread of consumer goods. 'In a country which has neither foreign commerce, nor any of the finer manufactures, a great proprietor, having nothing for which he can exchange the greater part of the produce of his lands, consumes the whole in rustic hospitality . . . The great Earl of Warwick is said to have entertained every day at his different manors thirty thousand people . . . A hospitality nearly of the same kind was exercised not many years ago in the Highlands of Scotland. It seems common to all nations to whom commerce and manufactures are little known.' The traditional barriers to development depended, therefore, on the great proprietors' hospitality; not on feudal law which was aimed, unsuccessfully, at controlling those same proprietors. 'But what all the violence of feudal institutions could never have effected, the silent and insensible operation of foreign commerce and manufactures gradually brought about. These gradually furnished the great proprietors with something from which they could exchange the surplus produce of their lands without sharing it with tenants or retainers. All for ourselves and nothing for other people seems, in every age of the world, to have been the vile maxim of the masters of mankind . . . For a pair of diamond buckles perhaps, or for something as frivolous and useless, they exchanged the maintenance of a thousand men for a year, and with it the whole weight and authority which it could give them . . . and thus for the gratification of the most childish, the meanest, and the most sordid of all vanities, they gradually bartered their whole power and authority.' It is an extraordinarily cynical picture of the 'bourgeois revolution', brought about by a combination of the 'childish vanity' of the great proprietors and the 'merchants' and artificers' pursuit of their own pedlar principle of turning a penny wherever a penny was to be got'. But that was always the point of Smith's miracle, that development is possible without any special transformation of human nature, without the need for education and without any exceptional skill or honesty in government. Instead it requires only two things: that government be effective in one limited sense, as an arbiter of disputes, and that there be some material incentive.

At one level, the freedom argument appears difficult to sustain in Darfur. Traditional society is not remotely restricted, indeed it is fluid and individualistic. Tribal, class and even racial boundaries are highly porous. Individuals from as far away as Nigeria have walked right across Africa and settled in Darfur and other parts of Sudan with little difficulty. Even within the family, affairs are organized in a way that most Europeans would find almost alienating in its independence. And, as emphasized so often here, land is abundant and free. It cannot be 'traditional barriers' that stand in the way of African development.

On the other hand, Darfur society does have similarities with Smith's description of feudal hospitality. Many traditional African societies revolve around the 'moral economy', in which the better-off maintain a large community of supporters and dependents. In Sudan tribal leaders use their resources in kind, principally cattle, to maintain their political position. Within the tribe, those leaders' principal function was to mediate disputes and enforce judgements (Cunnison, 1966: Ch 11). The clan chiefs of Scotland, who were just dying out in Smith's time, fed and judged their supporters in exactly the same way. Any European who has spent time in Africa will know personally the apparently illogical mixture of greed and generosity that is typical of such a society. Africans will give their last crust to an unknown passer-by, but they equally expect those who are better off than themselves to share their good luck without hesitation. The European insistence on drawing lines between 'mine and yours' seems bad-mannered and downright mean. Any African entrepreneur faces acute difficulties in his own homeland because his attempts to save and accumulate capital seem equally bad-mannered and mean. In essence, therefore, there is a strong presumption that the bulk of society's surplus will be distributed socially, not through the market.

In Chapter 2 the vent for surplus process was described, whereby access to consumer goods stimulates increased production in an area with unused land and labour. That concept was itself a development of Smith's ideas and his analysis of social change readily lends itself to an extension of the same concept: to what may be called the Vent for Social Surplus. Here the surplus does not consist of natural resources but is underused production, production that is surplus to subsistence requirements. The introduction of consumer goods releases that surplus which had, hitherto, been tied up in 'hospitality': the relatively sterile purchase of social authority. In this way, 'Commerce and manufactures gradually introduced order and good government, and with them, the liberty and security of individuals, among the inhabitants of the country, who had before lived in almost a continual state of war with their neighbours, and of servile dependency upon their superiors' (Smith, 1776).

A third facet can be added to the vent for surplus: X-efficiency, which emphasizes the importance of incentives in stimulating more efficient management and technological change. Consumer goods provide that incentive and so open what may be called the Vent for Intellectual Surplus.

Perhaps the central conclusion of this book is that aid distorts the processes of development by transforming the relationship between traditional élites and their retainers. Aid resources allow those élite to indulge their 'vanity' on consumer goods without paying the corresponding development price of sacrificing their authority. On the contrary, their power over the distribution of those aid resources actually bolsters their authority. What is more, the most effective tools the élite can use in this process are found in economic mismanagement. Licensing, monopoly, exchange rate manipulation, subsidy and the many other market distortions of the African state are all tools for political control over the distribution of resources. And those distortions serve to close off all three forms of the vent for surplus.

The Poverty of Nations

Adam Smith was trying to prove – most would say he succeeded – that man's self-interest can lead to the best of all possible worlds: the Wealth of Nations. The era of aid in Africa has come close to proving that when man tries to escape from his worse nature and act without self-interest the result is near enough the mirror image, the worst of all possible worlds – the Poverty of Nations.

Aid has contributed nothing to a solution of the fundamental problem of sovereignty. If anything it has made it worse, or at least delayed progress. Is there anything left, then, beyond the deeply unsatisfactory conclusion that all aid should be stopped; that the Puritan ethic is, in fact, correct and God helps those who help themselves? Should we conclude that Africa is poor and that aid makes it poorer and that even a reduction of aid will only slow the decline? If aid's attempt to create a development revolution, in the sense of an acceleration over evolutionary growth, is impossible, does this mean that there is no hope of Africa's ever catching up until it has grown through the earlier ages of man? The answer is no; or, at least, not necessarily.

The evidence of a potential for rapid growth may be found in the way the Sudanese and even the Darfuris, whose resources are among the poorest in Africa, saw rapid economic growth in a number of respects between 1900 and 1960. With variations, almost all African nations could say the same. In most cases that growth was the result of individual smallholders and pastoralists seizing the opportunities offered by access to outside markets. They received no financial aid and little or no technical advice.

Africa does have special problems. Transport is one. Modern railway and motor technology mean that it is possible to break this barrier, but roads and railways are particularly demanding on the states' sovereign capacities: to ensure regular maintenance, to fight off the demands of the railway unions and to resist its own desire to exploit these monopolies. African society also lacks that tripartite balance that helped to stabilize European societies through the 'bourgeois revolution': between landowners, wage-earners and merchants. The trading interest of the merchants has dominated most Sudanese governments and the only wage-earners who have won representation have been the modern-sector unions. The counterweight of landowners and rural smallholders is missing.

On the other hand, the range of cheap and attractive consumer goods available in world markets to encourage all sections of the Sudanese community to strive for better things is far, far greater than in Smith's time; and the scope for African products in world markets is an opportunity which could not have been dreamed of in earlier eras. There seems no particular reason why those incentives should not have very rapid results through the triple vents for resource, intellectual and social surplus. Provided, that is, that the central problem of sovereignty can be solved in a way that prevents the pressure of 'expectations and aspirations' from closing the vent.

Those pressures will get worse once development picks up speed. There will be an ever-increasing flow of choices that will need acceptable judgements. The temptation to try to avoid the conflicts that arise will be strong: to 'guide' or even stop development in order to avoid hard decisions. 'Change is not made without inconvenience, even from worse to better' and, as Smith pointed out, the inconvenience can be brutal and dispiriting. Even in his native Scotland, marginal areas like the highlands have less population now than they did in his time. The clearances that brought this about were inhuman. Darfur, especially north Darfur, is just such a marginal area as the highlands of Scotland. Nevertheless, these conflicts cannot be avoided. They will have to be faced and dealt with. Furthermore, disputes and conflict have an important positive side. 'Opportunism and argument are very human qualities. In many areas disputing is a normal form of social interaction, through which an individual tests his/her position and opportunities in the world . . . Conflict is not always negative; it is also the means by which groups can overcome inappropriate or "unjust" distribution of resources.' Above all, conflict is the natural way of testing the social implications of new technologies. 'Disputing and negotiation at least gives the opportunity to test the reality of suggestions made by water technicians' (Vincent, 1990). What is vital, of course, is that such disputes can be acceptably resolved. The central task is not to avoid conflict, but to manage it. Aid resources allow the African state great scope to avoid these potentially fruitful conflicts; as the Sudanese government did when it ducked the struggle over the division of profits on government and private irrigation schemes, to take but one example from Chapter 5. Instead of being forced to negotiate a deal that would ensure the future of their enterprise, the scheme owners were enabled to walk away while government bore the cost. Had the struggle been allowed to continue, both sides' wish for higher returns might have led to increases in efficiency and output. Instead the schemes have declined ever since.

Despite the recent optimism about multi-party democracy, it is difficult to see how the new African democracies will escape the central liberal dilemma: 'What if a majority of individuals, acting through democratic institutions, vote to "plunder" other members of the community, expropriating their property using the very coercive powers of the state that were instituted to protect property?' (Gamble, 1981). As the Sudan has shown, democracies are also exceptionally vulnerable to 'distributional coalitions'. It is perhaps no accident that many of the most successful non-European imitators of the west have a far from liberal tradition. Imperial Japan is the obvious example.

It is impossible to say what will be the most suitable form of sovereignty for Africa. The functions it will have to undertake are, however, absolutely clear. It must restore the value of money as a medium of exchange and as a store of value. This is far more crucial in an emerging economy with limited financial infrastructure and a restricted range of alternative investments than it is in the west. The control of inflation is more important than the IMF thinks, not less. It must re-establish taxation to measure the individual's commitment to the state and to value what the state offers in return. It must rigorously control the state's ambitions so as not to exceed its capacity. Above all, it must allow nothing to detract from its ability to serve its primary Hobbesian function, the defence of life and property. To the west property is tainted with the idea of wealth and riches. In the Sudan property is more often a few ill-nourished cattle or sheep and may be very close to life itself.

Conclusion

Aid is driven by First World concerns lightly modified by what the Third World recipients will accept. The result is deeply inconsistent. Aid agencies that are marginally accountable call for accountability, directives are issued against *dirigisme* and the very top of the aid business, the World Bank, appears to feel no embarrassment in calling for a 'bottom-up approach'. None of this reflects insincerity so much as the fundamental dilemma of trying to 'help people to help themselves' without infringing on their rights to self-determination. Aid is, by its very nature, a top-down exercise. The flow of resources is from top to bottom and there is no way known to man of making the initiative flow the other way.

Because aid is inconsistent and unable to reduce that inconsistency, it fails repeatedly. The result is increasingly feverish 'policy cycling'. Strategy after strategy is tried and abandoned, sector after sector is pumped up and then deflated because of failures that are not due to the inadequacy of the policy or the inappropriateness of the sector but are the result of overambitious targets and inadequate control. The insidious combination of sensitivity over control and aid's internal pressure to 'move the money', has meant that it does not just fail. It may actually retard the processes of development.

For the outsider, there are two questions: Can we help at all in building African sovereignty? and If we can, how? To say no to the first question and stop aid would only be the first step in a very long and possibly painful process. There is no way to predict how long it might take for the restoration of the normal pressures of taxation and undistorted markets to build a sovereign state which could provide the environment the Darfuri needs to be able to use his knowledge and ability to its full once again. All that can be said is that the potential is there and that, given the signal failure of aid to stimulate its realization, it is time to look for an alternative. Such an alternative might give very different results in different places. It might very well involve a period of instability. There is no reason, however, to believe that the outcome could not be quite positive, certainly better than the current dreary decline and possibly as good as the targets that aid has set itself and never come close to achieving.

A cessation of aid should not be dismissed out of hand. The ideal would be for an African nation to take its courage in both hands and decide for itself that it no longer wishes it. That is, however, unlikely. It is equally unlikely that the vast aid machine will accept its own redundancy or that its First World constituency will be willing to play the role of the Victorian parent, who is cruel to be kind. Are there, then, any ways to suggest a better form of aid?

There are three alternatives, representing varying degrees of infringement of the axiom that local control is inviolable. The most extreme of these is a return to colonialism, using the word to mean merely direct foreign control without the more complex associations. Before this is dismissed out of hand the dilemma of local control needs to be considered from a slightly different angle. Aid is always faced with a trade-off between immediate results and long-term capacities. The quickest way to help farmers may be to use the full battery of First World skills to breed a new maize variety, but this does nothing to develop a local research capacity. The quickest way to help the poor may be to allow foreign NGOs to feed them, but this does nothing for a balanced development in which both poor and élite play a role. The quick way in both cases is, in effect, micro-colonialism.

The case for a far more aggressive First World involvement in Africa at the national level depends on the urgency of this dilemma in the more disastrous areas. Is it really acceptable that quick results in these areas should be sacrificed to respect for local control, to the attempt to build up a more long-term solution? Is there an easy moral position on Liberia, and Burundi for example? Is the First World correct to respect local sovereignty if that leads to genocide? Is that any different from refusing to resist Nazism because it would mean infringing German sovereignty?

Food aid presents the opposite dilemma. It provides a short-term solution but not a long-term one. It may even delay the development of a long-term solution. But food aid springs from the same source: an unwillingness to abandon the control axiom and impose a solution. The droughts, wars and famines of the Horn of Africa present the best example. At the least, relief aid prolonged the various struggles in the area, in the sense that the pressures of outright famine would otherwise have so weakened the warring groups as to force them to settlement. This may seem very harsh, but it leads to a deeper question. Is it really moral to keep people alive in ways that do not solve their long-term problems, when that costs relatively little in the way of grain that is, in any case, surplus? Is it moral to do so, while avoiding the more difficult decision to impose a settlement by force of arms, merely because that second solution infringes sovereignty and will, incidentally, involve real costs instead of reductions of surpluses? (These words were written about a year before the much more aggressive intervention undertaken by the UN in Somalia.)

In short, the concept of local sovereignty, using the word in the modern sense for the right to block external interference, is used to cover up a deep moral problem for aid donors. Who do they really want to help, the people as a whole, the poor only or the state? The aid proposition is that assistance to the state can, by some trick of management, be made to help the people and the poor as well. The evidence is that it cannot and that in some cases it fails so disastrously that direct foreign intervention can no longer be excluded from consideration in extreme circumstances. Nevertheless, the 'new colonialist' solution is so antagonistic to the fundamental goals of aid that it can really only be considered in the direst emergency. (The Yugoslavia's and Somalia's have also demonstrated the enormous practical difficulties involved.)

A less extreme approach, the second of the three options, is to continue aid in more or less the same way as at present but to make a reality of the claims to transparent and effective accountability: to insist that recipient governments must earn the right to unsupervised control over aid resources. This policy would require three things. The first is a recognition that the volume of aid will have to be reduced, in the short run at least. The only way to ensure accountability is to cut off the aid immediately where audited accounts are not provided, inevitably reducing the flow of aid for a while. The second, which follows from the first, is the elimination or suppression of the political and bureaucratic pressures to 'move the money'.

The third is a reversal of the current arm's-length approach to knowledge. Money accountability is not the only requirement. A true measure of efficiency and impact is also required. That can only come from greater depth and width of understanding of what is feasible and what is actually desired in any given country. For this to be possible, donor agencies have to abandon the myth that the superficial techniques of social surveying can offer a substitute for the understanding that relatively long service in one country can provide. Donors must strengthen their staff on the ground and commit them to one country or to a limited number of countries for relatively long periods; long enough to justify their learning the language and genuinely coming to terms with the different culture. This has been recommended before, but the pressures that prevent it happening have always prevailed. Donor agencies are still highly suspicious of their own staff who become too committed to one country, who have 'gone native', and still more so of long-term technical assistance staff. This suspicion must be overcome and the emphasis returned to Knowledge in Place, knowledge that grows within its context rather than knowledge that is gathered and validated through the academic community.

This last recommendation wil be particularly difficult to accept. One thing that both donors and recipients will happily agree on is the low quality of techinical assistance staff, their excessive cost and their poor performance. The simple fact is that they do not cost very much relative to the market they are drawn from in First World countries. In 1990, a British lawyer cost some £150 per hour, about the same as a technical assistance consultant per day, and his living conditions are incomparably easier. The perception of excessive cost reflects the vast gap between local pay scales and TA rates, not the true value of First World skills in the market. The constant flow of trained Third World manpower towards the First World testifies to the same fact. Poor performance is mostly the result of the fairly impossible demands laid on TA, but the poor pay and conditions relative to First World markets also discourages the entry of top-class talent. It is worth remembering that the colonial Sudan Political Service was able to provide Sudan with an expatriate staff drawn almost entirely from the premier two universities in the United Kingdom, at a time when university education was rare even in the First World; a staff, moreover, that spent its whole working life in the remoter districts of Sudan.

One additional possibility is to require the donors who purport to be banks, and even some of those who do not, to act as real banks must do. This could be done by abandoning the restriction that they lend only to governments. Instead, their loans, especially those that are on very soft terms, would be linked to specific investments. If the investment did not pay off, then the loan would not be repaid. This introduction of an 'equity element' into aid-financed investment would resolve one of the most serious inconsistencies in project aid. Very many projects are planned and designed by the donors and tailored to their viewpoint, if not actually their requirements. It is wholly inequitable that the recipient government should bear all the risk of success or failure under such circumstances, however soft the loan terms. While this approach may not be applicable across the whole range of aid it would certainly help to bring at least part of it under the discipline of profit and loss. At the very least it might lead to the use of conservative estimates in project planning insterad of the optimistic ones that social cost benefit techniques usually arrive at, under pressure to 'move the money'.

Cost-recovery would be an important part of such an attempt to restore traditional disciplines of profit-and-loss. Repayment of development loans could be directly tied to cost-recovery. This would provide a direct link between the poor Third World farmer and the donor bureaucrat. If the farmer did not like the service offered then he would not pay for it and the bureaucrat that approved the loan would have to explain why it was not being repaid. Although the modern aid prescription lays some emphasis on cost-recovery it does not make explicit how important it could be as a means to restoring accountability, to re-establishing the consumer's willingness to pay as the primary discipline for all services. The difficulty aid has in supporting this kind of discipline can, however, be seen in the fact that every call for cost-recovery is accompanied by a warning against the social risks of too much cost-recovery.

It has to be admitted that it seems highly unlikely that the aid community will ever find sufficient unity of purpose to make a success of the approach described. The special economics of aid as a charitable gift mean that clear incentives to efficiency and accountability are just as lacking among the donor agencies as they are in the recipient countries. The likely reaction to the suggestion that the development banks should be more like banks may be seen in the World Bank's own recent analysis of its problems. It is reported that having admitted (at last) that a third of its projects run into major problems within five years, the bank criticizes its own staff for 'acting too much like bankers and too little like aid workers' (*New Scientist*, 17 October 1992).

The third possible approach is more radical than either of the foregoing. That is to distribute aid as a straightforward cash transfer but place it directly in the hands of the individual citizens of the developing countries. This would mean abandoning all attempts to identify from without what is the key sector, what is the culturally acceptable form of equity, what is a feasible structure of social organization. Instead the people of the country concerned would be given the money to buy exactly what they wanted. This method would restore taxation at a stroke to its rightful place as the means by which the individual citizen both buys the public services he wants and makes sure that it is done the way he wants it. It would allow the people of the country at all levels of society to decide how much consumption they could afford and how much saving was worth their while. At a stroke, it would free the theoreticians of aid from the treadmill of trying to decide between 'trickle down' and 'bottom up'.

To register all the citizens of African countries and ensure that they all got paid their rightful share would be a considerable practical task, but far from impossible with modern computing power. It is extremely unlikely that such a straightforward exercise would cost more than the overheads of the current aid machine; from the bureaucracies in western capitals through the warrens of academic endeavour to the miserable national staff trapped in misconceived projects in rural Africa, those are beyond calculation.

To conclude this exploration of the aid jungle, armed only with some experience, a little logic and Occam's Razor, I would suggest that there is only one truly 'bottom-up' approach and that is to place the money directly in the hands of the people of each developing society. The aid era to date has not been entirely wasted in that the essential commonsense and abilities of those people are now acknowledged. It is time to take the next logical step and hand back to them the complete freedom to make their own decisions; yes and to fight their own battles if necessary. Curiously, therefore, we arrive at the conclusion that Aid for Development is most likely to achieve its aims if it acts in exactly the same way as Aid for Charity.

BIBLIOGRAPHY

Adams, M. (1982). 'The Baggara Problem', *Development & Change*, vol 13, no 2, pp 259–89

Ahmad, A. G. M. (1974). *Shaykhs and Followers. Political struggle in the Rufa'a Al Hoi Nazirate*. Khartoum: Khartoum University

Anderson, D., and Grove, R. (1987). *Conservation in Africa. People, Policies and Practice*. Cambridge: Cambridge University Press

Arkell, A. J. (1952). *History of Darfur, 1200–1700*, Khartoum: Sudan Notes and Records, vols xxxii and xxxiii

Barnett, A., and Abdelkarim, A. (1988). *Sudan: State, Capital and Transformation*. London: Croom Helm

Bartels, G. B., Perrier, G. K., and Norton, B. E. (1990). *Applicability of the Carrying Capacity Concept*. London: Overseas Development Institute, Pastoral Development Network, paper no 29d

Bauer, P. T. (1976). *Dissent on Development*. London: Weidenfeld & Nicolson

Behnke, R. H. (1985). *Rangeland Development and the Improvement of Livestock Productivity*. Khartoum: Western Savannah Development Corporation

Behnke, R. H., and Scoones, I. (1991). *Rethinking Rangeland Ecology. Implications for Rangeland Management in Africa*. London: Commonwealth Secretariat

Bennett, J. W. (1984). *Political Ecology and Development Projects Affecting Pastoralist Peoples in East Africa*. Madison: Land Tenure Center, Wis consin University

Beshai, A. A. (1976). *Export Performance and Economic Development in Sudan*. London: Ithaca Press

Boserup, E. (1965). *The Conditions of Agricultural Growth: Economics of Agrarian Change Under Population Pressure*. London: Allen & Unwin

Breman, H. and de Wit, C. T. (1983). 'Rangeland Productivity and Exploitation in the Sahel', *Science*, vol 221, no 4618, pp 1341–7

Brown, R. P. C. (1990). *Sudan's Debt Crisis.* The Hague: Institute of Social Studies

Cassen, R. (1986). *Does Aid Work?* Oxford: Clarendon Press

Chambers, J. D., and Mingay, G. E. (1978). *The Agricultural Revolution 1750–1880.* London: Batsford

Chambers, R. (1983). *Rural Development – Putting the Last First.* London: Longman

Clapham, C. (1991). 'The African State', Royal African Society conference paper, Cambridge, April

Coase, R. (1960). 'The Problem of Social Cost', *Journal of Law and Economics*, October, pp 1–44

Collier, P. (1991). 'Africa's External Economic Relations: 1960–90', Royal African Society conference paper, Cambridge, April

Cunnison, I. (1966). *Baggara Arabs.* Oxford: Clarendon Press

Cunnison, I., and James, W., eds (1972). *Essays in Sudan Ethnography.* London: Hurst

Daly, M. W. (1986). *Empire on the Nile.* Cambridge: Cambridge University Press

—— (1991). *Imperial Sudan.* Cambridge: Cambridge University Press

—— ed (1985). *Modernization in the Sudan.* New York: Lillian Barber Press

Davey, K. J., ed (1976). 'Local Government and Development in Sudan. The Experience of South Darfur', conference report, Government Administration and Planning Conference, Nyala

Davies, R. (1957). *The Camel's Back.* London: John Murray

Department of Statistics (1956). *First Population Census of Sudan – 1955/56.* Khartoum: Ministry of Planning

—— (1968). *Census of Agriculture in Darfur Province – 1964/65.* Khartoum: Ministry of Planning

—— (1972). *Industrial Survey 1970/71.* Khartoum: Ministry of Planning

—— (1983a). *Industrial Survey 1978/79.* Khartoum: Ministry of Finance and Economic Planning

—— (1983b). *Household Income and Expenditure Survey.* Khartoum: Ministry of Finance and Economic Planning

—— (1983c). *Third Population Census of Sudan – 1983.* Unpublished preliminary data

Duffield, M. (1990). *Sudan at the Crossroads.* Brighton: Institute of Development Studies, University of Sussex, Discussion paper no 275

Eicher, C. K., and Baker, D. C. (1982). *Research on Agricultural Developments in Sub-Saharan Africa*. East Lansing: Michigan State University

Emmerij, L., ed (1987). *Development Policies and the Crisis of the 1980's*. Paris: OECD

Farmer, G., and Wigley, T. M. C. (1985). *Climatic Trends for Tropical Africa*. Norwich: University of East Anglia

Gamble, A. (1981). *Introduction to Modern Social and Political Thought*. London: Macmillan Education

Gillan, A. (1939). *Darfur 1916*. Khartoum: Sudan Notes and Records

Gillespie, I. A. (1966). 'The Nomads of Sudan and their Livestock in the 20th Century', *Sudan Journal of Veterinary Science and Animal Husbandry*, vol 7, pp 13–23

Gleichen, Lt-Col Count (1905). *The Anglo-Egyptian Sudan*. London: HMSO

Gould, J. R. (1972). 'Externalities, Factor Proportions and the Level of Exploitation of Free Access Resources', *Economica*, vol 39, pp 383ff

Grandin, B. E. (1987). *Pastoral Culture and Range Management: Recent Lessons from Maasailand*. Addis Ababa: International Livestock Centre for Africa, Bulletin no 28

Haaland, G., ed (1980). *Problems of Savanna Development: The Sudan Case*. Bergen: University of Bergen

Hamza, M. E. Z. (1979). *Fur Customary Law in Southern Darfur*. Khartoum: University of Khartoum, Customary law memorandum no 4

Hansohm, D. (1989). *The Potential of Small Industries in Sudan. Case Study of Nyala*. Bremen: University of Bremen

Hardin, G. (1968). 'The Tragedy of the Commons', *Science*, vol 162, pp 1243–8

Harvey, J. A. (1968). *Adaptive Research in the Jebel Marra Area from 1981 to 1986*. Khartoum: Jebel Marra Rural Development Project

Hayami, Y., and Kikuchi, M. (1981). *Asian Village Economy at the Crossroads. An economic approach to institutional change*. Tokyo: University of Tokyo

Hayami, Y., and Ruttan, V. W. (1971). *Agricultural Development. An international perspective*. Baltimore: Johns Hopkins University

Henderson, K. D. D. (1965). *Sudan Republic*. London: Benn

Hirschman, A. O. (1967). *Development Projects Observed*. Washington: The Brookings Institution

Howell, J., ed (1974). *Local Government and Politics in the Sudan*. Khartoum: University of Khartoum

Hunting Technical Services (HTS) (1958). *Jebel Marra Investigations*. London: HTS

—— (1974). *Southern Darfur Land Use Planning Survey*. London: HTS

—— (1976). *Savanna Development Project – Phase II*. London: HTS

—— (1977). *Agricultural Development in the Jebel Marra Area*. London: HTS

—— (1981). *Livestock and Range Development Programme 1981–84*. London: HTS

Ibrahim, F. N. (1984). *Ecological Imbalance in the Republic of Sudan. With Reference to Desertification in Darfur*. Bayreuth: University of Bayreuth

International Labour Organization (ILO) (1976). *Growth, Employment and Equity*. Geneva: ILO

—— (1987). *Employment and Economic Reform*. Geneva: ILO

Issawi, C. (1950). *An Arab Philosophy of History*. London: John Murray

Jewitt, T. N., and Ferguson, H. (1948). 'Soil, Agricultural Systems and Land Use in Darfur'. Unpublished technical note

Jewitt, T. N., and Manton, J. S. (1951). 'Soil Exhaustion in the Goz Sands of the Sudan'. Cutting from unidentified journal

Jebel Marra Rural Development Project (JMRDP) (1982). *Wet Season Survey*. Khartoum: JMRDP

—— (1983). *Crop Protection Report*. Khartoum: JMRDP

—— (1983). *Wet Season Survey*. Khartoum: JMRDP

—— (1984). *Wet Season Survey*. Khartoum: JMRDP

—— (1985). *Wet Season Survey*. Khartoum: JMRDP

—— (1986). *Wet Season Survey*. Khartoum: JMRDP

—— (1987). *Wet Season Survey*. Khartoum: JMRDP

—— (1987). *Pre-harvest Survey*. Khartoum: JMRDP

—— (1988). *Hydrogeology report*. Khartoum: JMRDP

—— (1988). *Irrigation Survey*. Khartoum: JMRDP

—— (1988). *Post-Harvest Survey*. Khartoum: JMRDP

—— (1988). *Wet Season Survey*. Khartoum: JMRDP

—— (1988). *Pre-harvest Survey*. Khartoum: JMRDP

—— (1989). *Pre-harvest Survey*. Khartoum: JMRDP

—— (1990). *P9 Survey*. Khartoum: JMRDP

JMRDP and Hunting Technical Services (1985). *Range and Livestock Development in the Jebel Marra*. Khartoum: JMRDP

Johnson, D., and Anderson, D. (1988). *The Ecology of Survival*. London: Lester Crook Academic Publishing

Kameir and Kursany (1985). *Corruption as the 'Fifth' Factor of Production.* Uppsala: Scandinavian Institute of African Studies, Research report no 72

Kapteijns, J. (1985). *Mahdist Faith and Sudanic Tradition. The History of the Masalit Sultanate 1870–1930.* Leiden: Africa Studies Centre

KTI (1985). *Evaluation of Jebel Marra Rural Development Project.* The Hague: Royal Tropical Institute

Larrouse (1964). *Larrouse Encyclopedia of Modern History.* London: Hamlyn

Lees, F. A., and Brooks, H. C. (1977). *The Economic and Political Development of Sudan.* London: Macmillan

Lele, U., and Stone, S. W. (1989). *Population Pressure, the Environment and Agricultural Intensification. Variations on the Boserup Hypothesis.* Washington: International Bank for Reconstruction and Development

Liebenstein, H. (1966). 'Allocative Efficiency Versus X-Efficiency', *American Economic Review*, pp. 393–415

Low, E. M. (1967). *Marketing Groundnuts in the Sudan.* Reading: University of Reading

Mahmoud, F. B. (1984). *The Sudanese Bourgeoisie: Vanguard of Development?.* Khartoum: University of Khartoum

Manger, L. O., ed (1984). *Trade and Traders in the Sudan.* Bergen: University of Bergen

Matthews, ed (1985). *Economy and Democracy. Proceedings of the Economics Section of the British Association for the Advancement of Science, 1984.* London: Macmillan

Maxwell, S. (1991). *To Cure All Hunger. Food Policy and Food Security in Sudan.* London: Intermediate Technology Publications

Morton, J. F. (1981). *Tractor Usage in Wadi Rima.* Taiz, Yemen: Agricultural Engineering Project

Nye, P. H., and Greenland, D. J. (1960). *The Soil under Shifting Cultivation.* London: Commonwealth Agriculture Bureau

O'Fahey, R. S. (1980). *State and Society in Dar Fur.* London: Hurst

O'Fahey, R. S., and Abu Salim (1983). *Land in Darfur.* Cambridge: Cambridge University Press

Pingali, P. L. (1987). *From Hand Tillage to Animal Traction.* Addis Ababa: International Livestock Centre for Africa

Pons, V., ed (1980). *Urbanization and Urban Life in the Sudan.* Hull: University of Hull, Department of Sociology

Quin, F. M. (1989). *Agronomic Research in the WSDC Area – 1976 to 1988.* Khartoum: Western Savannah Development Corporation

Samuelson, P. A. (1976). *Economics*. New York: McGraw-Hill

Sarsfield-Hall, E. G. (1975). *From Cork to Khartoum*. UK: Private publication

Schultz, T. W. (1964). *Transforming Traditional Agriculture*. New Haven: Yale University Press

Scott, M. F. G. (1989). *A New View of Economic Growth*. Oxford: Oxford University Press

Scott-Villiers, H. (1984). *Land Use Change in Qoz Ma'aliya*. Khartoum: Western Savannah Development Corporation

Shepherd, A., Norris, M., and Watson, J. (1987). *Water Planning in Arid Sudan*. London: Ithaca Press

Smith, A. (1776[1986]). *The Wealth of Nations*, Books I-III. Harmondsworth: Penguin

Sudan Government (1939). *Governor-General's Report – 1939*. London: HMSO

—— (1940). *Governor-General's Report – 1940*. London: HMSO

—— (1941). *Governor-General's Report – 1941*. London: HMSO

—— (1945). *Governor-General's Report – 1945*. London: HMSO

Tendler, J. (1975). *Inside Foreign Aid*. Baltimore: Johns Hopkins University

Tiffen, M. (1992). *Environment, Population Growth and Productivity in Kenya. Case Study of Machakos District*. London: Overseas Development Institute

Tothill, J. D., ed (1948). *Agriculture in the Sudan*. Oxford: Oxford University Press

Tubiana, M.-J., and Tubiana, J. (1977). *The Zaghawa from an Ecological Perspective*. Rotterdam: A. A. Balkema

Vetaas, O. R. (1992). 'Micro-site Effects of Trees and Shrubs in Dry Savannas', *Journal of Vegetation Science*, vol 3, pp 337–44

Vincent, L. (1990). *The Politics of Water Scarcity. Irrigation and Water Supply in the Mountains of the Yemen Republic*. London: Overseas Development Institute, Irrigation Management Network paper no 90/3e

VRA/RMR (1977). *National Livestock Census and Resource Inventory*. Khartoum: Veterinary Research Administration; and Nairobi: Resource Management and Research

Western Savannah Development Corporation (WSDC) (1983). *Farmer Survey 1983*. Khartoum: WSDC

—— (1983). *Settlement Survey*. Khartoum: WSDC

—— (1984). *Farmer Survey 1984*. Khartoum: WSDC

—— (1984). *Nomad Survey 1984*. Khartoum: WSDC

—— (1984) *Consumption Survey 1984*. Khartoum: WSDC

—— (1984). *NAGAA Survey*. Khartoum: WSDC

—— (1985). *Development in Darfur*. Khartoum: WSDC

Western Savannah Development Corporation and Hunting Technical Services (1989). *Monitoring Vegetation and Land Use Change in Selected Areas of Southern Darfur*. Khartoum: WSDC; and London: Hunting Technical Services

Winter, E. J. (1974). *Water, Soil and the Plant*. London: Macmillan

Woodward, P. (1990). *Sudan 1889–1989. The Unstable State*. London: Lester Crook Academic Publishers

World Bank (1981). *Accelerated Development in Sub-Saharan Africa*. Washington: IBRD

—— (1984). *Toward Sustained Development in Sub-Saharan Africa*. Washington: IBRD

—— (1989). *Sub-Saharan Africa from Crisis to Sustainable Growth*. Washington: IBRD

Yapp, M. E. (1987). *The Making of the Modern Near East 1792–1923*. London: Longman

INDEX